ST
IN CHINA

A PRACTICAL HANDBOOK FOR STUDENTS

Patrick McAloon

STUDYING IN CHINA

A PRACTICAL HANDBOOK FOR STUDENTS

TAKE AN EXTRAORDINARY EDUCATIONAL TRIP TO CHINA!

TUTTLE Publishing

Tokyo | Rutland, Vermont | Singapore

Published by Tuttle Publishing, an imprint of Periplus Editions (HK) Ltd.

www.tuttlepublishing.com

Copyright © 2014 Patrick McAloon

All rights reserved. No part of this publication may be reproduced or utilized in any form or by any means, electronic or mechanical, including photocopying, recording, or by any information storage and retrieval system, without prior written permission from the publisher.

Library of Congress Cataloging-in-Publication Data

McAloon, Patrick.
 Studying in China / Patrick McAloon.
   pages cm
 ISBN 978-0-8048-4281-5 (pbk.)
1. Foreign study–China. 2. American students–China. 3. China–Description and travel. I. Title.
 LB2376.6.C6M43 2014
 370.116'20951–dc23

2013040427

ISBN 978-0-8048-4281-5

Distributed by

North America, Latin America & Europe
Tuttle Publishing
364 Innovation Drive
North Clarendon
VT 05759-9436 U.S.A.
Tel: (802) 773-8930
Fax: (802) 773-6993
info@tuttlepublishing.com
www.tuttlepublishing.com

Japan
Tuttle Publishing
Yaekari Building 3rd Floor
5-4-12 Osaki, Shinagawa-ku
Tokyo 1410032, Japan
Tel: (81) 3 5437 0171
Fax: (81) 3 5437 0755
sales@tuttle.co.jp
www.tuttle.co.jp

Asia Pacific
Berkeley Books Pte. Ltd.
61 Tai Seng Avenue #02-12,
Singapore 534167
Tel: (65) 6280-1330
Fax: (65) 6280-6290
inquiries@periplus.com.sg
www.periplus.com

First edition
18 17 16 15 14   10 9 8 7 6 5 4 3 2 1   1404CP

Printed in Singapore

TUTTLE PUBLISHING® is a registered trademark of Tuttle Publishing, a division of Periplus Editions (HK) Ltd.

Contents

Chapter 1	**China Beckons** 9	
	Geography.. 10	
	5,000 Years of Chinese Civilization in a Nutshell 28	
	Going to China Can Change Lives 41	
Chapter 2	**Choosing a Program** 45	
	Tourism 45	
	Short-Term Educational Programs 51	
	Long-Term Programs 67	
	A Note on Accessibility 71	
Chapter 3	**Before You Go** 72	
	Mental Preparation 72	
	Language Practice 79	
	Polish a Performance Skill 82	
	Immunizations 85	
	Getting Your Visa 88	
	Arranging for Your Flight 90	
	Packing 94	
	Last Steps 97	
Chapter 4	**Getting There** 98	
	Money for the Road... 100	
	Airport Pick-Up 100	
	Getting from the Airport to Your Destination 101	
Chapter 5	**Settling In** 106	
	Campus Living... 112	
	Chinese Roommates 119	
	Host Families 124	

Chapter 6 — Being a Foreign Student in China 134

- General Expectations About Student Behavior 134
- Some Pigs Are More Equal Than Others 137
- Will This Be On the Test? 138
- Preparing for Class 140
- The Pros and Cons of Being a Foreign Student in China 140
- Do's and Don'ts of Being a Successful Student in China 141
- A Note About Teachers' Expectations for Foreign Students .. 143
- Social Expectations Outside the Classroom 144
- What a "Student" is in Chinese Culture 146
- Your Role as a Representative of Your Nation 148
- Your Role as an English Speaker 149
- Standing Out in a Crowd 151
- Wrapping Up 155

Chapter 7 — Daily Life 157

- Local Transportation 157
- Taxis 163
- Riding a Bicycle 170
- Scooters and Motorcycles 171
- Driving a Car 172
- Satisfying the Needs of Daily Life 174
- Leisure 196

Chapter 8 — Intercity Travel 205

- Rail Travel 205
- Seating Class 210
- Getting There, from Buying the Ticket to Leaving the Station .. 213
- Air Travel 221
- Travel by Long-Distance Bus 224
- Travel by Sea 226
- Private Taxi 227

Chapter 9 — Sightseeing 229

- Popular Tourist Destinations for Chinese and Foreigners Alike 230
- Places Chinese Tourists Like to Go 235
- Theme Tourism 240

Contents

Chapter 10	**The Key to Going Back: Making Friends**	253
	The Pillars of Chinese Relationships	254
	Banqueting	264
	Using Your Foreign Identity to Establish Reciprocal Relationships	266
	Relationships to Avoid	268
Chapter 11	**Trouble, or "Ouch," "Oh, No!" and "Sorry"**	272
	Ailments	272
	Medical Treatment	276
	Legal Issues	279
	Dangerous Events, Natural and Manufactured	281
Chapter 12	**Going Home**	286
Chapter 13	**After You Return**	297
Appendix A	**Measurement Conversion**	305
Appendix B	**Reference Books**	306
	Background	306
	Travel and Travelogues	308
	Phrasebooks	308
Appendix C	**Popular Chinese Movies**	309
Appendix D	**Useful Websites**	311
	China News and Background	311
	Chinese News in the Developed World	311
	English Language Information about Life in Specific Cities	311
	Travel	312
	Study Abroad Program Listings	312
Appendix E	**A Sampling of Language Programs**	313
	Short-Term English Programs	313
	Short-Term Chinese Programs	313
	Long-Term English Degree Programs	313
	Long-Term Chinese Degree Programs	314
	Index	315
	Photo Credits	320

Chapter 1
China Beckons

Congratulations! You are thinking about participating in an educational experience in one of the most historically and culturally fascinating places on earth. Either that, or you were looking for something on Chile and went one book too far to the right on the shelf. Welcome to you, too!

This book is written for people who may soon be going to the People's Republic of China for the first or second time as a student, as a curious adult, or as staff in a study abroad program. We will cover your experience from start to finish, beginning here with an overview of Chinese geography and history that will help contextualize your experience-to-be, followed by a discussion of why China is relevant to our lives and worth learning more about.

I recommend reading all the way through this book well before you leave so that you know what the experience may be like, as well as know where to flip to when you are actually doing things like packing, dining, studying, socializing and getting ready to come home.

If you are reading this, you probably have a fairly strong intention to go to China. If you still need convincing, here are a few facts that may tip the balance in favor of going:

- China is culturally diverse, with 56 official ethnic groups with their own traditions and customs. Within the majority Han ethnicity, there is tremendous regional diversity.
- There are eight named categories of cuisine and myriad others that offer an astounding variety of dishes and flavors.
- China has seven thousand years of art to appreciate, including china (go figure), paintings, embroidery, carvings,

Shanghai at night

castings, songs, plays, and on, and on, and on.
- China is a leader in world trade and has a burgeoning domestic economy that offers many opportunities to the quick and ambitious.
- You can get a fresh, filling and nutritious meal for two U.S. dollars.
- Chinese culture requires that hosts treat guests like kings and queens until they become good friends and no longer need the royal treatment.

These are just a few tasty morsels. A trip of any kind to China is unforgettable; an educational trip to China is often a life-changing experience. But don't take my word for it. Read this book and go!

For the remainder of this chapter, we will look at what defines the land that is now the People's Republic of China. It is a place with a long and complicated history, experienced on a swath of territory that is huge and diverse. Let's take a little time to get to know the place and its people so we can have a greater appreciation for the experience you are planning to have.

Geography

When Chinese people look at a map of their country, they see a rooster, with the Northeast its head, Hainan Island its feet, and the vast areas of Xinjiang and Tibet the rooster's body and wings. The rooster's breast has always been the heart of China, culturally and politically. As with any political map, China's borders have changed much over the years: at one point, the Korean peninsula would have been the rooster's beak while the areas of Mongolia, Xinjiang, and

Urumqi

XINJIANG

XIZANG (TIBET)

Lhasa

*Claimed to be part of Xizc
Governed by the Republic of In*

Tibet have floated in and out of central Chinese rule. The fluidity of the Chinese political map is an excellent metaphor for many things in China. When you ask a Chinese person what you think is a yes-or-no question, the answer is often some variation of "it depends." For example, you may ask, "what time does the hot water run in this dormitory?" and the answer might be, "6–9 a.m. and 6–11 p.m. ... and depending on when the solar-heated water is used up."

Since political borders change and even the notion of a "nation" is an invention of the European

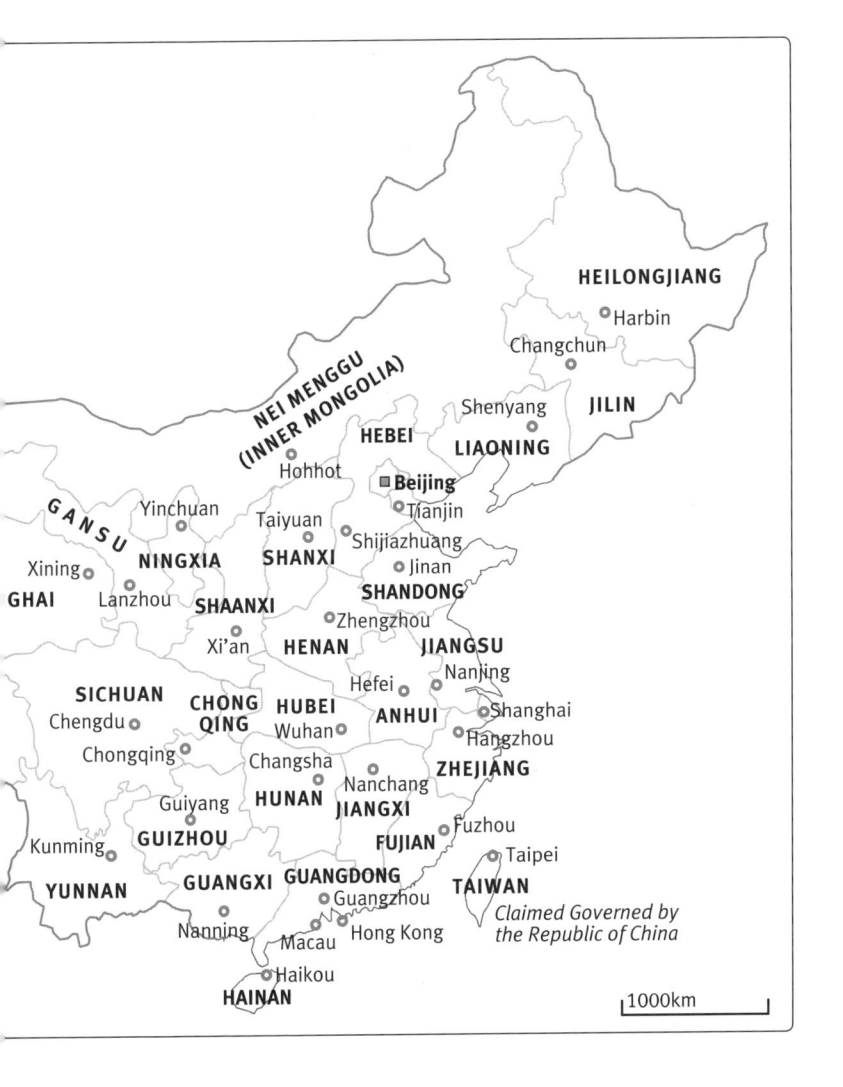

Romantic period, a more useful way to conceptualize "China" is to think of it as an area defined by people with shared interests, cultures, or both. As far as the Chinese are concerned, China is defined by areas inhabited by a socially-constructed ethnic group called the "Chinese" (**Zhōnghuá mínzú 中华民族**), which is composed of the 92% majority Han ethnicity and the 8% ethnic minorities who inhabit the areas around the Chinese heartland and who are called "Chinese" in order to fit the country-as-family model of Han Chinese political thought.

Let's begin this section on Chinese geography with a discussion of China's topography as it relates to cultural history and a look at China's political, economic, and cultural geography today. This basic understanding of Chinese geography will help you contextualize what follows in the sections on history and culture, and may inform your decision regarding where in China you would like to study and explore.

■ Topography and Worldview

While Plato was creating the basis for Western philosophy around 500 BCE, Confucius was doing the same for Chinese thought in what we now call China. Confucius lived in the northern portion of the Chinese heartland, the flat area bounded by the Chang Jiang (lit., Long River **cháng jiāng 长江**; what the Chinese call the Yangzi[1]) to the south, and mountains to the north and west. If you put a pencil on a map of China with the eraser somewhere in this heartland and point the lead in any direction, you will discover an interesting situation: from Confu-

---

1 The "Yangzi" is what inhabitants of the lower Chang Jiang once called that portion of the river, and the foreigners who popularized the name of the river happened to meet those inhabitants first.

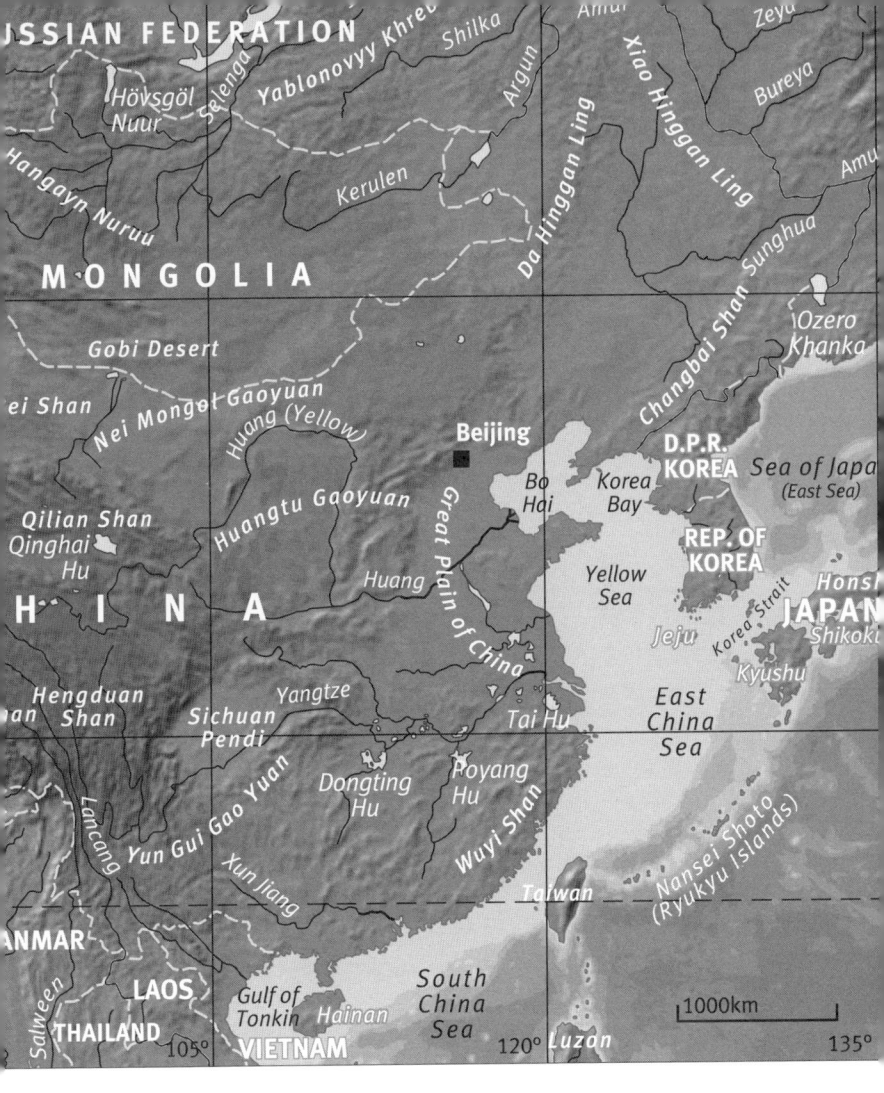

cius' time to only a couple hundred years ago, a traveler from the Chinese heartland going in any direction would likely have died before reaching a civilization as advanced as his/her own. Even the nearest candidate, India, is separated from China by the highest mountains in the world. The result of this is that Chinese civilization grew up in relative philosophical isolation; even when foreign ideas did reach ancient China—like Buddhism—they had to go through so many intermediaries that they acquired many distinctly Chinese characteristics by the time they reached the heartland. Imagine a very, very long game of "telephone," and instead of transmitting a single sentence, you are transmitting a profound religious philosophy.

As you might imagine, a civilization that develops surrounded by "less advanced" peoples tends to think of itself as the center of anything worth knowing; indeed, the Chinese name for China is "Middle Kingdom" (**zhōngguó** 中国). For centuries, the Chinese were inventing and using a great many things that no one around them was using, including the Europeans. You can learn exactly what these things were by reading Joseph Needham's *Science and Civilisation in China*. Alas, the Chinese were too satisfied with their situation for their own good. While they were using gunpowder for fireworks, the Europeans were refining its use for killing people; while the Chinese were using compass needles to make divinations, the Europeans were using them to find new people to use the gunpowder on, sailing on ships

Early Chinese compass, used for fortune telling

steered by rudders invented by the Chinese.

Not interested in the tributary relationship that the Chinese offered the other barbarians on their periphery, and even less interested in China's prohibition of the sale of their opium, the British violently interrupted thousands of years of Chinese regional superiority by attacking China in the 1850s.

French and British forces invading Beijing during the Second Opium War in 1860

■ Geography and Lifestyle

If you thought everyone in China eats rice like we eat bread and potatoes, get ready for misconception number one. Eating rice as one's staple carbohydrate is actually a Southern Chinese custom. As the climate map on the opposite page shows, there is great variation in Chinese weather patterns, which leads to important differences between northern and southern Chinese culture.

The dividing line between these two climates is roughly the Huai

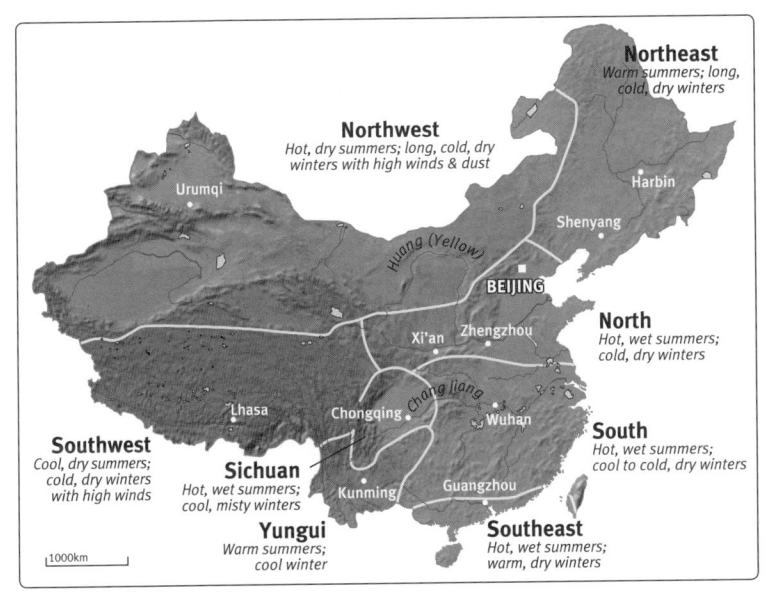

Climate map of China

Northeast Warm summers; long, cold, dry winters
Northwest Hot, dry summers; long, cold, dry winters with high winds & dust
North Hot, wet summers; cold, dry winters
South Hot, wet summers; cool to cold, dry winters
Southwest Cool, dry summers; cold, dry winters with high winds
Sichuan Hot, wet summers; cool, misty winters
Yungui Warm summers; cool winter
Southeast Hot, wet summers; warm, dry winters

River (**Huái Hé** 淮河), but you can easily substitute the Chang Jiang for this Chinese Mason-Dixon Line. First, you will notice that, in the Chinese heartland that composes the eastern 1/3 of territorial China, northerners live in a climate that is drier and colder than southern China. As a result, northerners eat wheat-based staple foods like noodles and dumplings, while southerners tend to eat rice. Most Chinese restaurants in the U.S. are run by southern Chinese, so it is easy for Americans to get the impression that rice is the staple food everywhere in China.

Surplus economies that led to urban development grew in areas where crops could be harvested more than once a year, farms could spread out quickly on flat land, and where it was far enough north that tropical disease was not an issue. Looking at the map, you might notice that these conditions exist in Henan, Jiangsu/Zhejiang and the Chengdu Basin of Sichuan Province. The *Sanxingdui* culture of the Chengdu Basin developed and disappeared before Chinese culture as we know it expanded from the east to include Sichuan, leaving

Bronze head from Sanxingdui culture

a brief but fascinating archaeological record unlike mainstream Han culture.

Another difference between northern and southern China is the ratio of mountains to flatlands. With the exception of the Xing'an and Changbai Mountains, northern China has a much more level topography. The south, with its mountainous topography, had much less regional communication, resulting in the great variety of dialects and cuisines that are found there. Northern Chinese speak some variation of Mandarin, the version of Chinese most commonly taught in schools; at home, many Southern Chinese speak a version of one of the other seven dialect families, all of which are mutually unintelligible without practice.

■ Political, Economic, and Cultural Geography Today

Today, there are 33 administrative divisions that answer directly to the central government in Beijing. Of these, 22 are provinces *per se* (e.g., Sichuan and Zhejiang); five are autonomous regions that are functionally provinces, but are set up to allow more minority involvement in government (e.g., Ningxia Hui Autonomous Region); four are province-level municipalities (e.g., Beijing and Chongqing); two are Special Administrative Regions (Hong Kong and Macao).

Provinces are composed of prefectural-level cities that roughly correspond to counties in the United States, except that in the U.S., counties may have cities located in the county that do not actually answer *to* that county. Below the provincial level of administration in China, each administrative division answers to the next-larger

Political map of China

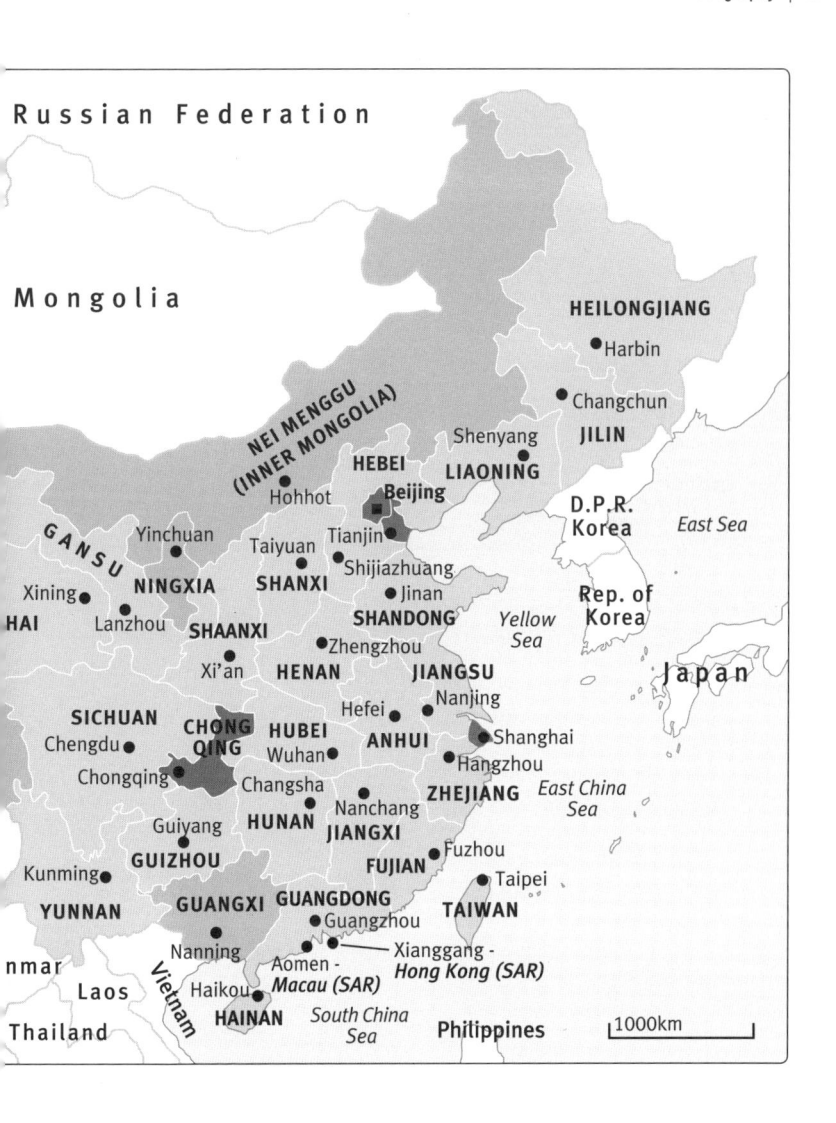

geographic division. Thus, there are counties and cities that report to prefectural-level cities, and townships that report to the counties and cities in which they are located. Each level answers to the next higher level in a theoretically straight line to Beijing, whether you are in the Department of Transportation or the Public Security Bureau.

The reality of this all-roads-lead-to-Beijing administrative structure is more complex; as the saying goes, "the mountains are high and

The National Grand Theater in Beijing

the emperor is far away" (**shāngāo huángdì yuǎn** 山高皇帝远). The further you get from Beijing, both in terms of geographic and administrative distance (there are offices of the Municipal Management Bureau at the national, provincial, prefectural city, and city levels), the more leeway is taken by those in positions of authority. Policies that are laid down at the central level are interpreted and re-interpreted at each lower level until the government officials interacting directly with their constituents have a lot of freedom in how they rule. When you have such a large population to administer, you have to expect and allow a certain amount of autonomy on the part of grass-roots officials.

All this autonomy at the local level leads to a great deal of competition between cities and provinces: if one city has something, peer cities want it, too. A Beijing taxi driver once said that Beijing built the impressive National Opera House on Chang'an Avenue because Shanghai had already built something similar. Currently, a city is considered amateur if it is not building a subway, regardless of the practicality of running a subway system there. Even Guiyang, a city built among moist karst limestone outcroppings, is building a subway. If Beijing, Shanghai, Guangzhou, or Shenzhen have something, it is usually only a matter of time before secondary cities have it, too. This situation works well for officials whose professional achievements are measured in terms of how much GDP has grown in their section. Though it naturally leads to a certain amount of redundancy, this system incentivizes construction projects that benefit many people.

China today is more like the European Union than the United States in terms of the relationships between different areas.

The Shanghai Opera House

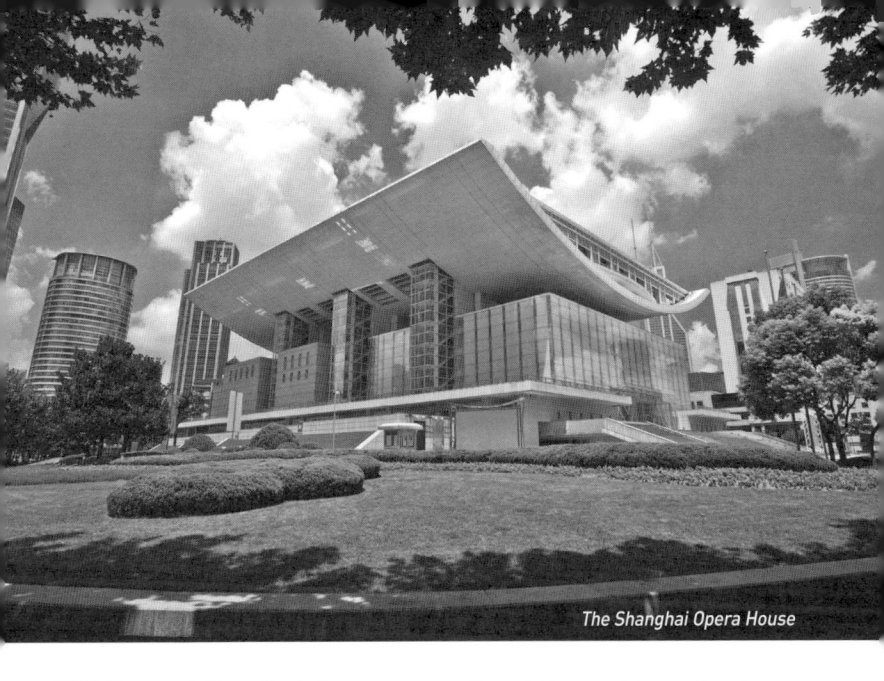

With the great diversity in language, resources, cultural artifacts and social expectations that exists between regions, provinces, cities and even localities, it sometimes seems like a miracle that the country remains whole, give or take a large island off the coast of Fujian Province. In this relationship-based social system, people seek partners they trust to do things professionally, and trust is most easily created on the basis of mutually-shared language and social expectations. Sometimes, Cantonese and Northeastern Chinese business people can feel like they are from totally different countries ... and at several times in Chinese history, they would have been! When you are in China, knowing your geography is not only the mark of an educated person, but it is also important for learning how interact with the locals in a way that makes them feel comfortable. Next, we will work our way from north to south and then east to west, using geographic divisions that are meaningful to the Chinese.

■ North and South China

"North China" (**Huáběi** 华北) refers roughly to the area north of the Huai River and east of the city of Xi'an. Each province in China is known for certain famous sites, foods, and customs. When Chinese people think of Inner Mongolia, they think of the grassy steppes; when they think of Shanxi, they think of coal and food made with flour. Overall, northern Chinese are thought to care more about face than Southern Chinese, to be able to drink more, to talk more about politics and less about private enterprise. After all, Shandong Province was the home of Confucius, who said that business is for petty people. That said, "China's Silicon Valley," *Zhongguan Cun*, is in Beijing, and two of China's best-known brands overseas (Tsingtao beer and Hai'er appliances) are based in Qingdao, Shandong. Though "Reform and Opening Up" started in the South, north China has come a long way in developing private industry, as well.

South China (culturally, if not geographically) extends from Guangxi in the southeast to Jiangsu in the east. People in this region live on rice-based diets, drink rice-based liquor more than sorghum-based liquor, and have traditionally been more isolated from one another than those living in the north, where there are expanses of easily-traversed land. The further south you go from the Yangzi River delta, the later that area was settled by ethnic Han peoples. Guangdong Province, one of the richest economic powerhouses in China today, was once considered a political and cultural backwater.

■ The Northeast

When Chinese people say the Northeast, they are referring to the three provinces of Heilongjiang (**Hēilóngjiāng** 黑龙江), Jilin (**Jílín** 吉林) and Liaoning (**Liáoníng** 辽宁). Northeast China's climate is similar to that of the upper Midwest: warm in the summertime and bitterly cold in the winter. As a result, central heating is found throughout the region (as opposed to southern China). Northeast China is known for producing a particular strain of rice, timber, chemicals, vehicles and people who can drink a lot of hard liquor. It was the Northeast's rich resources that led the Japanese to annex it in 1931, build modern American-gauge railroads across it to Russia, and build up the coastal city of Dalian before the Chinese won the area back in 1945. Today, Northeast China is home to factories that produce Audis, Volkswagens, BMWs, and Boeing aircraft. There is an American consulate located in Shenyang, the capital of Liaoning Province.

■ East China

When Chinese companies divide the country into sales territories, East China is one of the most coveted areas. "East China" is composed of the megalopolis of Shanghai

Snow sculpture in Harbin

West Lake in Hangzhou

(**Shànghǎi** 上海) and the provinces of Jiangsu (**Jiāngsū** 江苏), Zhejiang (**Zhèjiāng** 浙江), Anhui (**Ānhuī** 安徽), and sometimes Jiangxi (**Jiāngxī** 江西). Because of the fertile land found in the flat Chang Jiang river delta, Jiangsu and Zhejiang have traditionally been wealthy parts of the country; Anhui and Jiangxi are mountainous and are only now experiencing some economic growth as a result of public investment. A web of highways and rail lines connect the various population and manufacturing centers of Shanghai, Nanjing, Hangzhou, Suzhou, Kunshan, and Ningbo. People from East China tend to be of slighter build than Northerners, and their diet tends toward more finely cut dishes and sweeter flavors instead of salty ones.

All roads may lead to Beijing, but Shanghai comes in a close second. As a hub for international commerce and interaction since its creation in the 1800s, Shanghai is a mix of Western and Chinese culture. Shanghai is a modern cosmopolitan city, sometimes referred to as China with training wheels for newly-arrived foreigners. Because it has been on the vanguard of economic and cultural interaction with the West for decades, labor prices in East China have risen considerably, driving unskilled manufacturing westward, where such labor remains relatively plentiful and cheap.

Anhui Province's claims to fame are being the home of Yellow Mountain (**Huáng Shān** 黄山), a national park described in the travel chapter of this book and the headquarters of one of China's most successful home-grown auto companies, Chery. As the transplanted home of the University of Science and

Shanghai skyline along the Huangpu River

Province, to the south of Anhui, is best known as the home of the Jinggang Mountains, where the fledgling Communist army grew under cover from the Nationalists until forced out in 1929. Unbeknownst to many outside of Jiangxi, the province has produced many famous Chinese people, including scholar-officials Ouyang Li 欧阳理, Wang Anshi 王安石, and Yang Wanli 杨万里, philosopher Zhu Xi 朱熹, Nobel prize-winning author Gao Xingjian 高行健, and former Vice President Zeng Qinghong 曾庆红.

Technology of China (moved from Beijing in the 1970s), capital city Hefei is also a center for technological growth in the province. Jiangxi

■ Central China

Like the American Midwest and Plains states, "Central China" is a little harder to define than the other regions, but it generally includes

Blossoming Chinese mustard (油菜 brassica juncea) plants in Wuyuan, Jiangxi

Hubei (**Húběi** 湖北), Hunan (**Húnán** 湖南), and sometimes Jiangxi (**Jiāngxī** 江西). These provinces are mountainous with major rivers creating flat areas where agriculture and some manufacturing flourish. Central China is rich in history, covering territory once ruled by kingdoms who fought for control of larger portions of the nation; the city of Wuhan, in Hubei, has been a major river port for hundreds of years, and is one of the access points to the Three Gorges portion of the Chang Jiang river; today, Hubei is the focus for many foreign companies hoping to open up the populous markets of the region.

Food in this area tends to be spicy, with Hunan and Jiangxi representing probably the spiciest cuisines in China. Many readers may think that Sichuan food is the spiciest in China, but Hunan and Jiangxi cuisines focus on the use of red and green hot peppers, sometimes seeming to use the addition of other items simply as an excuse to eat hot peppers, like "pepper-fried watermelon rind," a traditional Jiangxi dish. Though less economically developed than the coast, Central China has traditionally produced talented scholars and warriors; you can hardly take a step in Central China without stumbling across a rural village that was home to some famous official or general.

■ Southeast China

This region is defined by the coastal provinces of Fujian, Guangdong and Hainan. Though Guangxi is technically in this area, there is so little commerce in Guangxi, that it is rarely mentioned in the same breath as the other three provinces that have thriving manufacturing industries that supply domestic and overseas customers. Fujian, as the province nearest to Taiwan, has received little direct investment from Beijing other than the installation of military equipment, and so the Fujianese rely on their own family and hometown relationship networks to invest in and develop private industry. As one factory owner in Fujian said, Fujian is like an orphan who has had to learn how to take care of himself. Fujianese entrepreneurs produce a wide variety of light manufactured products, from metal parts to clothing.

Guangdong, on the other hand, has grown as the gateway to Hong Kong and the rest of the world. The Pearl River Delta, extending from the capital of Guangzhou past the factory cities of Zhongshan, Dongguan and Humen to the South China Sea between Macao and Hong Kong, is now an important part of the world's supply chain for manufactured goods of all kinds. Proctor & Gamble's China headquarters are located in Guangzhou, reflecting the region's receptivity to Western-style business. Shenzhen, China's shining example of what can happen when you throw billions of dollars at a fishing village, is becoming south China's center for finance, a Mainland version of Hong Kong, located just over the border.

Dolce & Gabbana store in Shenzhen. Where is your nearest D&G store?

The island of Hainan was once part of Guangdong Province, but was separated as an independent province when the entire island was made a Special Economic Zone (SEZ), with special treatment for export-oriented businesses. The island has seen its share of ups and downs in terms of capitalizing on its SEZ status, but it remains a popular tourist destination as "China's Hawaii." After a few months in the smog and traffic in a city, a vacation to Hainan definitely feels like a tropical getaway.

■ Southwest China

When Chinese people talk about "Southwest China," they mean the three provinces of Yunnan, Guizhou, and Sichuan. This region is characterized by high mountains, numerous minority peoples, and more spicy food. With the exception of the Chengdu Basin and the banks of the Yangzi River as it flows east out of Sichuan and Chongqing Municipality, industry struggles to grow here, making tourism, natural resources, and agriculture the main sources of income. Sichuan province is one of the most populous in the country, its migrant workers driving the economic boom in low-wage manufacturing and construction jobs. You can hear Sichuan dialect spoken throughout China, and there seems to be a Sichuan restaurant on every street corner wherever you go. Guizhou is one of the poorest provinces in China, primarily because the beautiful Karst topography that dominates the region makes commerce difficult. Visitors seeking primitive "authentic" conditions (including "authentic" housing

Geography | 25

Sunny Hainan Island

conditions) will be able to get their fill in this province. Yunnan, on the other hand, has been developed into a major tourist destination with frequent flights between the capital of Kunming and the tourist hubs of Lijiang, Dali, and Xishuangbanna (Jinghong City). Throngs of tour groups inundate these places, but if you take a few steps off the beaten path, you can find many romantic alleys and villages that have been left alone by the masses on their way from one photo op to the next.

■ The West

Once you get west of an imaginary line that connects Xi'an and Sichuan, you are in a whole other China. From the Uighurs in Xinjiang to the Tibetans in Qinghai, Gansu and Tibet (which the Chinese call **Xīzàng 西藏**), western China is populated largely by ethnic minorities whose territory has been more or less under the influence of Han China for hundreds of years.[2]

Despite the limited human population of Western China (see map above), it has always been a highly strategic location: the Silk Road that connected Europe and Central Asia to the Chinese imperial courts ran through Xinjiang north and south of the Taklimakan Desert; there are

China population density

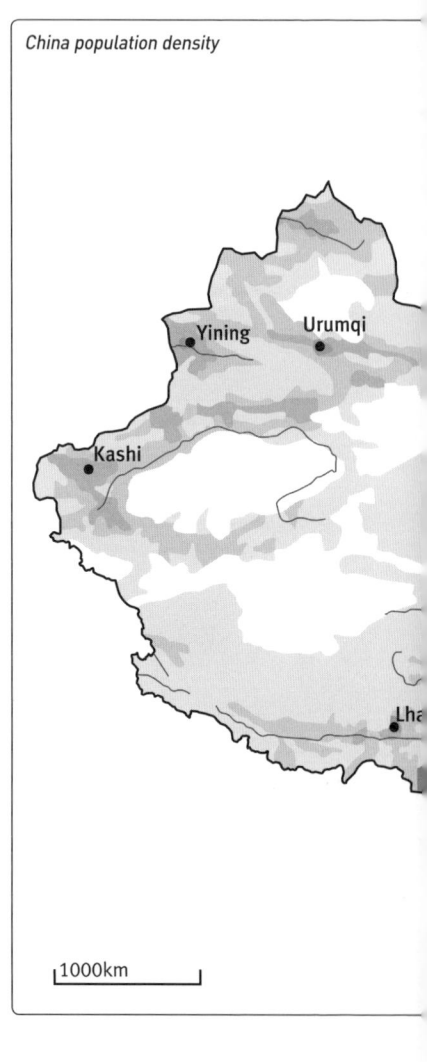

found there reserves of coal, natural gas, and petroleum; and, last but not least, Western China is a vast buffer zone between a wide variety of peoples who have had designs on the Chinese heartland. Unfortunately for China, the very reason that Western China is such a good

---

2 And, by "more or less," I really mean sometimes more and sometimes less. The Tibetans at one time conquered large parts of modern day Sichuan, Gansu, and Qinghai, as well as Tibet proper. Later, the tides turned and the Han Chinese exerted their influence over Tibetan-inhabited areas.

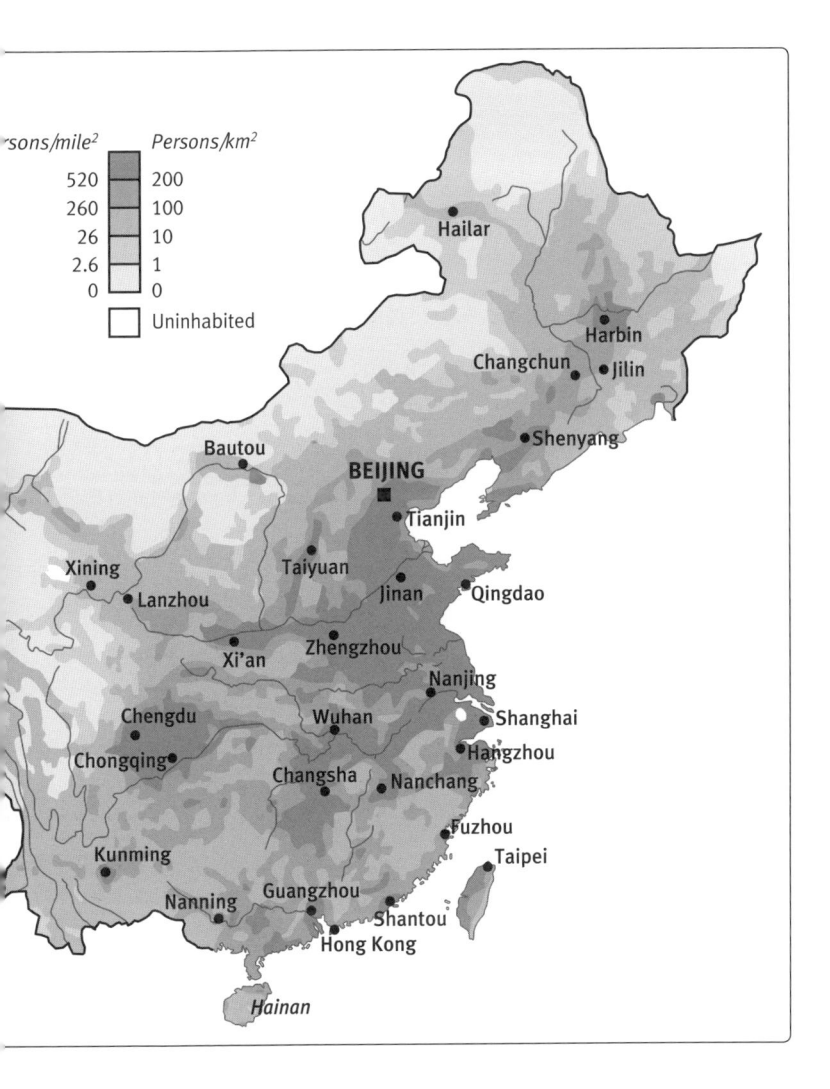

Persons/mile²	Persons/km²
520	200
260	100
26	10
2.6	1
0	0

Uninhabited

buffer makes it difficult to access its resources. As you can see in the population map above, there are large swaths of Western China in which there is an average of 1 or fewer people per square kilometer. This is not because there are no convenience stores there; the terrain and climate are so inhospitable that practically no one can live there. Thus, this region remains relatively unspoiled, from the Tian Shan and Altun Mountains in the north, to the Kunlun Mountains between Xinjiang and Tibet, to the Himalayas between Tibet and

India/Nepal. Punctuating the mountains are the Gobi and Taklimakan Deserts, and the Tibetan Plateau.

In the late 1990s, the Chinese government began a program to build up the west, including large-scale highway construction, urban renewal and growth, incentives for professionals who opted to move from the coastal urban areas to the interior, and even the establishment of sister-state relationships between the impoverished and technologically backward western provinces and the advanced eastern provinces.

While the "Develop the West" movement did result in the construction of many important infrastructure projects (like the controversial railroad to Tibet), the physical terrain seems to have been simply too much for even these concerted efforts. In the past few years, the central government has shifted its investment attention back east, to the non-coastal provinces that are convenient sources of land and low-cost labor for the bustling coastal zones.

Like the American West, Western China is a region of impressive natural beauty that is simply not found in the densely-populated east. Local minority cultures add to the sense that you are no longer in China proper, and the occasional ethnic unrest and/or freedom fighter[3] event adds to that feeling. Normally a safe place for foreign travelers, it behooves one to read the international section of the paper when planning a trip to Tibet or Xinjiang these days.

5,000 Years of Chinese Civilization in a Nutshell

The Chinese creation myth states that the world began when an egg formed in the previously formless universe. Inside the egg, the principles of Yin and Yang came into being and into balance.

Yin (dark) and Yang (light) counterbalanced and interdependent

From this egg sprang Pangu (**Pāngǔ** 盘古), a figure usually depicted looking like a monstrously hirsute caveman. With the help of his friends, Turtle, Qilin (a cross between a dragon, an ox, and a fish), Phoenix, and Dragon, Pangu spent 18,000 years making the earth and sky. Tired from his labor, Pangu died and donated his body parts to the physical world: his eyes became the sun and moon; his body the mountains; his blood the rivers; his muscles the soil, and so on. At some point—"history" is a little

---

3 Or, "terrorist," depending on your perspective.

hazy on this—a female figure named Nü Wa appeared and used Pangu's mud-flesh to make people. She also made people with her brother, Fu Xi, but we can skip the scandalous details of that maneuver.

Fast-forward to the thirtieth century BCE, and we encounter the slightly less exaggerated figures of Huang Di and Yan Di, the Huang and Yan emperors. It is more appropriate to think of these two fellows as nomadic clan leaders than "emperors," *per se*: keep in mind that people in the third century BCE thought the invention of fixed shelters was pretty neat and emperors were still a long way from building the Forbidden City. Nevertheless, Huang and Yan are considered the originators of the ethnic Chinese. Tracing the roots of an ethnic group is kind of like looking for the headwaters of a major river—everyone knows where it comes out, but which of the millions of feeder streams is the "first?" Yan and Huang are the Lake Itasca of the Han ethnicity: the Mississippi may have many sources, but Itasca is the one that gets the tourism. Today, the Chinese still refer themselves as the offspring of Yan and Huang... and their supposed hometowns have indeed become tourist attractions.

Perhaps Yan and Huang represent the beginning of the Chinese people because they became the first symbols of the Good Old Days in the Chinese tradition. Like anyone else, many Chinese throughout history idealized earlier historical periods and their political leaders. *Unlike* most everyone else, the Chinese have been wishing for the return of righteous leadership on and off for *five thousand* years. With the beginning of the Xia Dynasty around the twenty-first century BCE (yes, the other twenty-first century), began a pattern called the Dynastic Cycle. Depicted in the diagram below, the Dynastic Cycle is essentially a repeating cycle of people who are fat and happy and people who live in fear for their lives. Understandably, the latter tended to look back to the fat and happy times and wish those leaders could return.

As this cycle repeated itself every 20-400 years for 5,000 years, it became a part of the national

```
         New dynasty established by charismatic leader
              ↑                              ↓
Rebellion overthrows current dynasty    Time of prosperity
              ↑                          - Peace & stability
                                         - Infrastructure projects for economic growth
Natural disasters and/or foreign         - Makes sure people have necessities of life
invasion overtax dynasty's already
under-supported ability to                          ↓
provide food, security to people
                                        Decline
                                         - Over-taxation to pay for extravagant court
                                           lifestyle, defense from barbarians at the gates
                                         - Neglects safeguarding people's livelihoods
```

psyche—things might be good today, but you just know it's going to go south sooner or later. Compare this to how average Americans felt about their national security in August 2001, or about their financial security in 2007. If you knew that there is a statistical probability that your nation, your assets and your life could disappear as soon as the emperor decided being frisky with the concubines was more fun than making sure the barbarians stayed on their side of the Great Wall, you would probably develop a stoic attitude, too.

The first Chinese "dynasty" was the Xia (**Xià** 夏), which lasted from roughly the twenty-first to the sixteenth century BCE. There remains some discussion about the physical existence of the Xia as a political entity, but archaeological discoveries in Anyang, Henan Province in the 1960s and 1970s have convinced most scholars that the Xia did indeed exist where early Chinese histories placed them. As described in the Dynastic Cycle, the Xia was founded by a strong leader named Yu who successfully controlled flooding of the Yellow River (his father had been executed for failing to do so). Still following the cycle, the dynasty lasted through a few father-son hand-offs of power until the last emperor, Jie, completely alienated his people and was overthrown by the neighboring Shang clan-state, thus starting the Shang Dynasty (**Shāng** 商, about 1700–1027 BCE). You may be asking yourself why the Xia is considered the first dynasty when there were obviously other clan-states around at the same time (like the Shang). Indeed, there were at least seven civilizations coexisting with the early Xia as the Neolithic period became the Bronze Age. As is often the case, it doesn't really matter if the Xia was the most important or the most powerful or the most advanced clan-state of the period—modern people call Xia the first Chinese dynasty, so it is.

The Shang Dynasty is particularly important because with them, we move from early Chinese civilization to early Chinese history—that is, the first written record of Chinese civilization. The Shang left behind tens of thousands of inscriptions called oracle bones in English (**jiǎgǔ wén** 甲骨文, or 'shell-and-bone writing'). These materials were divinations inscribed on turtle shells and animal shoulder bones and then put over flame to induce cracking. The appearance of the cracks were interpreted by special officials who would then advise the king on matters such as when to go hunting, when to go to war, and what the weather would be like. With the king being the representative of Heaven on earth, if the rivers overflowed their banks and the government was not ready to help the peasants, it could be interpreted as a sign that the king had lost the Mandate of Heaven. Then, it was just a matter of time before the uppity neighboring clan-state decided they could build dikes better than you and your peasants helped them cut off your head.

The language on the oracle bones is a direct antecedent of contemporary Chinese writing. Though the characters have changed enough over the millennia that expertise is required to decode them, there are definite similarities between Shang characters and modern characters. Whenever one of these bones turned up in a Henan field, the local farmers would sell these mysterious artifacts (they called them Dragon Bones) to the local apothecary, who then ground them up into powders believed to have medicinal powers. It is not known how many oracle bones thus became health elixirs.

In addition to being the first to write Chinese characters on something that didn't disintegrate (who knows how long Chinese writing had been around before they started carving it on bones), the Shang also made great strides in the manufacture of bronze ware. These bronzes were used for ritual ceremonies and were cast with intricate designs. The skills required for designing and casting these vessels are testaments to the dynasty's technological advances. Spiritually, the Shang were a little more earthy. When the king died, his servants and horses were killed and buried with him so that he could still live the high life in the afterlife.

Going back to the Dynastic Cycle, you can guess how the Shang Dynasty ended and the Zhou (**Zhōu** 周, 1027–221 BCE) began. We can give the last Shang king a break, though, since he was only the second king to have this happen to him. Who knew at that early time that despotism and neglect was not the recipe for a smooth transfer of power?

The Zhou were a clan-state based to the west of the Shang, near Xi'an in modern day Shaanxi. During this time, Chinese political and social philosophy bloomed, with Confucius expounding his wisdom and the Mandate of Heaven formally coming into being. The Mandate of Heaven stated that the king/emperor was Heaven's representative on earth, but if he were to be successfully overthrown, that would be a sign that he had lost Heaven's support. This conveniently gives credibility to whoever wins a war between the central government and unsatisfied citizenry/gentry.

At the beginning of the dynasty, the Zhou was more a collection of family clan-states loosely confederated under the Zhou family from the capital at Hao. Over time, however, these states become increasingly tied together by central rule, including the establishment of dynasty-wide political institutions and unified agricultural taxation policies. Not all of the local lords were on board with the increase in Zhou family power, however, and in 771 BCE, rebel lords helped northern barbarians invade the Zhou territory, killing the king and forcing the Zhou family to relocate to Luoyang in Henan. With the barbarians and local lords in control of the western areas, the second half of the Zhou Dynasty (771–221 BCE) is referred to as the Eastern Zhou. Over the course of this 500 year period, the power of the Zhou court diminished and the semi-unified Chinese territory devolved into separate and competing states.

This period is further divided into two periods called the Spring and Autumn period (**chūnqiū shíqī** 春秋时期 770-476 BCE) and the Warring States period (**zhànguó shíqī** 战国时期 475-221 BCE). It was during the unstable Eastern Zhou that Confucius (551-479 BCE) began trying to peddle his political philosophy to his own regional king and those of neighboring states. His "can't we all just get along" message was not particularly popular with the expansion-hungry kings of his time, but it caught on later, when it was used to justify strict hierarchies under by strong rulers.

Mencius (372-289 BCE), a disciple of Confucius, also wrote during this time, developing the Five Relationships that are used to describe every human relationship, either literally or by analogy: ruler-official; husband-wife; father-son; older brother-younger brother; friend-friend. This remains with us today in the way that children are supposed to interact with their parents and how employees interact with their superiors (also the father-son model). Mencius believed that if each member of these dyads acted according to his role, one being in a superior position of responsibility and the other being in a subordinate position of loyalty, then the world would remain in order.

Unlike Mencius, who believed that man is essentially good, Xunzi (ca. 300-237 BCE) believed that man is essentially bad. In Confucianism, good leaders are models of propriety after whom subjects of the nation will want to pattern their behavior. Xunzi and his followers, especially Han Feizi and Li Si, were not ready to leave stability up to the masses' ability to appreciate the refined manners of a gentleman-official. Instead, he believed that a strong, authoritarian government was the best way to make sure that there would be peace in the land, a kind of "the best defense is a strong offense" approach to government. Perhaps not surprisingly, Xunzi's school of thought, called Legalism, was a little more popular in the rough-and-tumble Warring States period and immediately after, when the Qin unified the states under a single emperor.

In this time of intellectual diversity, Daoism[4] also took root. Attributed to the legendary Laozi and Zhuangzi (369-286 BCE), Daoism focused on the relationship between man and the natural cosmos, rather than among men on earth. This philosophy avers that the cosmos is, by nature, an integrated whole that is unnaturally broken up when man assigns names and categories to things we experience in nature. The Daoist sage is one who can push aside these artificial divisions and reconnect with the power of the universe that flows through its oneness, like Yoda and the Jedi in the Star Wars series.

It has been said that Confucianism is the philosophy of those in power, while Daoism is the philosophy of the powerless seeking

---

4 This is often spelled "Taoism," using the older Wade-Giles Romanization of Chinese characters, but it is pronounced the same.

solace. At the very least, both have made deep impressions on Chinese culture that continue to be felt today. Poor Mozi (ca. 470-391 BCE), on the other hand, always seems to be the footnote for this age of philosophers. Mozi advocated "universal love," a unity of spirit and purpose through which mankind would achieve many things while avoiding war and strife. The method in Mozi's philosophy is much like that of Christianity—if you treat your fellow humans like brothers and sisters, you can overcome many things. Where they differ, though, is that Mozi simply believed that unified action was the most efficient means of achieving social goals. To him, war was bad simply because it is an inefficient use of resources.

■ China Begins

The English word for China comes from the Qin Dynasty,[5] which began in 221 BCE when the king of the State of Qin beat the last remaining rival state from the Warring States period. Upon winning, the king gave himself the title "First Emperor" (**Shǐhuáng** 始皇) and is now referred to as The First Emperor of Qin. You can imagine what kind of guy names himself First Emperor after beating the last of his rivals.[6] First Emperor Qin immediately set about standardizing everything he could think of: writing, axle width (think about our interstate highway system), weights and measures, and so on. The First Emperor did China a huge favor in doing this, but his heavy-handed methods resulted in a rebellion during the reign of his less-charismatic son, thus ending the Qin Dynasty in 210 BCE.

Out of the ashes of the Qin arose the Han Dynasty (206 BCE-220 CE). A contemporary of the Roman Empire, the Han greatly expanded the territory that was administered from its capital at Chang'an (modern Xi'an). Under the Han, Chinese territory expanded to cover most of the places where ethnic Han Chinese populations are concentrated today.

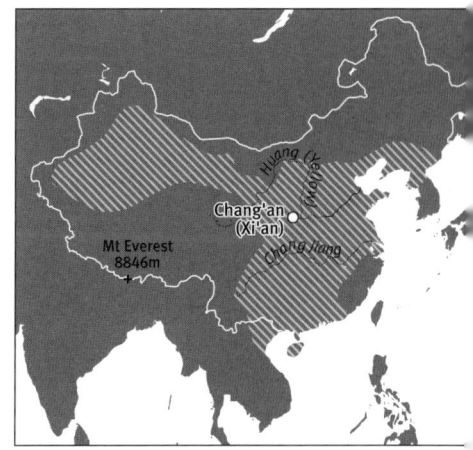

Extent of Han Dynasty territorial control

---

5 Spelled Ch'in using Wade-Giles, but, again, pronounced the same as Qin in modern Chinese pinyin.
6 Hint: The same kind of guy who commissions an entire army of terra cotta warriors, horses, and carriages to be crafted for his tomb, and then buries it.

It was during the Han that the Silk Road became an important artery of trade between Europe, Central Asia, and China. Many things traveled along this route, including fruits, spices, silk, porcelain, music and musical instruments, visual arts, and Buddhism. Buddhism had to take the long way into China, around the Himalayas, around the Taklimakan, and through the Hexi Corridor (Yellow River valley) to Xi'an and eastward. The things that traveled the Silk Road changed hands many, many times before reaching the other end; in the case of silk, this did not make much difference—it only cost more. In the case of abstract items like music and religion, by the time they reached the other end of the route, they had acquired new flavors and interpretations.

Achievements of the Han include the inventions of paper, porcelain, and the imperial examinations for official service. The latter, roughly equivalent to the American civil service exam, was important because it institutionalized the process for earning power and promotion through diligence and merit. The Han had a good thing going for a while, but a reformer-rebel overthrew the dynasty briefly from 9-24 CE, and even after the rebellion was suppressed, the Han never quite got back on its feet ... by Chinese standards, at least: the Han lasted another 200 years before completely falling apart.

■ Other Dynasties You Should Remember

The Dynastic Cycle was repeated several times from 220-518 CE, when the Sui Dynasty finally reunified China. Like the Qin, they shot their wad on unification projects (in this case, the Imperial Canal linking Northern and Southern China), and fell in 618 CE, when Li Shimin led a rebellion that overthrew the Sui and established the Tang Dynasty, the dynasty to which all subsequent dynasties aspired.

Lasting from 618-907 CE, the Tang was everything a dynasty should be—large, well-managed (at first), open to new and foreign ideas, a patron of the visual and written arts, and a stable environment for the growth of trade and technological innovation. During this time, it was considered classy for government officials to be able to write poetry at the drop of a hat. Centralized government was further improved under the Tang and, for a long time, things generally went well. Even Christianity, in the form of Nestorian "heretics" from central Asia, showed up in the capital at Chang'an at this time and was allowed to flourish among a variety of other foreign belief systems that the Tang found to be intriguing.

All good things must come to an end, however. In the 800s, economic difficulty at home, military losses to Arabs in Central Asia, and a concubine who people thought kept the emperor from getting work done led to domestic rebellions that opened the way for the ever-envious northern barbarians to invade and conquer the Tang.

After only about 50 years, the Song Dynasty (960-1279) was established, reuniting China and re-initiating a period of economic prosperity. The arts again flourished during the Song, but with the northern barbarians always knocking at the gates, Song arts tended to have a worried tone. And they were right to be worried. In 1127, invaders took over northern China and the Song court had to move to Hangzhou, where they stayed until Kublai Khan and his Mongolians came and become the first non-Han rulers of a unified China. Mongolian rule over China is referred to as the Yuan Dynasty (1206-1368), the dates overlapping with the Song because of the time it took to completely dismantle the Song.

In 1368, a peasant Han Chinese overthrew the now-Sinicized[7] Mongolian rulers and established the Ming Dynasty. If you have heard of "Ming vases," they come from this renaissance of Han Chinese culture. The Ming sent Zheng He on his voyage to Africa, achieved great heights in the arts and in government administration, and generally created an environment in which the citizenry felt happy. Beijing became the capital of China during the Mongolian Yuan Dynasty, but the Beijing tourists know today was built during the Ming.

As Lincoln said, you can make everyone happy some of the time or some people happy all of the time; in the late Ming, the emperors began alienating important sectors of the nation, and when the non-Han Manchurians from the northeast started knocking at the Great Wall, a disgruntled Ming general actually let them in. The Manchurians established the Qing Dynasty in 1644, moved their capital to Beijing, and made everyone grow their hair long and tie them in braids ("queues") like they did. Cutting your hair was interpreted as a sign of sedition and was sometimes punishable by death. Like the Mongols before them, the Manchus adopted many aspects of Chinese culture and allowed Han Chinese to hold many official posts.

When the British Lord McCartney offered the fruits of the industrial revolution to the Qing court and asked what they would like to buy, he was told that the Chinese had everything they needed, but if the British would like to become a tributary state, the Qing would be happy to offer their benevolent protection. The British, not being accustomed to being offered benevolent protection, left in a huff and started looking for a product that would reduce the incredible trade imbalance that had arisen between China and Great Britain.

By the early nineteenth century, the English and their former colonies had become addicted to something the Chinese could sell in abundance: tea. Think about it—there is even a time of day for consuming this beverage in the Commonwealth. Can you imagine if there were Coke Time or Gatorade Time in the early afternoon? Now

---

7 The Mongolians, like northern barbarian invaders before and after them, were interested in Chinese civilization and often picked up the language and customs over the course of ruling the Han Chinese.

imagine a world in which the British are buying loads and loads of tea with pounds sterling (real silver) and the Chinese are saying they wouldn't buy British-made goods for all the tea in China–literally. The British then sought a product that could likewise result in addiction and its attendant profits, and found it in opium. Opium addiction in China soon became widespread, with some households losing all their wealth to the opium dens. While helping to mitigate the trade imbalance, the opium trade also had the effect of irking the Qing court, which sent an official named to Lin Zexu to Guangdong Province (where foreigners were limited by law to live and trade) to take care of the problem. He took care of it by destroying the British inventory of opium. This, in turn, irked the British, who sailed the Royal Navy over in 1839 and bombarded Chinese coastal cities until the Qing agreed to sign the first of several "unequal treaties." As a result of this first Opium War, the Chinese lost their control over foreign trade in China, were forced to open more ports to foreign commerce, had to allow foreigners to manage customs duties, and had to surrender part of what is today Hong Kong to the British. A second Opium War (1856–1860) resulted in the opening of yet more ports to foreign trade, the loss of the rest of what became the colony of Hong Kong, and the destruction of the Old Summer Palace in Beijing at the hands of British and French troops.[8] The Chinese consider their modern history to begin with the First Opium War.

The importance of the Opium Wars cannot be underestimated. The European appropriations of territory and resources that followed the Opium Wars represent the first time in Chinese history that a foreign invader did not stop, take a look at the Chinese way of doing things and decide that they were superior to his own barbarian ways. The world as the Chinese knew it–Han civilization surrounded by envious barbarians–had come to an end. After a few very bloody and disruptive domestic uprisings and some more attacks by foreigners from all over the map (including Japan), the Qing Dynasty finally fell in 1911, when Han Chinese army units inspired by Sun Yat-sen overthrew the Empress Dowager and her court.[9]

The time between 1911 and 1949 is referred to as the Republican period, as the central government–when there was one–represented a

---

8 It is important to note that many Chinese differentiate foreigners based on skin color rather than nationality. As a result, Americans and French are considered variations on a theme.

9 The Empress Dowager was not technically the leader of China, but as the matriarch of the imperial family, she ran the show. Not exactly the best administrator, she blew one year's budget for the imperial navy on a marble boat in her Summer Palace compound. The imperial navy got a double whammy when they shot at Japanese warships during the Sino-Japanese War of 1893 and found that Chinese profiteers had sold them bum shells that did not explode.

nation called the Republic of China. Some felt that the Dynastic Cycle was just going through another run,[10] while others believed China was embarking on the establishment of an entirely new phase of Chinese history. The latter people can be divided into adherents of the Nationalist Party and members of the Chinese Communist Party, founded in 1921. Members of both parties believed they had the right vision for a post-imperial China that would be a member of the modern political and economic world. In addition to communism and democracy, self-determination was another Western political belief that stirred the Chinese. When the warlord in control of Beijing agreed to let the European victors of World War I give Germany's territory to Japan in thanks for Japan's participation in the war, protests broke out that became the May 4th Movement. This movement was led by Chinese intellectuals who felt that the time had come for a reimagining of what it meant to be Chinese, and how to create a new China.

The early Republican period was chaotic, with local warlords jockeying for regional and national power. Eventually, Chiang Kai-shek (**Jiǎng Jièshí** 蒋介石) emerged as leader of the Nationalists and he set about unifying China again under his party's rule, this time based in Nanjing. Jiang squeezed the idealistic Communists out of the picture–quite brutally–and received recognition for the Republic by 1928.

Between 1928 and 1937, the Nationalist Party under Jiang Jieshi consolidated its power in the cities while the Communists built their own base of support in the countryside. In 1934, the Nationalists pushed the Communists out of their base of operations in Jiangxi, and by the time the 100,000 men (and 35 women) found a place where they could settle down without the Nationalists on their heels, they had walked 12,500 kilometers (about 7800 miles) and lost almost 90% of their people. This exodus, called the Long March, ended in Yan'an, Shaanxi Province, and left Mao Zedong clearly in charge of the Party. While the Communists were learning how to institutionalize land reform to make life better for the destitute peasant class, the Japanese Army was working to increase its own influence in China.

The Japanese Army, working semi-independently of the Japanese government, essentially took over Manchuria (Northeast China) in the early 1930s. There, they built railroads and industry, moved Japanese citizens to Manchuria like colonists, and assassinated the local Chinese warlord. The spread of Japanese influence in China became a little too much for the Chinese to take in 1937, when a minor skirmish broke out on the southwest outskirts of Beijing (then called Beiping, as the capital, or "jing" was in Nanjing). Called the Lugou Qiao Incident,

---

10 Including Yuan Shikai, who made himself emperor after helping the anti-Qing and pro-independence movement. He died only a few years after he assassinated his way to the top.

after the bridge (**qiáo**) over Lu Gully (**Lù gōu**) for which it was named, the skirmish is considered the formal beginning of World War II for the Chinese, a good 4 years before Pearl Harbor.

The Nationalists and Communists fought each other and the Japanese from 1937 to 1945, with varying degrees of cooperation. At one point, one of Jiang Jieshi's generals kidnapped him and forced him to ally with the Communists to fight the Japanese. As far as Jiang Jieshi was concerned, the best of the Nationalist forces needed to be saved for the civil war he knew would come after the war with the Japanese. U.S.-China cooperation was very strong during World War II, with the volunteer Flying Tigers fighting from southwest China, supplies flying to China over "the Hump" (the Himalayas), and the bombers of Doolittle's Raid in 1942 crash landing (and just crashing) in China after bombing Japan. World War II, or the "War to Resist Japan" as it is known in Chinese, left a very deep scar on the Chinese psyche. If you research the Rape of Nanking or the human experiments carried out at Unit 731 in the city of Harbin, you can begin to understand why the average Chinese person becomes angry when contemporary Japanese politicians pay homage to their war dead–including war criminals–at Yasukuni Shrine.

From 1945 to 1949, the Nationalists (supported by the U.S.) and the Chinese Communist Party (with modest support from the Soviets) resumed their fight, but this time, the Communists, trained by eight years of war with the Japanese, were in a position to challenge Nationalist control of the country. As most Chinese of the time were poor and living in the countryside, the peasant-based Communist Party offered a more positive future than the Nationalist Party, whose power base was largely in the more affluent urban centers. In 1949, the defeated Nationalist Party moved the Republic of China to Taiwan and the Chinese Communist Party established the People's Republic of China on October 1st, a date that is celebrated as Mainland China's independence day.

The Maoist period in Mainland China lasted from 1949 to roughly 1976, when Chairman Mao passed away. Under his rule, China once again became a solidly unified country, and, for a time, the majority of the population enjoyed social equality, even if this mainly meant being equally poor. Beginning in the mid-1950s, China underwent a series of mass movements, culminating in the Great Proletarian Cultural Revolution of 1966-1976. These mass movements were designed to root out elements of old-fashioned Chinese culture and foreign ideas that the Party felt were holding back modernization and social equality. If you were a disenfranchised peasant, these movements were generally a positive event; if you were an academic, a business owner or a government official with the wrong friends, these movements could lead to public ostracism, poverty, and even death.

Mao Zedong proclaimed the founding of the People's Republic from above the position of his portrait on Tian'anmen.

Upon his deathbed, Mao Zedong named Hua Guofeng as his successor, but Chairman Hua was weak and limited by being the Great Helmsman's hand-picked man. To waver from Mao's policies would threaten his own credibility, but the country had just gone through ten of the most destructive years in its history, so to do nothing would have meant disaster, as well. Enter Deng Xiaoping, an early leader in the Chinese Communist Party who had studied in France during the Republican period and who had been struggled against during the Cultural Revolution for supporting reformist policies that Mao considered to be counter-revolutionary. Deng's own son had been rendered handicapped when Red Guards loyal to Mao forced him off of a fourth-floor balcony during the Cultural Revolution. With a background like this, Deng was a man who was not afraid to forge his own path for the country after Mao.

Though Deng never assumed the title of Chairman of the Chinese Communist Party, he was the de facto leader of the country until his death in 1997. Under Deng, reforms began in the countryside, where farmers were once again allowed to sell surplus crops and keep the profit for themselves and for increasing their production. This was followed by the creation of township and village enterprises, which were small businesses started by local governments to satisfy market needs not being efficiently met by the nationally-orchestrated command economy put into place in the early 1950s. Fast forward to the 1990s, and private enterprise really began to take off. People's lives were becoming materially more comfortable and, at the same time, urban residents began to wonder why "some pigs are more equal than others."[11]

In 1989, university students in Beijing started to ask–politely–for reforms in the way the universities were administered. In the beginning, democracy was not a part of the Tiananmen movement at all; some argue that the students were upset because the dismantling of the command economy meant the disappearance of the guaranteed lifetime employment that had followed college graduation. Of course, no major issue is simple: the Tiananmen protests became a movement supported by those seeking academic reform, employment reform, greater intellectual freedom, and, to some extent, greater political freedom. The central government was itself split on these issues. The lack of opposition parties in China does not mean China has no opposition groups; it simply means that heated debate takes place behind closed doors amongst the leadership, and when the debate is finished and a decision is made, everyone stands behind it in public.

Leading Chinese universities have traditionally been the locus of patriotic dissent, and they continue to be so today. They are walled-off mini-cities in which academics can work in peace and provide non-mainstream perspectives that trickle through to the leadership and the public consciousness. In the end, the hardliners won the internal debate regarding the role of the people in helping to guide reforms, and the decision was that the people–especially university students–had better keep their political thoughts to themselves. The imposition of martial law and the bloody crackdown that began on June 4th, 1989 put a serious damper on public political discussion in China, but Chinese universities today continue to fulfill the function of watchman of society.

A lot of water has passed under the bridge since 1989. The average Chinese citizen still complains about corruption in the Party, and many dinner conversations lead to discussions about the one party system, but the Communist Party has managed to change just enough to remain relevant and appreciated for guiding the economic "miracle" (not really a miracle, if you consider all the thought and unified action that is going into it). Today, China is a nation run under the system of "Socialism with Chinese Characteristics." There are enough differences between the relationship between the state and the market in Western capitalist economies and in the Chinese system that this is not simply a euphemism for free-market capitalism. State-owned enterprise continues to have an important role in China's economy, and the central government plays a tremendous role in finance and capital/infrastructure investment.

Government involvement in

---

11 Read George Orwell's *Animal Farm*, which describes post-Revolution China almost perfectly, right up to Deng's reforms. This book was published almost four full years before the founding of the People's Republic.

New light rail in Beijing

China's economy has had a large role in the country's meteoric pace of growth. Thanks to targeted investment, infrastructure projects, preferential lending policies, preferential taxation policies, and sometimes simple strong-arming, the government has been able to move the economy forward "for the good of the many," even if sometimes at the expense of the good of the few. Many Chinese cities today are literally unrecognizable to residents who return after ten or even five years away. Neighborhoods are razed and replaced, roads moved, subways installed, highways built, and parks established. In Chinese historiography, we are clearly in a period known as "**shèng shì**" (盛世), or a period of prosperity, growth, and greatness. Among those old enough to remember pre-Reform China, there is always a tinge of worry that all this prosperity and growth could come crashing down at any moment because of the numerous ills that the country is also facing, but they soldier on in the hopes that their leaders will find a way to resolve issues such as the real estate bubble, official corruption, and the large disparity in income and quality of life between city- and country-dwellers.

Going to China Can Change Lives

Depending on where you live and where in China you are going, getting there can take anywhere from 12 to 36 hours, so there must be some reason so many people travel this grueling route. Trips to China can affect you personally, can improve the lives of those in your community, and can improve the lives of Chinese people as well. There are many things that Americans and Chinese can learn from one another, and simply making friends across the two cultures is an important step toward a peaceful future for both peoples.

Humans share many things, including the need for food, shelter, and social companionship. How we express these needs and obtain them in a culturally-appropriate manner varies from place to place, and this is why traveling to China can be a positive and potentially life-changing experience for an individual. So many common needs are met differently that travel to China is an eye-opening experience that can show you the diversity of human lifeways. Take one example: many Americans grow up thinking that it is natural—e.g., instinctive—to shower in the morning after waking up. After a homestay in China, you learn that East Asians shower at night. The process of discovering why other people do things differently and then discovering that there may even be methods superior to one's own is an important growth experience. East Asians wonder why Americans shower in the morning, spend the day getting dirtier and dirtier, and then put their day-old dirty bodies in once-clean bed sheets. It is hard to argue with that kind of logic!

Travel to China is good for individual growth also because it is a necessary step in the process of achieving fluency in the language and culture. If you hope someday to apply what you learn about China and the Chinese language to a professional career, the more time you spend in-country the better. There is no substitute for personal experience when it comes to understanding what makes another culture and its people tick, seeing them live in their own environment, unaffected by foreign cultures except in ways that are mediated by their own cul-

Don't even think about messing up those white sheets.

ture. Chinatowns in the U.S. are in some ways close to life in China, but they are not the same.

Going to China also opens up important economic opportunities for your own community. As China continues to grow and the Chinese people have more and more spending power, their need for American goods and services also continues to grow. Travel to China allows Chinese and foreigners who would otherwise not meet each other be able to find areas for cooperation and mutual benefit. For example, many schools in China want native speaking teachers of English, from preschool through college; foreigners who travel to China can connect schools there with native speakers seeking employment. This virtuous cycle of employment and cross-cultural interaction benefits everyone. Teaching English is not without its challenges, but this is part of the learning process, as well. China is still a developing country, so people exploring business opportunities with Chinese partners must remember that if the country were already highly professional and in possession of all the comforts to which Westerners are accustomed, there would not be so many opportunities for your compatriots to provide goods and services!

Teaching English is the low-hanging fruit of providing services in China; there are many other areas in which foreigners and Chinese can work together, ranging from artistic exchange to exporting high-tech items and management expertise. There are many things that can be done more efficiently and professionally in China, which makes consulting and training fertile fields for international cooperation. A Chinese policeman once told me that on a business trip to Australia, he was amazed to see that there were traffic lights controlled by sensors imbedded in the road that told the lights when there were and were not cars waiting at the intersection. Things we take for granted in our lives can sometimes be a large-scale business if exported to China. Sure, after 30+ years of being open to the world, there are many fields that have been pretty well developed by Chinese and foreign organizations (good luck going head to head with Proctor & Gamble and Unilever in the personal hygiene business), but there are still many market segments that offer opportunities to enterprising communities and organizations. The key is wanting to take advantage of the opportunities and having people willing and able to follow up on them.

Finally, traveling to China brings new and interesting ideas to the Chinese community. Despite the great number of Chinese who live outside of China and who continuously share their experiences with friends and family back home, there are still many people in China who have little or no contact with people who live outside their country. When non-Chinese go to China to study, work, or even to only visit, they often unconsciously provide examples of how our cultures are different. For example, many Chinese people—especially those with little exposure to foreign culture (even if they live abroad)—are not accustomed to thanking service workers for their contributions, from janitors to bus drivers to wait staff at restaurants. The absence of thanking is not noticed by these workers because it is rarely done, but when they are thanked, they do notice that. On a grander scale, many Chinese today would like to see Chinese people see each other as members of one human family, to develop a sense of public responsibility that translates into environmental protection, avoidance of litter, responsible media and political behaviors, and many other things that go along with believing that you should treat all humans equally well, and not only people who are part of your in-group. Without literally preaching such behaviors, American visitors to China can be an example of how the Chinese concept of **rén** 仁, or human kindness, can surpass national borders. That will come in handy the next time the U.S. military bombs a Chinese embassy, as it did in 1999.

Going to China is often a life-changing experience for foreigners, and the longer they stay, the more life-changing it is. There are many reasons foreigners should go to China, from seeing firsthand what progress looks like at breakneck speed, to sharing cultures and perspectives. Most important of all, if you are thinking about going to China, you should *want* to go to China. If someone else wants you to go because it is "good for you," try to make your first trip a relatively short one. Anecdotally, maybe about 1 in 30 students goes to China for the first time and discovers that interacting with China on Chinese terms is so jarring to their sense of what is "right" and "natural" that they decide it is not for them. The other 29 students, though, discover that living and studying in a foreign country is a growth experience that they would not trade for anything else!

Now that you have decided if you are game for a trip to China, the rest of this book deals with practical aspects of getting there, living there, succeeding there, and then successfully getting home.

Chapter 2
Choosing a Program

Once you have decided that China is a place you'd like to visit, the next step is deciding what you want to do there. For this, you need to establish what you most want to get out of the experience.

- Do you want a set of exotic photographs?
- Do you want to build your resume for future employment at a company in your own country? At *any* organization (including Chinese ones)?
- Do you want to learn more about the history or material culture of China?
- Do you want to know China as the Chinese see it?
- Do you want to find out if China agrees with you before possibly embarking on a lifetime of becoming a Chinese-speaking expert on China, also known as a "China Hand"?

In this chapter, you will learn what kinds of programs fit which goals … and what budgets fit what kinds of programs. Your goals may change over time, and you may find yourself going to China in more than one role. Maybe someday, it will be *you* taking people to China!

Tourism

Any time you set foot in an unfamiliar place, you are embarking on a learning experience. Even if you simply buy a round-trip ticket to China, stay at the Portman Ritz-Carlton and wander around Shanghai for a week, you will see, hear, taste, and smell so many new things that it would still count as an educational experience. There are essentially three modes of tourism through which you can experience China: independent travel, group tours operated by travel agencies, and study tours operated by educational organizations.

■ Independent Travel

Independent travel, like the example above, is the least programmatic method of visiting China described in this book. There is no one paid to look after you, to answer your questions, and to arrange a bus that leaves when you are ready to go instead of when the schedule says it is time to go. What you get out of the experience is entirely based on what you put into it.

Traveling on your own can be very rewarding.

The main advantage of independent travel is that it is the cheapest possible way to have a Chinese experience. Many an intrepid traveler has bought a copy of the Lonely Planet or Rough Guide and followed the backpacker trail across China, hopping from hostel to hostel. You choose your travel dates, you choose your living arrangements, you choose your domestic modes of transport, you choose what you see and when.

When you are master of your trip, you can choose the US$3 noodles by pointing at the food on the table next to you instead of eating the US$10 meals that may be predetermined in group tours. You can also choose to take the hard seat train from Xi'an to Beijing and experience the masses, a test of endurance that no travel agency can afford to put their customers through.

Another benefit of independent travel in China is that you can spend as long as you want in one place before moving on. Maybe you get to Xishuangbanna in Yunnan, do all the typical tourist sites and then decide to rent a bicycle and ride out into the countryside to see how the ethnic Dai (Thai) minority people live. In the first village you come to, a bilingual child tells you that they will celebrate a festival the next day and that, if you come back, you will see something very special. Sure, you had planned to take a plane to Xi'an the next day to see the Terra Cotta Warriors, but they've been there for 2,000 years already—they can wait another day! When you travel in a group, not only can they not change travel arrangements at the last minute, but they would not be able to take you to a village that no other foreigner has visited before. If they did that, there would be too many question marks involved–can the bus get there? Do the locals have anything to show the group? Are there any flushing toilets for the inevitable emergency bathroom visit? Is the food safe to eat?

Of course, independent travel in a non-English-speaking country is not for everyone. In exchange for all this freedom, you have a lot of work to do, both before and during your trip. Without a team of people being paid to lay out your experience for you, you have to do the planning and then the gesticulating required for getting your point across to people whose language you do not speak. Admittedly, you can spend a week in Beijing and see all the main sights without ever feeling like you needed to be able to speak Chinese, but it costs more to experience China in translation.

■ Group Tours

Most Chinese people do their traveling–international and domestic–in groups. Joining a group tour makes it easy to visit new places because all the headaches associated with going where you don't know what's good and bad are already taken care of by someone else. Chinese group tours also achieve economies of scale by obtaining deep discounts from motels, tourist attractions and bus lines. American tour groups to China, on the other hand, lose much of this cost advantage in the higher expense incurred by hiring American or fluent non-native speakers of English to accompany the group.

Group tours of China tend to follow a few main routes that hit the sights that first-time visitors want to see, like the Great Wall, the Forbidden City, the Terra Cotta Warriors, Shanghai, Suzhou, Hangzhou and Yangshuo. These tours are sold in the US by American travel agencies that contract with Chinese travel agencies to deliver the tours. The Chinese travel agency will arrange lodging, domestic transportation, park/museum entrance fees, and, usually, three meals a day. Because they need to make sure that the pickiest foreign tourists in the group are happy, most tours use 4- and 5-star hotels and restaurants that are safe in terms of hygiene and flavor.

Thus, the advantage of joining a group tour is that you get to see many sights in China without having to bother with the logistics of travel. You will see the most famous parts of China, stay in comfortable hotels, eat delicious food that does not challenge your sense of what is edible, and the bus will always be there when you are done touring the temple. With a group tour, you will be able to do this without feeling at a loss for [Chinese] words. Even the schlock vendors at the places you visit on a group tour speak enough English to negotiate with you in your own language.

The main disadvantages of joining a group tour are cost (if that is a concern for you), lack of freedom (if that is a concern for you) and the fact that you are only skimming

Bargain hard!

the surface of China. A foreign-organized group tour gives you a sterilized experience that essentially creates a bubble of your own culture in which you float through China observing the country's "achievement culture"[1] and natural sights. Missing is the human element of Chinese culture—the polychronic time orientation,[2] the attention to hierarchy (would your tour guide hand out your hotel room keys to older and male tour members first?), the unpredictability of life in China that is purposely reduced or eliminated from the tourist experience.

In short, joining a group tour of China is an easy way for adults to see China and experience observable differences.

■ Study Tours

Study tours are designed to be just what they sound like—a tour that is more educational and interactive than the traditional **zǒu mǎ guān huā** (走马观花—look at the flowers from a speeding horse) style trip. The defining characteristic of a study tour is that there are classes built into the program. These classes follow a theme; some common ones include Chinese business, Chinese history (e.g., the Silk Road), Chinese law, and, often, simply "language and culture."

There are study tours designed for teenagers, with a visit to and classes in a Chinese high school and nights in a high school dormitory; there are study tours for college students, with lectures and language classes at a Chinese university and housing in a college dorm; and there are study tours for adults that often include lectures by subject matter experts talking about the history and culture of locations visited during the tour.

One way to compare study tours is to look at the ratio of "study" to "tour." Some study tours implicitly define "study" as "doing something you don't usually do," because it is

---

1 A term that linguist Hector Hammerly uses to describe artifacts of which a given culture is proud, artifacts that they consider to be cultural or national achievements. Chinese examples would include the gardens of Suzhou, the Great Wall, the Forbidden City, and so on.

2 The cultural tendency to subordinate on-time schedules to human factors and to feel comfortable with conducting more than one activity at the same time.

inherently educational to have new experiences. There is certainly some truth to this, and if the tour operator designs a program of visitation in which participants are exposed to things to which the average tourist is not exposed, the educational factor increases greatly. For example, the William & Mary in China language program at one time had a three-week study tour that preceded the 5-month traditional study abroad classes in Beijing. During this tour, students visited the usual tourist sites, but also visited factories, watched traditional artistic performances, took roads less traveled, ate foods that seriously challenged the limits of American gastronomy, and were given opportunities to learn on their own during free time. During that study tour period, the only formal daily instruction was in the form of a week of morning classes in Chinese art and *taiji quan* (**tàijí quán** 太极拳 AKA tai chi) at Suzhou University.

This could be you!

Other study tours have a relatively large classroom component,

No matter how you go, you will take a lot of photos like this.

The hard-to-find Qi State Wall in Shandong

essentially making them short-term study abroad programs with local or regional tourism added. These programs are commonly university-organized and often provide home institution credit for the courses taken in China. An increasingly popular form of study tour is one in which the overseas program is one or two weeks of inter-semester travel to China immediately following or preceding a term-length college course in the U.S. institution. Because participants in this kind of program are primed to focus on certain thematic aspects of the experience, these study tours are highly educational, regardless of the study-to-tour ratio.

In many study tours, formal instruction comprises no more than half of the program. Such programs can be excellent gateway experiences for those just dipping their toes in the Chinese pool. You still get the obligatory temple photos while also learning a little more than usual about the role of the temple in Chinese history and culture.

Factors you can look at when choosing any form of tourist program in China include:

- Cost—When comparing program prices, make sure you are comparing apples to apples. Does the program fee include international airfare? Meals? Entrance

fees? The more you pay, the nicer the hotel, the nicer the bus, and the nicer the decoration of the restaurants you go to. Usually.
- Sites—How many sites are included in how much time? Do you prefer a hectic schedule in which as many sites are crammed in as possible, or a more leisurely trip?
- Group size—How many people does the program need in order to for a group to go over? How large are the classes, if there are any?
- "Touristy-ness"—Does the group go to the Badaling Great Wall (very touristy) or Simatai (less touristy)? Does your Shanghai trip only include the Pearl Tower and Yu Gardens, or also the French Concession? A jazz bar at night? You will have to decide what you want, as there are pros/cons of each. Simatai is farther from Beijing proper and therefore means sacrificing a visit to somewhere else.

Short-Term Educational Programs

For a little greater time commitment, you can consider joining a short-term educational program. For the sake of discussion, we will define such programs as those in which formal instruction is the core of the program, and the program is at least one college academic term in length, and does not result in a degree. A tour or study tour may still be a component of the program, but regularly scheduled coursework with homework assignments is a core element, and possibly for graded credit.

Educational programs are most often tied to an educational institution, either in China or the U.S., and participants' performance in the program is a matter of record. This is in significant contrast to the tour-based options described in the previous section. Tour operators, as providers of a business service, must put short-term customer satisfaction ahead of long-term goals such as language or culture expertise, which require an investment of time and patience much greater than most tourists wish to make. In educational programs, there is an expectation on the part of both the teachers and the students that the program will—like a fitness club membership—force participants to do uncomfortable things in order to reach a difficult goal such as increased Mandarin ability.

■ Short-Term English-Language Programs

English-language programs in China of term length or more are increasingly popular means to study in China. Once upon a time, the majority of programs in China for American learners were Chinese language programs. Today, however, there is enough English-speaking expertise in China to offer term-length programs in English without breaking the bank.

Global Alliance for Education is a popular operator of short-term English language programs in China. They offer semester-length programs in Beijing, Xi'an, and Shanghai that award 15 credits for the study of business, globalization, politics, culture, and language, depending on the program. All programs have a language component, but prior language study is only a prerequisite for their intensive language program in Shanghai. As required by Chinese law, these programs are delivered in China through local partner universities and include study tour components. This facilitates the issuance of transcripts that are needed for credit transfer once a student returns to his or her home institution.

Global Maximum Educational Opportunities (g-MEO) is a new organization that has arisen to serve a portion of the students the U.S. Department of State hopes will contribute to fulfilling President Obama's goal of sending 100,000 Americans to China to study. This organization has partnered with organizations in Shanghai, Suzhou, Wuhan, and Chengdu to offer term- and academic year-length programs in all subject areas, some of which offer scholarship support by the Chinese government.

CIEE, an organization with over 60 years of experience helping people acquire international experience, offers three programs in China in which English-language subject instruction is offered. These semester-long programs are in the areas of cultural studies, business, and globalization... but the subject matter courses are held once a week, while Chinese language instruction occupies two-to-five hours per day. This schedule seems to imply that the program is primarily a language program with a subject matter component designed to attract students from certain high-interest majors such as area studies and business.

Short-term English-language programs have the advantage of being relatively easy to apply to one's home institution's graduation requirements. Many programs like CIEE and the Alliance for Global Education have already worked with major universities to establish appropriate credit transfer procedures, and even if a student's university has not worked with any of these organizations before, the institutional experience of these groups is such that it should be relatively easy to establish credit transfer procedures.

Some things to keep in mind when choosing a short-term English language program:

- Academic credit—Do you need it? If so, does the program website indicate how many credits they believe their program is worth (meaning that they have at least thought about it)?
- Courses—Will the courses count toward your major? Your graduation?
- Host institution—Is the Chinese host institution a re-

spected school[3] that should have quality teachers? If not, what does the program do to ensure quality?

■ Short-Term Chinese-Language Programs

The vast majority of learning programs in China for Americans are short-term Chinese-language programs. These are programs that offer Chinese language instruction to American students in a formal learning environment for one academic term to one year, and result in no degree. Until recently, short-term Chinese-language instruction in China was largely the purview of a few established Sino-foreign partnerships and a few well-known Chinese universities. With the world growth of popularity in learning Chinese, it has become popular for Chinese universities large and small to establish short-term Chinese-language programs for foreigners.

As you research which programs appeal to you, asking the following questions will be helpful in identifying which programs may best match your needs and interests.

The following are some questions to ask when choosing a short-term Chinese-language program.

Where is the program?
Basic as this question is, it is a good place to start. Using informa-

---

3 An easy way to check is if the school is one of the 100+ universities in China's Project 211.

Life in the big city (Beijing)

tion from Chapter 1, you can now differentiate between northern and southern China, urban and rural, "tier-one" cities and below, and coastal and inland locales. When choosing a program, you may want to go somewhere with as many comforts of home as possible (a coastal tier-one city), or you may want to try something new and adventurous, living like many Chinese people do, in a tier-two or -three city. There are few study abroad programs based in truly rural areas, but any tier-two or -three city-based program will put you within an hour's public bus ride of the countryside. Farms just outside of major cities are generally not the poor kind you see on charity specials, but the infrastructure there is still very different from rural areas in the U.S. and will provide an eye-opening experience when visited.

The vast majority of Americans

still go to Beijing or Shanghai, and these two cities have the highest concentration of top Chinese universities. These cities have many choices in terms of programs, housing, extracurricular activities, and also transportation. As major metropolises, there are many internationally-oriented businesses and NGO's that can offer jobs after graduation, and both have large expatriate communities that have created an American experience abroad for those who find themselves in China because they had to go, not necessarily because they wanted to. Guangzhou and Shenzhen are tier-one cities as well, but because they have much smaller foreign presences (companies and people), and are not traditional centers of Chinese academic accomplishment, there are fewer study abroad programs for Americans there.

Just as U.S. companies have turned their attention from the high-rent, high-wage Beijing and Shanghai metropolitan areas to tier-two and -three cities, so has American study abroad in China. Smaller cities can offer learners a more "Chinese" experience by putting them in a place with fewer opportunities to speak English, and, perhaps more importantly, fewer opportunities to interact with people who are able to adjust their behavior to accommodate Western expectations and customs. Learning how to negotiate life in a traditional Chinese city is a useful skill for any potential China Hand, and will also come in handy in major cities, where many inhabitants are originally from smaller cities and towns.

Finally, location affects the form

How many foreigners do you see in this Wuhan scene?

These folks in rural Sichuan are probably not speaking textbook Mandarin.

of Chinese to which learners will be exposed. Standard Mandarin is the lingua franca of all major institutions of higher education in China, so learners will be able to hear and practice standard pronunciation at universities throughout the country. What changes from place to place, however, is the form of Chinese most commonly spoken off-campus. Though standard Mandarin is based on the Chinese spoken in Beijing, it is commonly believed that the local form of Chinese closest to standard Mandarin (e.g., what is spoken by network news anchors and radio broadcasters) is found in Harbin, a provincial capital tier-two city in northeast China.

The farther you go from Harbin, the further the local speech gets from standard Mandarin. Mandarin is quickly replacing local dialects in much of China as children grow up speaking Mandarin (even if accented) at school and only listening to the local dialect at home, so local students at Chinese universities tend to speak Mandarin, even amongst themselves. Important exceptions are Shanghai and the provinces of Sichuan and Guangdong Province, where the locals are proud of their dialects instead of considering them to be a symbol of provinciality. Beginning learners may want to study in a location where the local dialect is at least a member of the northern Mandarin dialect group just so that off-campus interaction complements on-campus instruction. Intermediate and advanced learners, on the other hand, would benefit from practice speaking with Chinese whose Mandarin may be heavily accented and who may even prefer to speak a different dialect altogether when in the company of other locals.

How many years has the program been in existence?

There are many aspects of program administration that can only be learned by experience. Planning for a new or young program helps, but actual boots-on-the-ground experience helps avoid some problems, and, more importantly, helps program staff effectively deal with the one kind of problem that is guaranteed to pop up: one that has never been seen before. Repeat offerings of a program teaches the operating institutions important lessons about housing, pedagogical methodology, domestic travel, safety, and overall efficacy of the program. Experience means that when an unfamiliar medical condition appears, program staff can rely upon previous experience to react in a prudent fashion.

Simply being in existence for many years is not sufficient, however. In order to capitalize upon all these lessons, a program must maintain an institutional memory of these lessons. This can be achieved through personnel retention and/or easy-to-follow standardized processes (which businesses with high employee turnover, like fast-food restaurants, do). Programs in China that try to reduce the possibility of students encountering events outside of their control (e.g., last-minute schedule changes, cameos in local TV productions, etc.) create a bubble of American culture for their students' comfort. Learners wishing to have an authentic Chinese experience can research how many opportunities for community interaction the target program creates for participants. Each time a program sends or takes its participants out of the Chinese language classroom, it exposes them to the unpredictability of real life in China.

Keep in mind that China only opened up to the West in 1979, so there are few programs with very long track records.[4] A program with 10 years' experience in China can be considered as having had time to learn the ropes. Because few programs have staff that stay for ten years, you can find out how often the staff come and go and learn how continuity is maintained. Many university-run programs are managed by tenured professors who are around for a long time ... but who may have little to do with day-to-day delivery of the program in China. It should be fairly easy to tell how much experience a program's staff has with program delivery—one way would be to just look at the staff bios and photos. Staff in their 20s will be full of youthful exuberance while those in their 30s and 40s are more likely to have been around the block a couple of times.

What are the stated goals of the program? Are there any implicit unstated goals?

As you research different language programs, it will be helpful to see if the program's goals for its participants and yours align. Many programs state their goals explicitly, for example:

---

4 CET would be one of these, having started in 1982 as China Educational Tours.

The Princeton Chinese Language Program has established its own distinctive pedagogy ... based on the belief that a strong foundation with an emphasis on accurate pronunciation and grammar is absolutely necessary for language mastery[5]

or:

Objectives: Develop appropriate cultural behavior, ability to perform effectively in frequently encountered cultural contexts, and interpersonal communication skills.[6]

Based on these two goal descriptions—and other information about the programs on their websites—one can tell that there are some real differences between different programs' intended outcomes for their participants. The important thing is to establish whether or not a program's goals align with your own goals for learning Chinese, and these goals may change over the course of your language learning career. For instance, the Princeton in Beijing program explicitly states above that it focuses on building a strong linguistic foundation, and participants in this program consistently demonstrate excellent skills in the target areas of pronunciation and grammar. Having built this foundation, an advanced learner may wish to switch gears and join a program such as Ohio State's, which trains learners to accomplish tasks with locals who are not paid to communicate with them and who judge the foreign speakers of Chinese by Chinese standards.

Some programs do not have stated goals, but the program design can still tell you the designers' unconscious (or at least unarticulated) objectives. Here is the text from one program's "overview" page:

CCIS Nanjing, China Program Students study on a semester program at Nanjing University in the city of Nanjing, about 200 miles west up the Yangzi River from Shanghai.

First as China's capital of six ancient dynasties including the Ming dynasty (A.D. 1368–1644), then as the capital of the Republic of China from 1911 to 1937, and now as the capital of Jiangsu Province, this bustling city of six million is rich in scenic and historic sights. Major historical sights in Nanjing include: the tomb of Sun Yat-sen, remnants of one of the best preserved ancient walled-cities in China, the tomb complex of the founding emperor of the Ming dynasty, and the Presidential Palace of Chiang Kai-shek (which was also the palace seat for the Taiping Kingdom of Heavenly Peace).[7]

As soon as you find that a program's description consists primarily (or in this case, only) of a

---

5 From Princeton in Beijing's website, February 17, 2014.
6 From Ohio State University's Office of International Affairs website, February 17, 2014.

7 From CCIS Nanjing website, October 6, 2011. www.ccisstudyabroad.org/program.php?link=china_nanjing

There is a lot to see and learn in Nanjing.

description of the program's geographic location, the next stop should be the program's "academics" or "curriculum" page. In this case, the academics page first describes the host Chinese university, implying that local Chinese faculty comprise the core instructional staff of this program.

There are two common threads in traditional teaching of Chinese as a foreign language in China: 1) The belief that if a foreigner learns enough characters, he or she will be able to read and understand written Chinese discourse and also be able to use those characters' spoken forms to engage in culturally-appropriate dialogue with native speakers; 2) No foreigner can really master Chinese, so good enough is good enough. Nanjing University, the host university in the preceding example, happens to be a leader in the field of teaching Chinese as a foreign language, so students there have access to highly effective teaching methodologies.

Under the description of Nanjing University, the "academics" page goes on to describe the courses taught in this program. Listed as a language program on www.studyabroad.com, it is a combination of language courses and courses taught in English about Chinese topics. The curriculum also includes local excursions and a one-week study tour to Beijing. Hence, the unstated goal of this program is to give American learners a managed initial exposure to China. This is also reflected in the alumni feedback that the program chose to post on the website. This kind of program would be perfect for learners whose goals at the time of application are to have "my view of the world and my country expanded enormously," as one alumnus put it.[8]

Does the program offer the level of language instruction that you need?
You may need to take (and sometimes ask for) a placement test to let the program know where you fit. Experienced administrators can often do this after only a brief phone call and perhaps an email or a scanned handwriting sample. Some programs used standardized tests such as the HSK or online tests such as BYU's Computerized Adaptive Test for Reading Chinese and OSU's Computerized Adaptive Listening Comprehension Test.

Programs can be found for students at all levels from true beginner to truly advanced. Many educators caution against beginning foreign language study *in* the target country because the extracurricular experience often becomes an exercise in futility or at least avoidance. If a learner can only use the target language in a classroom setting because he or she has too few linguistic tools, that learner might as well stay in the U.S. and build up the requisite foundational skills. At the other end of the spectrum, truly advanced learners need to leave the classroom-based instruction model and learn to conduct projects in the local community. ACC and Ohio State do this through community research and volunteering projects; Ohio State and EducAsian also do this through internships.

When looking at internship programs, keep in mind that in China, there are both Chinese-language internships and English-language internships. Offices in China in which the language of work is English offer a lower barrier to entry and a nice line on your resume, but they also represent a relatively limited increase in your ability to work on an equal basis with Chinese professionals (ostensibly why you are considering an internship in China instead of at home.). An internship at a Chinese organization, which requires a fairly advanced level of Chinese language ability, does much to teach you how to work in China and with Chinese people. You can intern in China with any level of Chinese language ability, but the more language skill you have, the more you will get out of an internship there.

Is there a resident director who works for the program? Is that person a program employee or an employee of the foreign affairs office at the host institution?
A resident director is someone on-site whose job it is to handle most or all aspects of the program that take place outside of the classroom (and often inside, too). This includes, but is not limited to, coordinating living arrangements and excursions, making sure students are fed and healthy, and resolving interpersonal issues involving students and

---
8 Ibid.

instructors, peers, and locals. Resident directors also play the roles of psychologist and parent-away-from home for students who need it.

In programs with a resident director, students' needs are attended to and the students have a mediator to whom they can turn when resolving sensitive issues. In programs without a resident director, students are largely on their own for day-to-day living, and their success in dealing with issues that arise depends on their own resourcefulness and the willingness of the host university's foreign affairs office (**wàibàn** 外办 or **wàishìchù** 外事处) to get involved.

The difference between having a resident director and having only a foreign affairs office to help is illustrated by the following true story. An American student rented an Internet router from the foreign affairs office to be able to get online in her dorm room. She changed the settings on her laptop as instructed but still could not connect to the Internet. She asked classmates for help, tried changing cables, changing the settings, and everything else she could think of. A good student of Chinese, she then tried to resolve the issue herself through the foreign affairs office. They told her that she should contact the university-contracted Internet hardware maintenance person, a man who also owned the bar/Internet café in the foreign student dormitory. That man was also unable to make the router work with the student's computer, though the student tried many different methods. After about a month, a solution was finally found. At that point, the student went to the foreign affairs office (which collects money on behalf of the contractor when renting out routers) to ask for a refund of the router rental fee she had paid up front for the first unsuccessful month of service. The office told her to talk to the contractor. She talked to the contractor, and he said he only serves the hardware and that she should talk to the office, as they collect the money. When she went back to the office (which, as is custom, is closed for two or more hours every day for lunch and siesta, making it sometimes difficult to find someone to get help from), they told her they would not issue any refund. She then asked the resident director to intercede, which he did... and was given the same response as the student received. He talked to the contractor who, using his own perspective of the situation that involved the student taking too long to bring up the problem to the office (because she was trying to solve it herself), said that the young lady was not entitled to much of a refund at all. Between the student and the resident director, a partial refund was obtained and the negative experience was duly noted. For this and other similar experiences with that host institution, the program was moved to another university the following year. That following year, the program's relations with the foreign affairs office was excellent and the resident director was able to resolve all the issues involving that foreign affairs office that the office was capable of resolving.

Because they play so many roles—many of which are performed differently by natives of China and the U.S.—the origin of the resident director can have an impact on the participant experience. Again, the difference may not be one of "good" vs. "bad" or even "good" vs. "better," but one of personal preference regarding the difference. A Chinese resident director will often be skilled at negotiating the "system," from dealing with the foreign affairs office to negotiating good deals with external service providers. A Chinese resident director may also have a more conservative take on "security" than an American one. For instance, one program in southwest China would not allow the American students to conduct community surveys on academic subjects for fear that the surveys would be political, or at least, perceived as political. At another program in southern China, the idea of Chinese and American students rooming together in on-campus dorms was considered too radical and an invitation for cross-cultural friction.[9]

The ideal situation may be for a program to have both American and local Chinese staff on site. This is not always possible for personnel or economic reasons, but this mixture allows them to play good cop-bad cop, to play the "foreigner card" when something uncomfortable needs to be said, and to apply their relative strengths to the student experience. If you want someone to tell you to drink hot tea and get an IV drip when you're sick, go to the Chinese staff; if you want someone to tell you to drink orange juice and take a pill, go to the American staff.

What are the living arrangements?
In the "old days," foreign students lived insulated from the Chinese experience, even on campus. Of course, Chinese-as-a-foreign-language classes only had foreigners in them, but the living arrangements were particularly segregating: there were foreign student dormitories where non-Chinese students had to live, and where Chinese people had to sign in and out when they visited. At the time, the foreigners were told that such arrangements were for their own security, but there was always a suspicion that it was the Chinese who were being protected from us, rather than vice versa.

Today, the situation is much improved in some places and about the same in others. Some programs now arrange for Chinese roommates who live with the foreign students; others build in homestay experiences that substitute for Chinese roommates where such an arrangement is not allowed or practical. It should be noted that programs that do have Chinese roommates for the foreign learners tend to have achieved that by expending a great deal of energy and goodwill to overcome the local host's unwillingness to entertain such an arrangement.

---
9   Having a Chinese roommate is increasingly common in American programs in China, but many Chinese schools are still not comfortable with this arrangement.

The gate at Jinan University's Zhuhai campus

The most common living arrangement on Chinese campuses is still for the foreigners to live with a foreign roommate in a dormitory specially set aside for non-Chinese. In some cases, these dorms double as campus motels, and thus accept Chinese guests, as well. Though these guests do not live with the American students, they do allow a Chinese environment to permeate the living facilities.

Living in foreign students' dormitories on campus may be fine for students whose goal is to hone linguistic skills in classes, but for those who want to be part of the local community, it is useful to know that Chinese universities themselves are not exactly part of the communities in which they are located. They are essentially self-sufficient walled compounds that a student could stay inside for the entire semester and never lack anything (except for a change of scenery). Students hoping to experience a landlord-tenant relationship, or to learn what it means to visit neighbors simply for the sake of maintaining the relationship through conversation (**chuànmén 串门**) would be hard-pressed to do so from an on-campus base. For younger undergraduate learners who may need some convenience and comfort (and for their resident directors' sanity), on-campus living would be appropriate. For programs in which learners are being trained to be independent foreign members of Chinese society, a break from the campus cocoon is an important component of the process.

As you research the location and living arrangements of short-term Chinese language programs, be aware that it became fashionable

University towns look something like this these days.

about ten years ago for Chinese cities to move their flagship universities to "University Towns" in the outer suburbs. This initiative resulted in many universities having an old downtown campus right in the middle of things but stripped of the main academic departments, and having one or more suburban campuses far away from anything except villages and farm fields. Find out if your program is based in a remote island of Chinese academe, or if you are a hop, skip and a jump away from the myriad learning opportunities that downtown campuses provide. Also find out what public transportation is available at the location of the target program. Ten years from now, the university cities may be the centers of thriving business districts, but for now, they are not.

Some programs provide homestays for part or all of the duration of the program. Homestays are exactly what they sound like–living with a local family. Learners who have positive experiences during their homestay swear by their effectiveness in exposing the foreigner into Chinese culture. Learners who have neutral or negative experiences also appreciate the learning value of the homestay, though for different reasons. Managing homestay experiences is very time consuming for a study abroad program, and some programs believe that the positive outcomes achieved by some homestay students can also be achieved in a well-run dormitory-based program. The primary challenge in offering a homestay component of a study abroad program is that there is a relatively narrow demographic that makes a good host family: wealthy enough to not do it for the doing homestays, the larger their pool of potential homestay families, and the more likely it is that they will be able to place students with good homes. That said, "good" for one student may be not so good for another. Like roommates, homestay families represent a chance at an amazing experience, but come with no guarantees.

Hosts participating in long term homestays often become "expert" in dealing with American youth. That manifests itself in the ability to anticipate and avoid potential problems their student guests might encounter. The result can be that the guests are in their comfort zone more of the time, or it can be that the guests never learn to negotiate the discomforts of living in another culture.

Is there a U.S. partner? If so, is there a credit transfer process in place? If not, can the program provide paperwork that you can use to apply for home institution credit?

An increasing number of Chinese universities are marketing their language programs directly to foreign students, without going through an intermediary such as an American university or organization that aggregates students and then delivers them to the Chinese program providers. Applying directly to a Chinese university is much cheaper than going through a U.S.-managed program … because you don't have the overhead that comes with hiring U.S. staff, including an American or U.S.-trained Chinese resident

Maybe you can stay in a new neighborhood like this one in Guizhou.

money; available to be active hosts during the entire homestay period; conveniently located near program activities; and have personalities that will make for a positive experience. In order to meet the volume needs of each cohort of students, study abroad programs sometimes must recruit homestay families that do not meet all of their criteria. The longer a program has been director. See the section on resident directors (page 59) to determine whether you would mind not having a U.S.-trained staff member on site. Some American students go to China on a U.S.-managed program for their initial trip, and then either return or simply stay for a Chinese university-managed program because they are comfortable enough in the language and culture to handle a less mediated Chinese experience.

Programs with a U.S.-based partner will not only have representation in the United States that can be contacted for answers to all your questions (in understandable English and without the delay of time-zone shifted email receipt and response), but who can also facilitate credit transfer if you need it. Some U.S.-based programs already have U.S. institution credit built into the program: the Inter-University Program for Chinese Language Studies (IUP) awards Indiana University credit that can be transferred among institutions in the U.S. with relative ease. Other U.S.-based programs can work with their Chinese partners to produce transcripts and other documentation necessary for credit transfer. This is useful because many American universities require documentation for credit transfer that Chinese universities do not normally produce for their own courses, including course syllabi, grading rubrics and distributable copies of exams.

Is the program designed for a particular U.S. school's domestic Chinese program? If so, how are outside applicants handled?

Among American-managed study abroad programs, you will find non-profits that serve students from anywhere, consortia of smaller colleges that primarily aggregate member school students, programs contracted to Chinese universities for individual U.S. universities' students, and programs delivered in-country by a combination of U.S.- and China-based staff. For any program that is institutionally housed at a single American university, it will be helpful to ascertain how much that program is simply an overseas component of a unique domestic U.S. Chinese program, and how well that program can accommodate students from outside that U.S. Chinese program.

If you are considering a program that was designed for a single American university's students but that also accepts outside students, how does that program:

- Evaluate skill level pre-program for appropriate course placement; re-evaluate placement post-arrival, as necessary?
- Ensure that all students are treated like part of one community?
- Process requests for credit that can be transferred?
- Deliver pre-departure orientation information and materials (including insurance cards)?
- Obtain participants' passports for visa processing? Return those passports?

If you fall in love with another school's program, but find that they are not experienced in handling non-local students, do not despair. Reasonable and intelligent program administrators can figure all these things out if they are new to accepting outside applicants.

Is there a language pledge, and how do you feel about that?
One of the most controversial aspects of overseas study program design is whether or not a program should have a language pledge. A language pledge is a promise made by the students and teachers not to speak the students' native language for the duration of the program. Proponents of the language pledge system say that it is the only way to create an immersion environment for students who are going to China on a program, which, by definition, is populated by other English speakers whose natural inclination is to speak English with one another. On the other side, program managers who decline to institute a language pledge believe that 1) practicing Chinese with other non-native speakers often leads to the use of Chinese words as a cipher for English sentences and intentions instead of culturally-appropriate Chinese ones, and, 2) refusing to speak English in China reduces the population of China to the role of language study servant for the Americans, rather than language study partners who engage in relationship-building exchanges of language.

Proponents of each method will swear up and down that the other side is pedagogically unsound in this regard, and both can provide ample anecdotal evidence supporting their positions, so you will have to make up your own mind on the subject. If you are interested in a program that does not have a language pledge, but do not trust yourself to seek opportunities to speak Chinese with Chinese people, you can consider suggesting to your classmates a modified language pledge. Some study abroad programs begin with an opportunity for their participants to draft their own behavioral expectations document. At this time, you could create a language pledge that requires program participants to:

- Speak Chinese whenever possible.
- Speak Chinese with fellow Americans as long as the communication follows Chinese standards and thus could be repeated with a native speaker for effective communication.[10]
- Speak English with Chinese natives when it serves a strategic, relationship-building purpose.[11]

---

10 Unlike the "joke" I once heard an American student say to his classmate: "什么上, 医生?" Translated literally, this is "What's up, doc?," but to a native speaker, it is completely gibberish.

11 Many Chinese parents want their children to practice English. An American student who helps a Chinese child practice English will then enter into a cycle of friendship-building reciprocity with the parents...who probably cannot speak English, thus drawing the student into a Chinese-speaking community.

Long-Term Programs

We defined a short-term program as one lasting one academic term to one academic year and resulting in no degree. Most programs in China for foreigners fall under that category, but as American Chinese language education and Chinese higher education develop, there are more and more offerings of one year or more that result in a Chinese degree for foreign learners. These programs can be divided into degree-granting programs delivered in Chinese and degree-granting programs delivered in English.

■ Long-Term English-Language Programs

From 1979 to now, Chinese industry has been busy learning Western business and manufacturing practices so as to be able to compete on the world market for increasingly higher segments of the value curve. Chinese manufacturing capacity has moved from making cheap teddy bears using the foreign customers' designs, right up to the complex business of airplane design and construction. Now, Chinese education has gotten on board with learning foreign practices in order to compete internationally.

An increasing number of Chinese universities have started degree-granting programs delivered in English that are designed to attract foreign students, the idea being that world-class American and European universities attract students from around the globe, so Chinese universities should learn to move into this space, as well. Universities that have gotten into this field include (but are not limited to): Beijing University of Aeronautics and Astronautics, People's University, Beijing Normal University, Central China Normal University, Fudan University, Southwest Jiaotong University, Zhengzhou University, and Xiamen University. These programs include four-year undergraduate programs, as well as graduate programs of anywhere from two-to-three years in length. Majors offered include math, engineering of all kinds, economics, law, medicine, business/management, and physics. Many of these classes are taught by "sea turtles," a homonym for the Chinese word for 'overseas returnee'—Chinese natives educated overseas who return to China to work.

The advantage of joining these English degree-granting programs is twofold: price ... and price. For most Americans, obtaining an English language degree in China is not as attractive as earning one in the U.S., so we will focus on graduate programs. The average tuition in an English-language graduate degree in China is about ¥30,000/year for a three-year program. In late 2011, this was about US$5,000/year. By comparison, a master's degree from the Ohio State University cost $29,000/year in 2011. Before anyone starts drooling over the price difference, remember that a master's degree in petrochemical engineering from Beijing University of Aeronautics and Astronautics carries a different weight on the international labor market (or even just the American labor market) than a similar degree from a U.S. institution does.... which is exactly what Chinese universities hope to change as they learn how to build and run first-rate English language programs.

The other price advantage is that the Chinese government is throwing cash at the development of world-class degree programs, and part of this cash is available to foreign learners in the form of scholarships and graduate assistantships. At the People's University MS in Finance program, for instance, foreign students can earn a 50 percent tuition waiver in return for part-time work as English instructors. The availability of scholarship funds, rather than (currently nonexistent) prestige associated with the degree is what currently draws Americans to these English-language Chinese university degree programs. Many Americans want to return to China for further study after completing their undergraduate study but do not want to go back as an English teacher. The English-language degree programs' scholarships make it possible for Americans to return to China on the Chinese government dime, while at the same time adding another degree notch to their belts, which could, in fact, be useful if they end up working in China and have gone to a respected Chinese university. A good listing of this type of program can be found at www.cucas.edu.cn.

■ Long-Term Chinese-Language Degree-Granting Programs

If your goal in going to China is to improve your Chinese and you can obtain funding for a Chinese language degree-granting program, you can now direct-enroll in regular university classes at the undergraduate and graduate level at a growing number of Chinese universities. It is still no walk in the park for a foreigner—especially one who is not ethnically Asian—to register for and then attend Chinese classes for Chinese students, but some universities already have experience doing this, and many others are open to the idea even if they have never done it before or know how to do it, institutionally.

One of the earliest programs allowing direct enrollment in a Chinese university was not degree-granting, but it got the ball rolling. The Chinese Flagship program's Nanjing Center, originally run by Brigham Young University, helped Americans enrolled in Chinese Flagship programs around the United States take classes in their field at Nanjing University alongside their Chinese peers. Perhaps recognizing the trend toward more foreigners reaching a level of Chinese ability that would allow them to take classes about other subjects in Chinese, Chinese universities began opening up certain majors to foreign students.

Currently, the field that most commonly sees foreign students taking classes in Chinese is medicine. A significant number of students from developing countries in Africa and South Asia go to China to earn a medical degree because Chinese education is more advanced and/or more accessible than in their home countries. Enrolling in programs with existing foreigner enrollments is easier because there are people you can ask for advice.

If you are interested in a major that currently has few or no foreign students pursuing it, you will have to learn how to find out what classes are offered when there may not be a course catalog. You will have to learn who teaches the classes you want to take so that you can earn their permission to take the class. Again, because many schools do not regularly publish course offerings, and who will actually teach a course can change at the last minute, this can be difficult, too.

Once you are in your classes, you will need to figure out what is required of students in the class. Many expectations in Chinese classes are unspoken because they have been learned prior to college. There is usually no syllabus, rarely are there any articulated reading assignments shorter than entire books, few homework assignments, and the final grade may be based on only one or two exams. All of this must be ascertained by a proactive student. The professor has enough to do already without spoon-feeding Chinese education culture to a foreigner who was crazy enough to take his class for Chinese students.

Despite all the challenges, the advantage of having a Chinese degree, especially a Chinese graduate degree that follows an American undergraduate degree in the same field, is that you are eminently employable to organizations on both sides of the Pacific. This assumes that your degree is from a major university in a major city, but few Americans have considered any other kind of Chinese degree. If you are applying to be a retail store manager in Wyoming, a Chinese degree will not be very helpful, but if you are applying for a job with an international NGO or a multinational corporation, a Chinese degree in your major field means that you not only know your stuff in your field but that you can talk about it in Chinese, as well. There are currently very, very few Americans who can say this about their Chinese ability, and most of them have either spent decades in China or are graduates of a Chinese Flagship program at Brigham Young or Ohio State.

There are many ways an American can get to China for an educational experience, from brief skips across the surface of the culture to full-on immersion in the Chinese education system. The type of program you choose to join in order to go over depends on your personal goals for the visit, both short-term and long-term. For many people, they do not even know if they will have long-term goals that include China until they have gone a first time. For this reason, it is usually recommended—and research supports the idea—that first-timers do not spend too long in-country on their first visit. All but the most insular and sterile programs in China will provide first-time visitors with many sights, smells, tastes, sounds and, most of all, ideas that will challenge an American's sense of what is "normal."

Some find this challenge exciting and want more; others find it annoying at best or downright upsetting at worst. Finding out if you are excited or put off by experiencing China is best done on a program no more than a semester in length. Going home after a few weeks or months gives you an opportunity to recharge or reevaluate. The recharged ones will have a chance to brush up on things they need help with while they have the benefit of a U.S.-trained Chinese language teacher; the re-evaluators will have a chance to compare experiences in China that seemed negative at the time to real life in the United States (as opposed to an idealized recollection that may have come to mind while in China). When the author first went to China in 1997, he spent a summer and a semester there; when he reached LAX on the way home in December, he was overjoyed to be back. After a month in Virginia, however, he was itching to go back to China.

Use the Internet and the list of programs in Appendix E (page 314) to find programs that are attractive to you. Then, use the checklist of questions in this chapter to evaluate the suitability of those programs to your personal goals. You may have to send an email to a program coordinator or two to get all the answers you want. Sometimes the lack of an answer or the incomprehensibility of an answer is answer enough for the purposes of deciding to which programs to apply.

In the next chapter, we will assume that you have been accepted to the program of your choice and it is time to get ready to go. What do you need to do to get ready? What shots do you need? What should you pack? How do you get your mind in the right place (just as important as packing deodorant)? It is during the activities described in Chapter 3, "Before You Go," (page 72) that you slowly come to realize, "Hey, I'm going to CHINA!" We'll help take the edge off of the anxiety that can crop up when you get to that point.

A Note on Accessibility

If you have a physical handicap, you need to know at the very beginning that China is not a handicapped-accessible country. As sweeping as this statement sounds, it is simply reality. There are a limited number of handicapped-accessible facilities in the tier-one cities of Beijing, Shanghai, Guangzhou and Shenzhen, but in tier-two cities and smaller, handicapped accessibility is limited to curb cuts where the sidewalk meets the street, and a strip of raised bumps in sidewalks for blind people to follow. The bumps are a noble thought, but they often end abruptly, sometimes lead straight into trees, poles, electrical cabinets and dangerously high curbs. Ramps in front of buildings are almost always put there for aesthetic reasons and not accessibility ones, so even if a wheelchair-bound person went up the ramp toward a building's entrance, there may still be a step to go up to actually enter.

If you have a handicap, ask programs in which you are interested if and how they can accommodate it. If they cannot, it is not their fault. China simply is not a handicapped-friendly environment yet, and there is only so much that one program can do to change that. Handicapped or not, China is not going to change for foreigners and foreigners will have to adapt to China. If you have a handicap, you will not have the range of freedom in China that you do in the U.S. You may be limited to living and taking classes in the same building; you may be limited in the hotels in which you can stay; you may be limited in the restaurants you can frequent; you will be limited in your transportation options.

If you have a handicap and still go to China, consider it as an opportunity to show the locals by example what handicapped people can do, rather than as an opportunity to criticize them for not having something comparable to the Americans with Disabilities Act.

Just crossing the street can be a challenge.

Chapter 3
Before You Go

There are a few things you need to do before you make a successful trip to China. First, you will want to get your mind in the right place. Then, you may want to work on your Chinese skills a little, even if you already speak some Chinese. While you are doing that, you will be getting your travel ducks in a row with immunizations, your visa, airplane tickets, and, finally, packing. This chapter will guide you through these steps, passing along the collective experience of many people who have gone through this process before you.

Mental Preparation

On trips of a month or more, it is likely that you will experience some form of culture shock. Culture shock is the feeling that you are in a foreign environment and the physical effects this conscious–and subconscious–realization can produce. This can happen in your native country as well as in a foreign country: one friend of the author described his moves from Philadelphia to bayou Louisiana to Charleston, West Virginia, as bringing on culture shocks almost as great as international moves. Knowing ahead of time that you are going to experience culture shock makes it easier to recognize when it hits, which, in turn, allows you to take measures to deal with it when the shock results in discomfort.

Culture shock comes in phases (see chart below); the time it takes to go from phase to phase varies from person to person, but it is rare to skip a phase entirely.

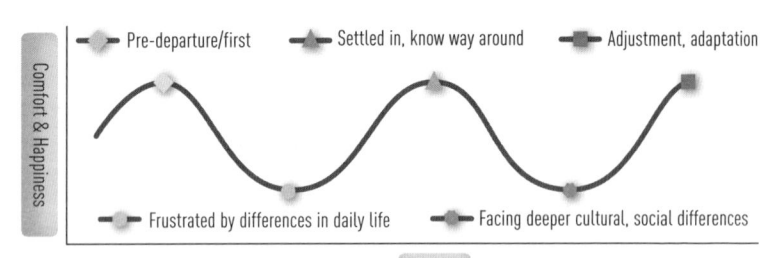

The cultural adjustment curve

I sent a postcard all by myself!

Except for those who go against their will (like some expatriated employees and their dependents), most people who travel to China begin their experience feeling the elation of seeing and doing completely new things. For those who studied the language and are finding that their use of Chinese leads to the anticipated result, the satisfaction is tremendous. The "I did it!" times make you feel like China is a place where you are realizing your full potential as an explorer of exotic places. This feeling of success also leads some people in this stage to feel qualified to explain all kinds of cultural differences based on a very limited number of data points. Even if you are not in a position to be trying out Chinese language skills, you will also experience the honeymoon phase as you visit temples, ride through villages and valleys unlike anything at home, and try foods that, even if you do not enjoy them, are so far outside your comfort zone you feel like you are in a movie. In these early days when you feel on top of the world, take advantage of the feeling to reach out and make new friends and do and see even more new things.

After some time–again, this varies from person to person–the feeling of elation begins to wear off. This happens when things you expect to happen don't and when things you do not expect to happen, do … and not in your favor. When you first arrive, these experiences are just part of the excitement of being in a new place, but after you settle into a routine, you start to expect that your routine in the new country should be as reliable as it would be at home. And then, the Internet goes out. Or the hot shower turns cold while you are in it. Or

If you have a sensitive stomach, don't buy snacks from the back of a tricycle.

the teacher of your class does not follow the syllabus handed out at the beginning of the term, and you don't know what to prepare in order to keep your 4.0 GPA. This is the shocking part of culture shock.

When too many of these things happen in one day, some expats call it a "China Day." This is a little unfair, since we have bad days in our own country when things don't go as planned. The difference is that in a foreign country, we start by blaming the foreign country for being foreign! When a non-Chinese person complains about the hygiene in a hole-in-the-wall US$3/entrée Chinese restaurant, the Chinese there wonder why the foreigner chose to be there. Indeed, if you choose to go to China—and you have finished this book—you should have an idea of what you are in for before you arrive. So, if you need to let off steam because you've had a "China Day," think twice before you complain to a Chinese person, no matter how "international" he or she seems to be.

Cross-cultural travelers compare the host culture to their own in an attempt to frame their understanding of the new culture, as well as to be able to explain the host culture to friends and family back home. It is very useful to engage in this activity of comparison and analysis, but it is important to make these comparisons carefully. During low periods in the cultural adjustment cycle, sweeping generalizations come all too easily.

Perhaps you are taking a taxi through suburban[1] Shanghai, late for an appointment, and you see an

---

1 What Chinese people call "suburbs" are farms and relatively dense but not high-end residential and business real estate found outside a major city.

old woman helping her grandchild use the gutter as a toilet. If you are having a bad day, you might think, "what a filthy country." Certainly, using public areas to relieve oneself is not very hygienic (for others), but it would be grossly inaccurate to deduce that the entire country is filthy and Chinese people do not have any regard for cleanliness. If you stop to think about additional supporting as well as counterexamples, you can start to reach a more nuanced understanding of the situation. What kinds of people make potty in public? Are they from urban professional or rural peasant backgrounds? Are public areas treated differently from private areas? Are individual apartments cleaner than the buildings in which they are located? Do you need to take off your shoes in Chinese homes? Shower before bed? If Chinese are so concerned about having a clean home, why are public spaces often dirty?

If you can put your observations in perspective, not only can you avoid potentially inaccurate stereotypes, but you may also reach an understanding of the situation that is based on the native experience instead of one framed by your own experience. Using American standards, you might assume that a grandmother who directs her grandchild to pee on the street lives in a dirty home. However, further reflection based even on limited experience in China will show that there is an important difference between public and private space in how some portions of Chinese

Hanging out with other foreigners sometimes is normal and healthy, but do try to branch out and socialize with locals who usually socialize with other locals.

society view the world. At the same time, there are other groups in Chinese society who are brought up to treat public space more like private space, even if not to the same extent that Americans are used to. There is probably a doctoral dissertation on this topic somewhere, if you are interested.

During the period when you are adjusting to life in China and its attendant unexpected events, it is natural to have a physical response to mental discomfort. Some people feel insecure in their daily lives and want stay in bed longer than before; others find that this insecurity leads to insomnia. Some people who try to isolate themselves from Chinese culture during this phase of adjustment seek out expatriate companionship in order to reassure themselves that "normal" life still exists. Ideally, these foreign friends—usually program classmates—will help each other get through the frustration and avoidance phase of cultural adjustment. Sometimes, however, the group simply closes itself off from the local environment, frequenting establishments designed for foreigners and continuing to complain about how foreign the foreign country is.

This is as close to jalapeños as you are likely to get in China.

After a visitor to China overcomes the initial frustrations of adjusting to normal daily life, there is a period during which daily routines are no longer a challenge and the stay becomes relatively comfortable. This phase, called surface adjustment by some, may last for the remainder of the program, depending on the design and length of the program. If the program has created a relatively isolated community for its American/foreign participants, dealing with differences in daily life may be the only thing its students need to do to become comfortable before going home. In programs with more interaction between participants and local culture, however, another "shock" phase in the cultural adjustment process is common. This is a time when deeper cultural differences begin to cause discomfort. In the first low phase, the problem was simply finding a way to have a chimichanga when you just absolutely had to have one. In this second low point, you encounter deeper challenges that may lead you to ask yourself if you picked the right culture/language to study.

It is one thing to be challenged by a lack of Tex-Mex food; it is another one entirely if you discover that personal time and space are very important to you, and that your definitions of these things are different from those of mainstream Chinese culture. To rise out of this phase, you basically have three choices: quit and go home; limit your interactions in China to foreigners and like-minded locals; or adapt. Quitting your program mid-stream is an expensive choice but preferable to having a nervous breakdown. Limiting your interactions in China to other foreigners would stunt your growing understanding of Chinese culture and language but would have a minimal effect on your grades in most study abroad programs. Adapting to the situation will make your experience more enjoyable, more educational, and prepare you for a lifetime of repeated cultural adjustment cycles.

It is important to understand that adaptation does not require discarding your beliefs. Rather, it means finding ways to accommodate the host culture instead of making them accommodate yours. Accommodating someone else's culture is essentially a test of patience, and it is up to those of us who choose to study and work in foreign cultures to accommodate ourselves to the host culture and not vice versa. We visitors must accommodate the hosts not only because it is culturally appropriate (more on this in the dining section), but because host country nationals who are forced to adjust their behaviors to suit visitors' behaviors will start avoiding the foreigners or expect to get something in return for their patience. If you want to have an equal adult relationship with local natives, you will need to accommodate their behavioral and social expectations. These adult relationships are absolutely necessary for your continued study of Chinese language and culture, and, eventually, for applying your knowledge to professional interactions with Chinese natives.

Adapting to Chinese culture means finding culturally appropriate ways to achieve your goals while still protecting your personal interests. Take the personal space example: success in most sectors of Chinese society requires expanding and cementing personal relationships through frequent shared experiences (often dining), as well as through reciprocal doing of favors (even if not asked for or required); all this eating and favor-doing takes a lot of time, time that some Americans might like to have spent climbing a mountain alone or building a ship model. What is an introvert to do? You could find a Chinese model shipbuilding club... but then you would find that Chinese model shipbuilders are still Chinese, and so seek to build and expand social networks. You can adapt by learning how Chinese people protect their time while maintaining positive social relationships. Like new parents watching the DVR after their toddler has gone to sleep, you might find new times of the day during which your pursuit of model shipbuilding (or whatever) is unlikely to conflict with Chinese relationship building. You could do this early in the morning, late at night, or simply apologize to your potential dinner host for having another engagement that evening, but you would love to get together any other day that week. Sure, China is not going to change for you, but in a country with 5,000 years of philosophy and 1.3 billion people, you can find Chinese ways of doing what *you* want to do. If you want to do or say something, a Chinese person has probably done it in a Chinese way before.

You can work together with your program-mates to get back to peaks on the curve, but there are things you can do on your own, as well. Furthermore, the basic act of taking charge of your situation will also have a positive effect on your feelings:

- First, make sure you are exercising. You should be doing this at home, too, but when you are abroad, it is especially important because keeping fit will help you fight the new viruses and bacteria to which you are being exposed, and exercising also makes your body produce endorphins, the chemical that makes you feel good. If you are not accustomed to exercising, start out light and work your way up.

Be forewarned that you may need to adopt a new exercise regimen if you were accustomed to working out before you arrived in China. Fitness centers have become much more common in first and second tier cities over the past ten years, but it may take a bus ride to reach your nearest one. Having to wait for a crowded public bus to travel forty minutes to a gym when you only had a ten-minute drive in light traffic back at home can itself lead to culture shock if you are not prepared for it, but now you are!

- Second, make sure you get outside. Force yourself to leave the comfort of your dorm room and go for a walk. See the sights. Smile at people. Be smiled at.

Go for a walk and chat with friendly people.

- Third, make a Chinese friend. Having a friendly relationship with a local who you are happy to see and who is happy to see you gives you a whole new outlook when you're abroad. You will then have someone to practice your language with, someone to learn the culture from, someone you look forward to sharing things with, and, most importantly, someone who can introduce you to other Chinese people. As your relationship network grows in China, so will your attachments and your comfort level.

Also, be forewarned that Chinese expectations regarding friendship can be different from American ones, so this important method for reducing culture shock itself involves some culture shock. Your new friend(s) will eventually start asking you for help—probably involving some child's English skills—which just means that you can ask them for help when you need it, too. Maybe you need help finding a good gym! This is friendship in China.

There are many different visual representations of the cultural adjustment process. Some of them are like the curve shown above; others are a simple U, with the visitor only feeling good again when it is time to go home; yet others are an elongated version of the W-model we are using, with the visitor's mood going up and down over and over until repatriation. A fourth model has the curve going up and down during the duration of the visit, but flattening out over time, with the visitor experiencing periodic swings in his or her feelings toward the host country, but generally feeling like he or she is on an even keel. It is hard to say which of these models will fit your experience, but you and your program mates will experience some form of one or more of them. Now you know what to do when it happens.

Language Practice

It is a good policy to know some of the language of your target country any time you take a trip abroad. If you are already a student of the Chinese language, continue using your class materials to prepare. If you are going without any previous language study, use the phrases inserted at relevant points throughout this book, and create for yourself a program of study using commercially and/or freely available materials.

Chinese language educators tend to have self-study materials they prefer and materials they feel are ineffective. Perhaps language self-study is similar to exercising–there are more and less efficient ways of reaching your goal, but if you maintain a rigorous program of practice and have someone ahead of you on the curve to provide feedback, you will make useful progress no matter what. As you review your options for purchase and/or download, keep in mind the following questions:

Is an audio program provided?
You really cannot learn to speak Chinese without native speaker audio input. There are Romanizations of spoken Chinese, but they are simply methods of putting Chinese sounds on paper using the alphabet that English speakers use. For example, the capital of China is written 北京 in Chinese, but Romanized as "Beijing" in *hanyu pinyin* and "Pei-ching" in Wade-Giles Romanization ... all with the same pronunciation in standard Mandarin. If you do not know how to make the sound that is written with a "j"in pinyin or "ch" in Wade-Giles, seeing these letters on paper will not teach it to you; you need an audio input to learn that sound because it does not exist in American English. The same situation applies to many sounds in Mandarin.

If no audio program comes with the materials, ignore the set and move on.

What is the basic unit of communication assumed by the authors?
You can find many learning materials that take words or even individual Chinese characters as the basic unit of communication. Adults expect other adults to speak in complete, even if simple, sentences. If you are going to spend time learning some of the language, you might as well learn how to speak like an adult. After all, people who speak like two-year-olds tend to be treated like two-year-olds. Once you have a foundation of culturally and linguistically appropriate sentence-level utterances for use in human dialogue,

then you can plug-'n-chug new words into those complete sentences.

When are reading and writing introduced?

An early or immediate reliance on Chinese characters for delivering new material makes it difficult for new non-native learners to access the content and can cause self-study to come to a premature end. Learning Chinese characters is fun, but getting to the point where you can communicate with them takes time to reach. Chinese people learn to speak Chinese *for years* before they learn to read or write, so look for materials that start with—or even stay with—pinyin Romanization in volume one.

Do the materials teach reading and writing of the things that a new arrival would have cause to read or write?

People who go to China with limited previous language study will have limited reading needs and even less need to write right out of the jetway. Items you should be able to read include: *man* 男 **nán**, *woman* 女 **nü**, *toilet* 厕所 **cèsuǒ**, *exit* 出口 **chūkōu**, *entrance* 入口 **rùkōu**, *tickets* 票 **piào**, *east* 东 **dōng**, *south* 南 **nán**, *west* 西 **xī** and *north* 北 **běi**,[2] common last names, professional titles, and phone and fax numbers. Things that you do not need to learn to read or write when cramming for a trip to China include: dialogues about likes and dislikes, paragraph-length letters or stories, comic strips written for beginning learners of Chinese, and so on.

Pedestrians crossing the street; please use the underpass.

Do the materials teach Wade-Giles Romanization and traditional characters (used in Taiwan), or pinyin Romanization and simplified characters (used on the Mainland)?

Many native speakers will tell you that the ancestors are rolling in their graves every time someone learns one format instead of the other, but as far as non-native speakers are concerned, it is a practical question instead of an emotional one. If you are going to the Mainland, start with pinyin and simplified characters; if you are going to Taiwan, start with Wade-Giles and traditional characters. If you intend to stick with Chinese for professional use, you will eventually want to learn to read both forms of writing. Wade-Giles Romanization was the most popular form of Chinese Romanization for about 100 years, and traditional characters were used to write over 2,000 years' worth of Chinese documents; pinyin is now the official Romanization

---

2   Chinese lists the cardinal directions in clockwise order starting from East, not up-down-right-left, as in English.

黄鹤楼送孟浩然之广陵
故人西辞黄鹤楼
烟花三月下扬州
孤帆远影碧空尽
唯见长江天际流

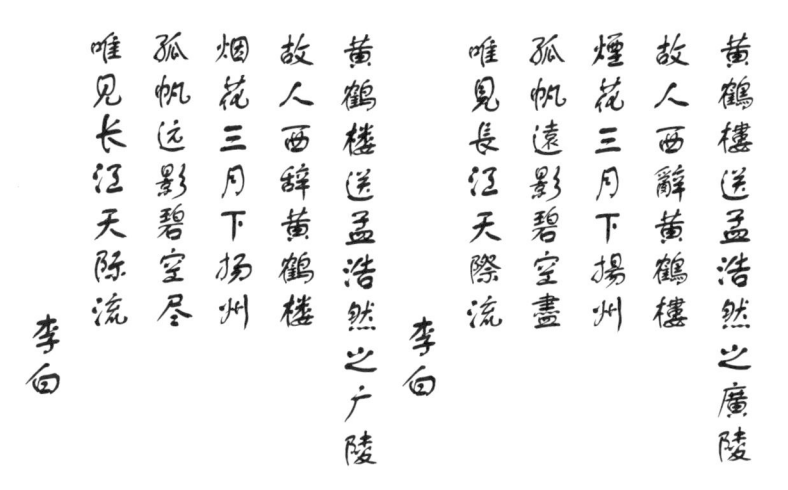

李白

黃鶴樓送孟浩然之廣陵
故人西辭黃鶴樓
煙花三月下揚州
孤帆遠影碧空盡
唯見長江天際流

李白

A poem by Li Bai in traditional (right) and simplified (left) character calligraphy

for both the Mainland and Taiwan (though in the latter, Wade-Giles remains the de facto Romanization), and simplified characters are the official form of writing for the PRC and Singapore. Educated Chinese of any origin can read both simplified and traditional characters, even if they cannot write them both.

Are the topics in volume one such that you can talk to native speakers in a way that leads to further friendly exchanges?

This means being able to meet people, introduce yourself, say who you are and where you come from, ask simple questions of your conversant, and express positive—even if limited—opinions. Phrases for "survival" in China are peppered throughout this book, but as one wise Chinese language educator once said, he "survived Vietnam without speaking a word of Vietnamese." You can find a restroom in China without speaking the language, but making friends requires more than hand gestures.

Is there a mechanism for self-evaluation?

Some materials provide self-tests and even built-in software for recording your language production for playback and comparison with native-spoken samples of the same material. These are useful for gauging your language production and progress. The more the self-evaluation is based on real-life skills, the better. For instance, it is more useful for you to be able to answer questions (in English) about the content of a subway announcement (in Chinese) than it is to do fill-in-the-blank items that test your understanding of word class or syntax. Self-evaluation tools are something of an icing-on-the-cake item, as you can get feedback from native speakers in your community and online.

Now that you know some things to look for in self-study Chinese language materials, you can hit the Internet and your local bookstore. Once you have chosen a primary set of materials and can pronounce pinyin Romanization accurately, you can also use one of the phrasebooks designed for travelers listed in the appendix to expand your repertoire. Below are some recommended materials for beginner self-study of Chinese (in no particular order):

- *Chinese: Communicating in the Culture*, by Galal Walker and Lang Yong. Created by the National East Asian Language Resource Center at the Ohio State, this series is designed for both self-study and classroom use. The workbook comes with audio instructional materials in MP3 format and there is an interactive CD-Rom that can be used with or instead of the workbook. The materials are designed for adult interaction with native speakers, starting with very simple exchanges. Professor Walker is internationally known within the Chinese language instruction and cross-cultural exchange communities.
- *Basic Spoken Chinese*, by Cornelius Kubler. Like CCC above, this is designed by and for American learners of Chinese. It includes a CD-Rom with videos of language use by native speakers from many different Chinese-speaking areas, giving learners practice listening to a variety of native accents. Professor Kubler is well-respected in the Chinese language instruction community.
- ChinesePod.com. An extremely popular online set of materials that is kept up to date by staff in Shanghai and is highly portable for the modern wired learner.

Polish a Performance Skill

If you thought the Chinese are a shy, demure people, get ready for a news flash: Chinese people tend to be quiet when people of authority are speaking, but there are many times when artistic performance is expected. If you are going to China as a student, you should prepare some kind of performance that you can whip out when needed. Being ready for it will make you less uncomfortable, score you brownie points, and also help avoid the confusion that many Chinese people feel when the famously outgoing Americans are asked to perform something but we just sputter and blush. The good news is, there are only a few set times that performances are expected, and only a limited set of performances are commonly seen at those times. The bad news is, American students in China are almost certainly going to encounter at least one of these situations, whether you like performing or not.

As long as your program is designed to expose you to authentic Chinese culture, your Chinese host institution should have a welcome party when you arrive and a going-away party shortly before you leave. The welcome party may be a tame banquet at which your teacher does most of the work, chatting up the host institution's leadership. If Chinese people play roles in your program other than instructional staff (e.g., roommates, home stay families, language partners, etc.), the welcome banquet may also involve a variety show ice-breaker. When Chinese students think of "party," they generally think of these planned, programmed variety shows in which groups of students take turns going in front of the others and do one of the following:

- Sing a song
- Perform a skit
- Tell a joke or a story
- Dance
- Lead the group in a game; losers of the game must do something performative.

Such events usually have two emcees, one American and one Chinese or one male and one female. Their job is to keep the show moving along, introduce the acts, tell jokes between acts, and generally keep the audience entertained/informed.

The going-away party will probably look very much like the welcome banquet, except now everyone has become friends and the skits and songs are based on these new friendships. During the program, there may be similar variety shows put on for visiting dignitaries, or if the group goes on a trip and there are times when a Chinese party is needed (like if a combined Chinese-American group is spending the night in a middle-of-nowhere town on the way to somewhere famous, and you must entertain yourselves).

So, how can you prepare for these parties? You only need a repertoire of one to three performances to get through your program. In fact, that should be enough to get you through most of your involve-

Sean Keith reciting poetry at a banquet

A duet of international friendship in Mengyin, Shandong

ment with Chinese culture, unless you go into television or a performance profession.

The easiest performance to pick up is singing a song to karaoke. Multimedia classrooms and halls often turn into karaoke clubs for these variety shows; if you can sing a song or two, no one will bother you if you stop after that. Learn at least one English language song and, if you can, learn at least one Chinese song. The best songs to learn depend on your age group. Here are some safe recommendations based on what kinds of songs are commonly available in China, though there are, of course, many other options:

It is also a good idea to learn at

Age Group	English	Chinese
Born in 50s		Revolutionary ("red") songs
Born in 60s or 70s	"Country Roads," "Changing Partners," "Hey Jude," "Yesterday," "Yesterday Once More," songs by Michael Jackson	Anything by Deng Lijun, Zhang Xueyou, Liu Dehua, Zhou Huajian
Born in 80s	Mostly same as above	Taiwanese pop music
Born in 90s	Top 40 music since 2005	Top hits you can find on Sogou*

* Sogou.com 歌曲 Top 100, music.sogou.com/song/topsong.html.

least one song well enough that you can perform it without reading the lyrics, and without any kind of musical accompaniment. The City of Columbus, Ohio once held a welcome banquet for a delegation from its sister city, Hefei, Anhui, at which the Chinese asked that one person from each side give a performance to break the ice. The Chinese, being used to this, pointed to one of their delegates who, in addition to being a government official, was also an amateur singer. She had no problem singing at the drop of a hat. The Americans, on the other hand, nervously looked at each other and took turns averring that someone else in the group should sing. Finally, someone suggested that all the Americans join together and sing the Ohio State University alma mater... except no one knew all the words! Finally, someone produced a smart phone, found the lyrics online, and was able to share with the few people who could see the little screen. The Chinese were definitely entertained! This anecdote also goes to show that any social event involving Chinese people can turn into a performance venue, so be prepared.

Skit performances are usually saved for farewell variety shows, when there is humorous material that would be understood by members of the audience that had participated in the program. Over the years, there have been reenactments of program excursions, friendly imitations of certain instructors' classes (and the students in them), and so on. If you

It's your turn next.

already have a performance skill, such as playing the piano or guitar, or doing magic tricks, by all means, continue to do those—they will set you apart and help people remember you. It takes time to reach the point at which you would be comfortable performing something for an audience, so start practicing as soon as you know you're going.

Immunizations

About three months before your anticipated departure date (even if you have not yet bought your tickets), schedule an appointment with your doctor to find out what immunizations you should get. If you do not have a family doctor, you can start with your campus clinic and they can refer you to an appropriate service provider. This book cannot tell you which immunizations you should or should not get; this is entirely between you, your family, and your doctor. However, we can tell you about some of the things to expect so that you can plan accordingly.

While you wait for your doctor's

appointment, you can begin doing some research on the Centers for Disease Control and Prevention website: wwwnc.cdc.gov/travel/destinations/china.htm. Here, you can find suggested vaccinations and current health warnings. Without getting too melodramatic, information is not freely exchanged when illnesses with the potential to become epidemics break out in China. Chinese health officials are nervous about reporting cases involving avian ("bird") flu and H1N1 ("swine flu") because it could have a negative effect on their employment. Thus, by the time we hear about Chinese epidemics in the West, it is because the cases are being found in major cities where foreign reporters are. If your program is canceled due to health concerns, chalk it up to modern life and look forward to going the following year. Count your blessings that you have a choice!

Assuming you do not engage in high-risk behaviors, your main health concerns in China will be digestive in nature. There is no vaccine for diarrhea, so your doctor may offer you prescription-grade medicine to bring with you for this. Your next main health concern will be respiratory ailments caused by poor quality air. Common colds can take a very long time to get over in China, but there is no vaccine for colds or long-term coughing and phlegm, either. The Centers for Disease Control provide a list of vaccines which they suggest physicians give to travelers to China. This list can be found on the CDC website (www.cdc.gov); it is reproduced below for your benefit.[3]

Routine Vaccines
Measles/mumps/rubella (MMR) vaccine, diphtheria/pertussis/tetanus (DPT) vaccine, poliovirus vaccine, etc.

Hepatitis A or immune globulin (IG)
Recommended for all unvaccinated people traveling to or working in countries with an intermediate or high level of hepatitis A virus infection (see the map on the CDC website) where exposure might occur through food or water. Cases of travel-related hepatitis A can also occur in travelers to developing countries with "standard" tourist itineraries, accommodations, and food consumption behaviors.

Hepatitis B
Recommended for all unvaccinated persons traveling to or working in countries with intermediate to high levels of endemic HBV transmission (see the map on the CDC website), especially those who might be exposed to blood or body fluids, have sexual contact with the local population, or be exposed through medical treatment (e.g., for an accident).

---

3 This is a reproduction of the list as provided on the CDC website on December 18, 2011, and is only provided as a reference. Only your health care provider can tell you definitively which vaccines to take prior to your trip.

Typhoid
Recommended for all unvaccinated people traveling to or working in East Asia, especially if staying with friends or relatives or visiting smaller cities, villages, or rural areas where exposure might occur through food or water.

Polio
Recommended for adult travelers who have received a primary series with either inactivated poliovirus vaccine (IPV) or oral polio vaccine (OPV). They should receive another dose of IPV before departure. For adults, available data do not indicate the need for more than a single lifetime booster dose with IPV.

Japanese encephalitis
Recommended if you plan to visit rural farming areas and under special circumstances, such as a known outbreak of Japanese encephalitis.

Rabies
Recommended for travelers spending a lot of time outdoors, especially in rural areas, involved in activities such as bicycling, camping, or hiking. Also recommended for travelers with significant occupational risks (such as veterinarians), for long-term travelers and expatriates living in areas with a significant risk of exposure, and for travelers involved in any activities that might bring them into direct contact with bats, carnivores, and other mammals. Children are considered at higher risk because they tend to play with animals, may receive more severe bites, or may not report bites.

There are some parts of China where cases of malaria are found. These are *rural* parts of Anhui, Guizhou, Hainan, Henan, Hubei and Yunnan provinces and some high altitude (over 5,000 feet) areas of northern China. Even if your program does not take students to such rural or high-altitude places, you may decide to go on your own during vacation time. It is up to you–and perhaps your program or insurance provider–what vaccines you get, but if malaria medicine is optional, you might as well bring it with you, just in case you make a last-minute decision to hit the semi-tropical areas of southwest China.

Insurance
Your program will let you know how they want you to handle your health insurance coverage while in China. Your regular domestic health insurance provider may cover you while abroad, but many programs require participants to purchase supplemental health insurance specifically for travel abroad. This allows the program to maintain a single procedure for what to do in an emergency, and it makes sure that everyone has a certain basic level of coverage, regardless of what the individual U.S. health insurance providers provide for. The Ohio State University has used HTH Insurance for many years with positive results. HTH's supplemental health insurance (supplemental to your regu-

lar U.S. provider, which you keep while you are away) covers the usual items related to health care as well as travel-specific items such as flying you to a specialist; flying a specialist to you; flying a parent to your bedside and, heaven forbid, flying your remains back to the U.S. Ask your program coordinator for how they handle health insurance issues.

Getting Your Visa

A visa for the PRC

There are two main types of visas for which student travelers to China apply: long-term student (X), and short-term student/tourist (L). The latter is commonly referred to as a "tourist visa," but it is also the appropriate visa for students spending less than six months in-country. Your program will tell you for which type of visa you will apply, and will probably provide you with directions for completing the application. As someone who has helped many cohorts of students complete their visa applications, I can tell you that it cannot hurt to have a primer in applying for a Chinese visa.

Step One: Complete the appropriate visa application form. Your program will probably provide this to you; if not, be sure that you download the right version. There is more than one version available on the Internet, and, sometimes, more than one version available on official Chinese embassy/consulate websites. If you must obtain your own visa without program assistance, get your application form from the website of the consulate responsible for the state in which you live. To find out which consulate is responsible for your state, visit the website of the Chinese embassy in Washington, D.C.[4] The Chinese embassy and consulate websites are not designed for user-friendliness, and finding what you want can be very difficult. When you find something, it may be out of date and the only way to find out the current situation is by calling the consulate or embassy itself. It is also very difficult to speak to a knowledgeable human being if you do call with a question... which is why so many people prefer to handle business with the Chinese embassy or consulate via people with inside contacts. Such people may be found in your program, or at visa application agencies.

Your application form should be completed in capital English letters; if you can complete it using a fillable PDF form, that would be even

---
4 The map showing the geographical divisions of the Chinese consulates is currently found at www.china-embassy.org/eng/hzqz/t84229.htm, though this may change at any time.

better. Applications completed in upper- and lower-case letters are often accepted, too, though. The application form has a space for a passport-style color photo. You can have this kind of photo taken at most drug stores. Be forewarned that the space for your photo is sized for Chinese ID card-sized photos, not international passport photos. Do not worry about this—just staple your photo to the printed form in such a way that you do not cover up any of the other information fields around it (e.g., sex, current nationality, etc.).

If you are going to China for short-term study, ask your program if you should check "旅游/Tourism" instead of "留学/Study" as the "major purpose(s) of your visit(s)

The east of obtaining a multiple-entry visa varies by visa type and the current visa policies in effect. Multiple-entry visas allow you to go in and out of the country as many times as you wish during the validity period of the visa (usually one year). As of the time of writing, holders of tourist visas issued outside of China were issued multiple entry visas with a 90-day limit on each visit. This means that a holder of this visa must leave the country at least once every 90 days. Hong Kong and Macao count as leaving the country, and they are very easy to reach from southern China. If you are in the north, you can still go to Hong Kong, or you can go to Korea, which is closer. At the time of writing, these options compared as below:

Route	Cost (round trip, USD)	Time (one way)
Beijing–Hong Kong train	$260	24 hours
Beijing–Hong Kong plane	$600	3.5 hours
Beijing-Seoul plane	$300	2 hours
PRC-Inchon ferry (over 10 ports of departure)	$200-$400 (depending on ticket class)	12-28 (depending on ports)

to China." As noted, short term study requires an L tourist visa, while long-term study requires an X visa … and more paperwork from the Chinese host institution. If you check "study" for a short-term program, you may be asked to produce the supporting documentation that is only required of students in long-term programs.[5]

The further south you are, the more cost-effective it is to go to Hong Kong for your 90-day ejection from China. And, your Chinese money, English, and Mandarin skills work there. It is hard to say how much English signage there is

---

5 PRC visa procedures change often, so check with your program, your regional Chinese consulate or a visa agency for current regulations. Frustrating as these changes can be, they are still simple compared to the complicated process Chinese citizens go through in order to get a visa to the US.

when you step off a Chinese ferry in Inchon, Korea, or how much English the taxi drivers speak.

Be careful to note that there is a section in one version of the visa application form related to your attractiveness as a visa applicant in which the "right" answers to the first four questions are "no," while the fifth question (have you ever visited China before?) has no right answer. Do not go running through questions one through four checking "no-no-no-no" and then check "no" to number five because it looks like it is just another answer-no-if-you-want-admission question. Be careful again to note that question six refers to questions one through four and has nothing to do with question five, which falls in between. This goes against American form design principles, but it allows the Chinese form to keep all the yes/no questions together and put an open-ended question at the end of the section. Finally, note that the format of the date field next to your signature at the end is Chinese style, from large to small: year-month-date.

Step Two: Submitting your SIGNED application (some people forget to sign it), attached photo and SIGNED passport (even more people forget to sign their passports) to your relevant embassy or consulate. If your program does this for you, note whether they require a separate payment for the visa fee (currently $140 for non-rush service), or if it is included in your program fee. If you are submitting your application yourself, it is important to note that all visa applications must be submitted in person...though that person does not need to be you or someone you know. It just means that you cannot mail your application in. If you do not submit your materials in person yourself, you will need to submit your materials through an agent or through a friend who lives near the consulate. National agencies such as TraVisa, and MyChinaVisa can do this, as can local travel agents who specialize in China travel. Most major metropolitan areas in the U.S. have one or more such travel agents; you can ask your local university Chinese department for recommendations. Whether you go through an agent or a friend, expect to give something extra to that person for submitting the materials for you. Agents have a set fee, your friend should get a gift.

As of October 2011, the Chinese consulate in New York was no longer processing visas with super-rush one-day service, even though this choice remains on the application form. Do not make a trip to New York expecting to get your materials back the same day.

Arranging for Your Flight

Once you are admitted to your program of study in China, it's time to determine the best way to fly to your destination. Flying to China is much like flying into any major airport anywhere in the world, especially now that all of China's international airports with connections to the U.S.

Shanghai Pudong International Airport

have new terminals. If you have not flown before, don't worry—a little common sense goes a long way.

There are several North American cities with direct flights to the People's Republic, and an even smaller number of cities in China to which those flights go. As of mid-2013, you could fly directly to China from:

- Vancouver, BC
- Toronto, ON
- New York (JFK and Newark)
- Washington, D.C. (Dulles)
- Atlanta
- Detroit
- Chicago
- Los Angeles
- San Francisco
- Seattle

These direct flights all terminate in Beijing, Shanghai, Hong Kong, or Guangzhou. Many other cities in China are reachable via direct international connections to Asian cities such as Seoul, Inchon, Tokyo, and Taipei.

As you choose your itinerary, look into what services and amenities each airline offers—it's going to be a long flight, so you should look for the best value. Things to ask about include:

- **Checked luggage allowances.** Who lets you take the most? Does the airline limit you to a certain number of bags? A certain total weight? A certain weight per bag? This last one can be very troublesome, as you may be under the total weight limit (= allowable weight/bag x number of bags), but if your packing is such that one bag is over by 3 pounds and another is under by 10, you will still either have to repack your luggage at the check-in counter or pay through the nose in overage fees.

- **In-flight entertainment.** Does each seat back have its own LCD monitor on which you can choose movies, TV shows, or games? Or is the in-flight entertainment projected onto a movie screen attached to a bulkhead?
- **Is alcohol is provided gratis (if you are over 21)?** Once upon a time, all alcohol on international flights was free, but hard liquor and liqueurs now commonly cost money.
- **Are there electrical sockets available for your laptop?** Once an amenity limited to business and first class, some flights now offer this in economy.
- **What is the seating arrangement of the aircraft?** How many seatmates' knees will you have to bump or jump in order to get to the restroom? In a row of four seats, you will only have to get past one person, at most; in a row of three, you may have to squeeze past two people ... one of whom may be asleep!
- **What kind of compensation is offered if you volunteer to get bumped from an overbooked domestic flight?** For example, at the time of writing, one airline gave $400 vouchers good for domestic travel within one year; another asked its volunteers to bid to get bumped, with the lowest bidder winning the compensation for which they agreed to take the later flight.

On international flights–and even on some domestic ones–you do not need to bring your own headphones, as the airline provides free ones to you. Once upon a time, some airlines flew aircraft whose audio programs were delivered via hollow tubes to your headphones, thus preventing the use of regular audio jacks–or your own headphones. This era seems to have passed, but you may run into an old jet with this set up.

Round-trip airfare during the busy season (summertime) is currently $1,500 to $2,000; in the off season (the rest of the time), it can be anywhere from $700 to $1,500, depending on dates and airports.

If your program is not in one of these cities, you will need to continue your travel in China by air, train or long-distance bus. You will save money if you book Chinese domestic airplane tickets on a Chinese website instead of getting one package deal on an American website through to your destination. You need to pick up your checked luggage upon arrival in your first Chinese airport anyway; if you transfer to a separately-booked domestic

A large Cathay Pacific Airbus at Hong Kong's Chek Lap Kok International Airport

Chinese flight, you should still be allowed the international flight's amount of luggage as long as you continue your trip within 24 hours. Check with your intended airlines before booking, to make sure.

The best place to start researching airfare is the Internet. Popular sites include Kayak.com, flychina.com, orbitz.com, Travelocity.com, and expedia.com. Even if you do not purchase your tickets here, it is a good idea to start looking at prices weeks before you are ready to buy so that you know what a reasonable rate is. You should also use this opportunity to start learning how to use Chinese travel websites so that you feel comfortable booking on one if you decide to do so. The most popular ones are ctrip.com (available in Chinese and English), qunar.com and elong.com (the latter two are only in Chinese). You can buy tickets on ctrip.com using a foreign credit card, but you need a Chinese contact phone number for the registration process. If you do not yet have any friends in China, your program may be able to provide a number you can use.

Booking a domestic flight separately from your international itinerary can save you up to 80% on the domestic airfare, but discount tickets can be difficult to change if something happens on the way to China. Booking one solid airplane itinerary from home to your destination city gives you the flexibility that comes with buying full-price domestic airplane tickets. Some people miss their international flight when a domestic flight is delayed or canceled; if you book all the way through to your final destination in China, it may be easier for customer service to help you rebook those tickets.

Generally speaking, the food and the service is better on Asian airlines that are not Mainland Chinese (e.g., Asiana, Cathay Pacific, Korean Air), while prices are better on U.S.-flagged carriers and Air Canada (via Toronto and Vancouver). At the time of writing, some flights to China on former Northwest Airlines routes out of Detroit and Minneapolis via Narita Airport in Japan ran older 747s with projection-screen in-flight entertainment and smaller overhead bins. These old behemoths also have five seats in a row in the center section, which means that the poor soul in the middle has to wait for his/her seatmates to go to the restroom or else engage in a feat of acrobatics to get there. Newer aircraft such as the 777, with large overhead bins, rows with no more than four seats and personal in-flight entertainment systems are found on most of the other routes to Asia.

Finally, when you fly to China from North America, you lose about 12 hours because of the time difference: if you leave the U.S. on Saturday afternoon, you will arrive on Sunday afternoon, even if your flight was only 13 hours long. You make it up when you come back, however: depending on your final destination, it is possible to arrive on a date and time earlier than when you left China! These are just neat trivia unless you are expected to meet up with someone in your destination city and you have miscalculated your arrival date. Be sure to check your arrival time *and date* twice before you book.

Packing

There are a number of things to keep in mind as you pack, but the one piece of advice that trumps all others is: pack no more luggage than you can move 60 feet across pavement without help. Everything else is secondary. Sticking to this rule will help keep you under airline baggage limits, make sure you can get from flight to flight, terminal to terminal and vehicle to vehicle even when no one can help you, and prevents you from being "that person" in your group that everyone rolls their eyes about because you always need help to get from point A to point B. Also, be sure to find out the carry-on and checked luggage restrictions of the airline on which you are flying. Going over weight is extremely expensive.

■ What to Bring

So, what should you bring? Here's a quick checklist:

- **Clothes for two weeks without doing laundry.** How many pieces of clothing this actually means depends on you—how comfortable you are re-wearing items of clothing before you wash them, and how often you think you will be able to/want to do your laundry. Remember to bring something to wear *while* you are doing your laundry, which may not be inside the building where you live!
- **One Xerox copy of the information page and the visa page of your passport in each piece of your luggage.** This is handy if the luggage gets lost, if you lose your passport (things move faster at the embassy if you have a copy of the lost passport), or if you needed your passport during a trip, but forget to bring it (!).
- **Pepto-Bismol tablets.** Easier to pack than liquid and they taste good, too.
- **Medicine** for cold, fever, stomach upset, allergies, etc. Chinese medicine works fine and is often much cheaper than American medicine, but most people prefer to stick with brands with which they are familiar when they are sick and unhappy.
- **Any prescription drugs you need,** in their original bottles so you can prove they aren't illegal, if necessary. Don't mix drugs in one bottle.
- **A copy of your glasses/contacts prescription.** If you need to get replacements, you can skip the vision test. You can also get great-looking glasses for cheap in China.
- **Fancy toiletries,** if you are so inclined. You can find most cleansers and facial creams,

etc., in China, but if you are wedded to a particular brand, bring some of your own.
- **Deodorant** that you like. You can find deodorants in major Chinese cities now, including foreign brands. If you particularly like a specific brand, bring your own supply.
- **Season-appropriate clothing.** If you are going in summer, bring warm weather clothes plus a pair of pants and a jacket in case of cool or rainy weather, which you can still experience at higher altitudes. If you will be in China during the winter, you can buy reasonably-priced winter coats and long underwear there and avoid taking up all that luggage space. You may need to shop around to find a coat with longer sleeves appropriate for Americans, but you should be able to find some styles that work.
- **One set of clothing you would wear to a reception** (like slacks/khakis and a tie for men, a skirt or pantsuit for women).
- **Optional: A money-holder that goes under your clothing around your waist or hanging from your neck.** Some travelers swear by these things; others can't stand them and stick with just using their wallet so that they do not need to lift up their shirt all the time.
- **Locks for your luggage.** These can be found at hardware stores and most places that sell luggage. Get the ones that are TSA (Transportation Security Administration) approved. When you leave valuables in your luggage, either in your dorm or in a motel, you can lock them up. Do not assume that every housekeeper in China is satisfied with her paycheck.
- **One hundred dollars U.S. in cash** that you can exchange for Chinese *renminbi* at your destination airport to handle initial expenses before you can find an ATM: taxi, hotel deposit/pre-payment (if necessary), food/drink. Before you go, tell your bank that you are going to China and for how long. If they see charges appearing on your card in China and you did not tell them to expect it, anti-fraud measures may kick in and you may find yourself with a debit card that is useless until you can call your bank ... which means trying to make an international call without any money! Alternatively, you can exchange money at your local bank, but it may take two days or more to get the RMB back.
- **Your laptop, if you have one.** Most laptop power cords have converters that will allow you to draw power from the 220V sockets they have in China. You will need to buy an adapter to fit Chinese sockets, though. These can be bought cheaply in China, but it may be some time before you have a chance to find one in your city's electronics market or at a department store. Just pick one up at a big box retailer or electronics store

before you go. Do not pack your laptop in checked luggage—it may disappear or get smashed.
- **An Ethernet cable.** Wireless access is not as widespread in China as it is in the U.S., and you may be able to save yourself some time if you have your own cable handy.
- **Gifts for people who help you.** If you don't know who may help you, bring gifts for five people. If you go over that, you can get the gifts in China. Good, easily-packed items include paperback fiction for learners of English, trinkets related to your hometown or state (only these things may be made in China), and items with your university's logo on them.
- In your *carry-on luggage*, not checked luggage (which can get lost when you need it most), bring:
  - **A written copy of your in-country English-speaking program representative's contact information**, including cell phone, as office phones won't be answered in the middle of the night.
  - **A written copy of the Chinese and English address for where you are expected to go when you arrive.** Even if you are supposed to be traveling in a group, there is always a remote possibility that you will be separated and need to get there alone.
  - **Your program director's estimate of about how long a taxi ride from the airport to your destination would take, and about how much it should cost.**

Do not rely on this data being stored in a laptop, smartphone or similar device. These things break, get lost, stolen, and more commonly, simply run out of electricity.

■ What Not to Bring

Here are some items that are best left behind:

- **An umbrella.** Just buy one for a few dollars as soon as you arrive and put it in your room. This saves luggage space and saves you money, as umbrella prices sometimes go up when it rains.
- **A lot of cash or traveler's checks.** Those days are past. Nowadays, American travelers to China use their U.S. bank debit cards to withdraw Chinese RMB from roadside ATMs. It is convenient, safe, and no more expensive than the service fees and/or mediocre exchange rates involved in exchanging cash or traveler's checks inside a bank.
- **AA or AAA batteries.** They weigh a lot and you can buy them in China, even if the quality is sometimes low.
- **Tissues.** They are available everywhere.
- **Stationery.** It's available cheaply on or near all college campuses.

- **Illegal substances of any kind.** Chinese law enforcement does not look kindly on the use of drugs, and they are even more unhappy with those who distribute them. This goes for marijuana, as well.
- **A lot of electrical devices.** They are heavy, and each one will need a plug-socket converter, a current converter, or both.
- **Intent to have a summer romance with a local.** This is sometimes controversial advice, but from my experience having led numerous groups of American students to China and worked with people who have taken even more, I can tell you that two things cause the most problems for Americans in China: alcohol and hormones. Problems with the locals mean problems for the program, and problems for the program mean problems for future participants. Try to have at least a year in China before you even think about dating a Chinese national. There are simply too many differences in how Chinese and Americans communicate for either side to understand the other's intentions right off the bat. Do everyone a favor and learn more about Chinese culture before you start dating. Her[6] parents will thank you for it.

Last Steps

You're really going! Your visa is affixed inside your passport, you have booked your tickets to China, your suitcases are ready to be packed … now it's time to let Uncle Sam know where you'll be in case they need to pluck you off a rooftop with a Huey helicopter. Or, at least know if you're in another part of the country when an earthquake strikes. Go to https://step.state.gov/step/, the State Department's Smart Traveler Enrollment Program, to tell them where you are going and when. Your program will be able to provide you with specific in-country contact information.

Now, all you need to do is wait for the big day when you get on that plane. In the next chapter, we'll get you on that plane, off of it, onto various other forms of transportation, and leave you standing in front of your hard new bed.

So long!

---

6 Most issues involve American boys and Chinese girls.

Chapter 4
Getting There

Most flights take the "great circle" route to China, that is, up and over Alaska or the north pole instead of "straight" across the Pacific. The curvature of the earth actually makes it shorter to fly north over Alaska or the North Pole and then south to China. Below are Chicago-Shanghai and San Francisco-Hong Kong examples of the great circle route to China, as created on the Great Circle Mapper website (www.gcmap.com).

While you are on the plane, be sure to get up and walk around periodically: it is good for your circulation. If you can, use the restroom during a movie: in between movies, there is a rush on the use of the toilets and you may have to stand in line... except that U.S. Federal law prohibits the formation of long lines on U.S.-flagged aircraft, so the flight attendants do not let many people wait at once.

On some Delta routes, you will connect to another flight in Tokyo's Narita airport, at which time, you will need to go through security again. If this is your first time abroad, you may be intimidated by having to go through security screening in a foreign country, but it is the same as in the U.S., and the staff speak enough English to get you through. Be sure your carry-on luggage strictly meets size requirements—I once had a Japanese screener tell me my camera tripod was 1 inch shy of being too long to fly when no U.S. TSA or airline personnel had ever brought it up before.

Shortly before you land, the flight attendants will distribute your arrival forms for Chinese Immigration & Customs. Complete this form on the plane and ask a flight attendant for another if you make a mistake. If you are flying to a Mainland Chinese airport, it can sometimes be difficult to find blank forms to fill out in the airport itself. That is often an American visitor's first experi-

Arrival/departure card for going through border control

ence with TIC, or "This is China," as expatriates in China say.

Regardless of your destination city, upon arrival in China, you will immediately go through two procedures: Border Control (AKA Immigration) and Customs. At Border Control, give your passport to the official when it is your turn, putting your arrival/departure card in your passport on the page where your current Chinese visa is affixed. Once in a while, the border control agent notices that you have done this and appreciates the gesture.

Many border control agents in China look bored and glum. Don't take this personally. Just smile and wait patiently for your passport to be scanned and a visa page to be stamped with arrival date/place information. Unless you speak Chinese well, I recommend against trying to "help" the border control agent find a good page to put the arrival stamp on. What makes sense to you (e.g., a blank spot near the visa you are using for entry) may not make sense to him or her (e.g., the first page he or she opens your passport to, even if that page is labeled "notes" instead of "visas").

After border control, follow the monitors (or your plane mates) to find your luggage carousel, just like in the U.S. Unlike the U.S., luggage carts in Chinese airports are almost always free. Grab one, stake out your spot next to the carousel and wait.

Once you have your luggage, you're ready to go through customs. Also unlike the U.S., going through customs in China consists of walking past a sign that says "Customs, Nothing to Declare" and a couple uniformed customs agents standing near dusty x-ray equipment.

Rumors about arriving travelers being taxed for bringing expensive items like iPads and iPhones into China have been circulating since around 2010. So far, enforcement appears to be lax or non-existent, but be aware that there is a possibility that China may soon start enforcing customs duties on valuable items, as the U.S. reserves the right to do.

After you push your cart past the customs agents and through the large doors to the terminal area, you're in China! If you are connecting to a domestic flight, follow signs (or ask how to get) to the transfer connection check-in counters that will be located after customs. Be sure to allow a good two hours between your scheduled arrival time and your domestic departure, as a lot can happen in between that can delay your forward progress.

For more information about flying domestically in China, refer to the intercity airplane travel section in Chapter 8 (page 221).

Money for the Road

Exchanging USD for Chinese RMB is always more expensive at an airport money exchanging service than it is outside, so only exchange US$100 in the terminal. This will be enough to cover ground transportation and one night's lodging, if necessary. If you can find an ATM in the terminal, your U.S. ATM/debit card should work there, but if not, you still have that $100 bill we told you to bring with you in Chapter 3. Remember, before you left the U.S., you should have called your bank to tell them when you will be in China so that they do not refuse your transactions there.

Airport Pick-Up

If you are traveling with a group or with a program director, your ground transport is probably pre-arranged. If you are being picked up, there should be someone holding a sign with your or your program's name on it standing in the terminal area just beyond the doors after customs. If someone was supposed to be waiting for you but no one is, wait for 15 minutes within sight of the passenger exit door you came out of and the people standing there holding signs with names. Your ride may have gotten stuck in traffic, or gone to the wrong terminal. Give him or her some time to find you before you make them lose face by calling the boss....

If your ride does not appear after 15 minutes or so, call your in-country program representative using a pay phone in the terminal. Many Chinese airports have mini convenience stores with a phone on the counter that serves as a public phone. They only take cash, so this is where your RMB pocket money comes in handy. It should only cost a couple *renminbi* ("people's money," also known as **kuài**, literally "chunks"–like our "bucks" for dollars). Your program representative should be able to contact your ride by cell phone. Your public phone should have a phone number at which your program representative can call you back. If not, make sure to describe a specific place where you will wait for the driver, e.g., Arrivals Exit 3 in Terminal 2.

If your flight is delayed and you end up arriving in the middle of the night and none of your in-country contacts answer the phone, you can either slum it in the terminal until regular services resume in the morning or ask someone at an

Grab one—they're free.

information desk to help you book a room at a motel near the airport. If you are at an international airport, these motels often have shuttle service to and from the airport, and you can come back to the airport after catching a few hours' sleep.

Getting from the Airport to Your Destination

At all Chinese airports, you can get downtown by taxi or airport shuttle bus, and all Chinese international airports with direct service to the U.S. have subway or light rail access to downtown. Each of these forms of transportation is described generally in the following pages, as each airport is different and your best source for current information is the signage you find in the airport. After reading this section, you will at least know what kinds of options you can ask about.

■ Taxis

By far, the easiest—and usually most expensive—way to reach your check-in address is to take a taxi. After 13-24 hours in the air and you're pushing a cart full of unwieldy luggage around, many people will pay just about anything to reach their final destination. Because of this, it is very important that you follow the signs in the terminal to taxi stands.

On your way to the taxi stand, where people wait in line for taxis to be arranged by uniformed airport staff standing at the head of the line, strangers may walk up to you and ask if you need a ride or need a taxi. *Do not* accept! These are drivers of unregistered taxis (e.g. random guys who own cars) who want to avoid waiting in the taxi line for a fare and want to avoid the costs associated with becoming a legally registered taxi (e.g., insurance, meter installation, city taxes, etc.). Sometimes, the fellow asking if you need a ride isn't even the driver, but just a salesman who gets a cut. These taxis do not give

There is a phone on the far right counter at this convenience store in the Zhuhai airport.

formal receipts and you have no procedural recourse if you are overcharged. Politely tell these people you do not need a ride, thank you, and continue to the taxi stand.

When you get to the head of the taxi stand line, the uniformed airport employee will probably give you a card with your taxi's license plate number written on it. This employee usually asks passengers where they are going, but only in Chinese. If he asks you something in Chinese, that is probably what it was. If you do not understand, just say, "Sorry, I only speak English." He will point to the car in line that he wants you to get in; go there and the driver will probably help you with your luggage. Keep in mind that many Chinese taxis now run on liquid propane gas, which is stored in a cylinder in the trunk. The cylinder reduces the amount of storage space available, so if you were planning to share a cab with three or even two other people, there may not be enough room for your luggage.

It is not rude to sit in the back of the cab, even if you are alone. Once you are seated, the cabbie will ask you where you are going. There is a slight possibility that your cabbie will ask you in English, and an even slighter possibility that he will understand an answer given in English. Just show the Chinese address of your destination to the cabbie, and off you go. Your driver should flip down the meter within 30 seconds of pulling away from the taxi stand. Once you are clear of the messy traffic at arrivals, if your driver has not yet turned on the meter, you can ask him to do so politely by pointing to it and saying "please?" Or, you can say it in Chinese: **Qǐng nǐ dá biǎo** 请你打表.

Most Chinese airports are connected to their cities by an expressway, some of which may still have tolls. The cost of the toll will be added to your fare upon arrival and will be ¥5-20. Chinese taxis do not take credit cards, though some major cities' taxis can swipe transit cards … which you are not likely to have, yet. Most Chinese cities' taxis now also charge a "fuel surcharge" of ¥1-3 that is also added to the metered fare. If you are being reimbursed for this trip, be sure to get a copy of the toll and fuel surcharge receipts as well as the taxi receipt when you pay.

If the driver cannot give you a receipt, you are not legally obligated to pay. However, sometimes cabbies honestly run out of receipt paper in the middle of a shift. Consult your program director's estimate of time and cost for your trip and decide for yourself if the cabbie was simply unable to produce a receipt for a trip that costs about what it was expected to.

■ Airport Shuttles

Chinese airports have shuttle buses that run regularly between the airport and one or more points in the city. These buses cost around ¥20 per person, including the airport expressway toll. It is common for arriving passengers to take the bus downtown and then take a taxi to their final destination, saving a lot of money. The main drawback is that information regarding the bus is in Chinese, including bus stop locations. If you are feeling adventurous-or if your budget requires you to-you can ask people around what stop you should go to in order to take a taxi to your final destination. Make sure your driver knows where you are getting off so that he can call on you if you don't catch the announcement. Shuttle buses at major cities have luggage compartments under

Taxi line at Qingdao's International Airport

the seating compartment, but some small cities' buses only have on-board luggage storage, which leaves only the aisle for storing large international-size luggage.

- **Subways and Light Rail**

Beijing Capital International, Shanghai Pudong, Guangzhou Baiyun, and Hong Kong Chek Lap Kok Airports all have subway or light rail access to downtown. Beijing and Hong Kong have airport express trains that run on dedicated tracks while Shanghai and Guangzhou have stops on the regular subway system. Hong Kong's airport express was designed for airplane travelers, with easy entrance and exit and on-board storage areas for luggage of all sizes. The Hong Kong subway, on the other hand, is designed for commuters and is not very convenient for people with a lot of luggage. You can expect similar situations with other subways that serve the airport. Like the taxis and buses, follow airport signage to the light rail and subway stations.

- **Public Bus**

Though you can take a public bus from the airport and it is definitely the cheapest way to get to/from the airport, it is not a practical choice for travelers with luggage who do not speak Chinese well.

- **Maglev**

For about ¥30, the Shanghai Maglev whisks you (at 300 km/h) from Pudong Airport… to a subway station in the suburbs of the Pudong side of Shanghai. It is a fun experience once or twice, but you might want to consider giving yourself a lot of extra time to figure out how to use it when you are not fatigued by a long flight and just starting to figure out how things work in China. If you choose to take the Maglev upon arrival in China, you may be looking at a trip that involves 1) Taking the Maglev to Longyang Metro Station 2) Transferring to the #2 subway line 3) Taking the #2 to whichever line goes to where you're going 4) Transferring to that subway line 5) Exiting the station nearest your destination 6) Possibly still needing to hail a taxi to get you and your luggage "home." *Caveat emptor.*

- **Hong Kong—Mainland Coach Service**

Special to Hong Kong, there is coach service from Hong Kong's international airport directly to cities in the Mainland, with minivans going to destinations in Guangdong Province and larger coaches going to destinations such as Nanning in Guangxi and Xiamen in Fujian. You purchase your tickets and board in Terminal 2. Make sure you have your PRC visa lined up already before you get on!

- **Rental Car**

Forget about it. There are now international rental agencies in tier-one

An airport shuttle bus in Chengdu

cities, but you really need to have lived in China for some time before considering driving there. It is possible for Chinese people to get a driver's license without knowing how to drive, and I don't mean that in a figurative sense. They literally do not need to know how to drive in order to obtain a driver's license. 'Nuff said.

Most foreigners going to China for the first time without pre-arranged ground transport treat themselves to a taxi ride, regardless of how far it is or how much it costs. It is hard to describe how exhausted you can feel after this international flight, and trying to negotiate a new environment is tiring enough without having to lug around your luggage. So, budget ¥200 for your transportation from the airport to your destination. It costs about this much to go from Pudong Airport to Hongqiao Airport (Shanghai's domestic airport), and about ¥150 to get from Beijing Capital Airport to downtown.

In the next chapter, we talk about what to do when you step out of the taxi at your destination, be it a hotel, university or homestay family's home.

Chapter 5
Settling In

In this chapter, we will get you settled into your living space. Most students in China live in a dormitory or a hotel. A small but growing number are living with host families, even if for a short time during an otherwise dorm-based program. Each living arrangement has its own characteristics that add to the study abroad experience. Some are positive, some are neutral, and some try your patience, but all are important parts of learning to live in a foreign environment.

Once you have arrived at your immediate destination in China, whether it is a hotel, dorm, or host family, one of your first tasks is to find a way to let your parents know you are safe. A cascade of other things leap onto your to-do list as soon as you walk through the door of your lodging–not the least of which is taking a shower–but getting a message to your parents or guardians needs to be near the top of your list. It may be as easy as booting up your laptop and getting on free hotel wireless, or you may need to hunt down an Internet Café and learn how to rent computer time. Worst-case scenario, you pony up some tens of RMB for a three-minute international direct-dial call from a pay phone at a time when your parents are awake at home. Don't scare them with a call in the middle of the night (the middle of the day, for you)! And, don't scare them with stories about the illegal taxi drivers you avoided, or how every car in China appears to be driven by a sociopath, or the quality of the air. For one, you don't have time to do this during an expensive phone call and, more importantly, the point of the call is to put your family's minds at ease. You can tell them scary stories later, when they understand that the stories are entertainment and not cries for help.

Now that letting your family know you arrived safely is on your to-do list, let's get in the door and settled down. Many American students in China spend at least one night in a hotel, even if they will eventually be living in a dormitory, and checking into a Chinese hotel involves some things that an American visitor needs to know.

When you arrive at the hotel, it is unnecessary to tip your taxi driver unless he helped you get heavy luggage out of the car. If that happens, a ¥5 or ¥10 note is sufficient. Your driver may even refuse it, as tipping is uncommon for taxi rides. On the other hand, tipping of bellhops at five- and some four-star hotels is not uncommon. If you want help with your luggage, let the bellhop put your luggage on a luggage cart, and be ready to tip him ¥5-10 per bag. If you do *not* want help with your luggage, then make sure you beat the bellhop to getting your bags to the front counter. If you hesitate, he may take that as a sign of acceptance.

If you are traveling at a busy time—perhaps there is an industry convention in town—the front desk may be swamped with people trying to check in, check out, or take care of myriad other issues. You may see some elbow their way to the desk and try to get service before others who have been waiting patiently. If there is a line, stay in it and wait your turn and fight the urge to join the ranks of what the Chinese call "uncivilized" people who do not care about others. If you form a line of one and observe that the only people the harried desk staff can serve are those who have made space for themselves at the counter (like at a bar), then you may have to just join the fray.

At the hotel counter, the level of English ability will depend on where you are and the star level of the hotel: the larger the city, the better the English; the nicer the hotel, the better the English. If you know that some form of the following dialogue will take place upon check-in, there should be few surprises in either language.

Dialogue	Notes
English	
Check-in counter person: Hello.	As long as you look foreign, the counter staff will lead with English. If you can actually do this in Chinese, do not be offended, as most foreigners in China cannot complete the check-in process in Chinese, so they are trying to be helpful.
You: Hello. I have a reservation.	
Check-in: Passport, please. (You give your passport, the counter staff scans or copies it and begins filling out the registration form for you)	The Public Security Bureau requires that hotels have a record of the foreigners that stay there. You cannot get around this requirement.
You: I can fill that out.	

Check-in: Thank you!
(You fill out the registration form with your name, home address, passport number, and visa number)

Some staff will try to fill out the registration card for you, but it is usually faster to do it yourself because you can find your name, passport number, and visa information faster than they can. Be prepared for them to rewrite numbers you write, though, as Chinese people write some numbers differently from us.

Check-in: You are staying for one night. The deposit is 428 yuan. Will you pay cash or credit card?

You: Credit card.
(Check-in swipes card, asks you to sign)

The "deposit" is really pre-payment. Unlike in the U.S., where your credit card is scanned at check-in and charged at check-out after adding any incidental expenses, most Chinese hotels need you to pay for your entire stay at check-in. If they take credit cards, you can charge it and hold on to your cash for places that do not take credit.

Check-in: Your room is 315. Your breakfast ticket is with your key card. Breakfast is 6:00 a.m. to 9:00 a.m. on the third floor.

You: Thank you.

You may be given a ticket for breakfast. Be sure not to lose it, as you need it to gain access to the breakfast buffet. If you have a short stay, they may give you enough tickets for the duration. Otherwise, you may need to ask the front desk for a new ticket every day.

Chinese check-in dialogue	Pinyin	English translation
服务员: 您好。	Fúwùyuán: nín hǎo.	Front desk: Hello.
客人: 你好。我订了房间。	Kèrén: Nǐ hǎo. Wǒ ding le fángjiān.	Guest: Hello. I reserved a room.
服务员: 请出示护照。	Fúwùyuán: Qǐng chūshì hùzhào	Front desk: Please give me your passport.
客人: 我可以填登记表，没问题。	Kèrén: Wǒ kěyǐ tián dēngjì biǎo, méi wèntí.	Guest: I can fill out the registration form, no problem.
服务员: 不好意思！您住几天？	Fúwùyuán: Bù hǎo yìsi! Nín zhù jǐ tiān?	Front desk: Sorry ... How many days are you staying?
客人: 一天。	Kèrén: Yī tiān.	Guest: One.

服务员: 您的押金是428元。您刷卡还是付现金?	Fúwùyuán: Nín de yājīn shi sìbǎièrshíbā yuǎn. Nín shuā kǎ háishì fù xiànjīn?	Front Desk: The deposit is 428 yuan. Will you be swiping a [credit] card or paying cash?
客人: 刷卡。	Kèrén: Shuā kǎ.	Guest: Swiping a card.
服务员: 早餐票夹在房卡套里面。早餐在三楼荷花阁, 6点到9点开。	Fúwùyuán: Zǎocānpiào jiā zài fángkǎtào lǐmiàn. Zǎocān zài sān lóu Héhuā Gé, liù diǎn dào jiǔ diǎn kāi.	Front desk: The breakfast ticket is in your room card envelope. Breakfast is on the third floor in the Lotus Flower Pavilion. It is open 6 to 9.
客人: 谢谢。	Kèrén: Xièxie.	Guest: Thank you.

Variations on this dialogue will depend on how much information the front desk clerk needs to get from or confirm with you. This may include the length of your stay, the size of your room (e.g., standard double, suite, minimalist "business room," dormitory style room), if you are staying at a youth hostel, and if your reservation includes breakfast. If you are checking into a five star hotel in a major city, there may be nothing for you to do once you hand over your passport other than pay for your room *and keep your deposit payment receipt.*

There was once a day in China when couples could only get a room together if they showed a marriage certificate. It is up to the hotel's discretion whether or not they allow unmarried couples to room together, but very few hotels–if any–care anymore.

With your room keycard in hand and your luggage trailing you under your or a bellhop's power, you can take the elevator (if there is one) or the stairs up to your room. Unlike U.S. motels, some Chinese hotels of up to five floors have no elevator. One such hotel in Taishan, Shandong, numbers its floors 1, 1a, 2, 2a, 3 and 3a, so those on the third floor think they only need to lug their baggage up three flights of stairs, but it really works out to six. This is when you will be glad you followed the packing advice in Chapter 3!

What your room contains will depend on the kind of establishment you are staying in. There are a limited number of hostels in China (you can look them up on the Youth Hostels Association of China website www.yhachina.com), and an astounding number of regular hotels. Chinese do not differentiate between "hotel" and "motel" to the extent that Americans do, though the words exist. International brands such as Shangri-La, Hilton, Holiday Inn, Mariott, Sheraton, Days Inn, and Super 8 are found in China, and they are all quite nice. There are also popular Chinese chains that cater to frugal travelers with basic but economical rooms, including the

Chapter 5: Settling In

A 4-star hotel in Nanjing

An affordable 3-star chain motel in Beijing

168 and 268 chains (named after the number of RMB one night's stay costs www.motel168.com), Home Inn (www.homeinns.com), Jinjiang Inn (www.jinjianginns.com), and 7 Days Inn (en.7daysinn.cn).

As soon as you step into your room, look between shoulder and eye level on the interior wall next to the door for a slot to put your room card key in. Most hotels conserve electricity through a system in which you must insert your key card in a slot to turn on the master power to the room. When you take the key out to leave, the power then goes out immediately or after a minute or so. This is a great way to conserve energy. Unfortunately, it means being unable to recharge your electronics or keep the room air conditioned or heated while you are out. If you need to, you can often substitute a credit card-sized item from your wallet to keep the power on while you are out of the room. Some older slots are even wide enough for the complimentary comb in the bathroom to fit into and keep the electricity on.

Many older hotel rooms' lights and other electrical devices are controlled by a console of switches built into the nightstand next to a bed. Here, you may find dimmers for the over-bed lights, on-off switches for the night-light built into the nightstand, the TV's electricity, the hall light, and some other lights and electrical sockets. It sometimes takes trial and error to find out whether the electrical socket into which you have plugged your laptop isn't working because the connection is bad or because you haven't flipped the right switch on this console.

At the minimum, a dorm-style room will have a bed (possibly a bunk-bed) and a table. A standard hotel room of any class will have a bed, a bathroom, a cable TV, and a desk. Included with the room are a hot water thermos or electric kettle, a pair of tea mugs, shampoo, a comb, and a toothbrush & toothpaste set. To refill the thermos with boiling water, put it in the hallway next to your door for a one-day turnaround or ask the front desk to have it refilled.

Some hotels put two bottles of mineral water on the coffee table; there should be a note somewhere near the bottle or elsewhere in the room indicating if they are complimentary or not. If there is no note, assume they are not free. In-room bottles of water cost two-to-three times as much as on the street outside the hotel. Nicer hotels will also place convenience items such as instant noodles and snacks in your room. These are definitely not complimentary and cost much more than on the street. Some mainstream Chinese hotels also have adult products in the bathroom, and these also cost extra.

A typical bathroom in a nice Chinese hotel

It is not uncommon to find on the nightstand a placard advertising services that the hotel offers, including haircuts, mahjongg parlors, poker tables, karaoke, and massages. If you are in a four or five star hotel, these services will be above board and pricey. If you are in a lower-level hotel or a lower-level city, be careful. The people playing mahjongg and cards will be gambling (common, but still illegal), the karaoke may offer post-crooning services that are identical to the services that are euphemistically advertised as "massages." If you are not at an international brand hotel chain, save yourself some trouble and do not partake in these services on the placard. Likewise, if you get a phone call to your room offering massage service, politely refuse for the same reason. These phone calls are in Chinese, so if you do not speak Chinese, you can just say "sorry" and hang up. If you do speak Chinese, the question will be something like **xiānsheng, nín xūyào ānmó fúwù ma?** 先生, 您需要按摩服务吗? (Do you need massage services?) A polite answer would be **bù xūyào, xièxiè** 不需要, 谢谢。(No, thank you.)

High speed Internet is now standard in Chinese hotels of three stars and above, with top-tier hotels offering wireless services as well. If you do not have an Ethernet cable to connect your laptop to a wall socket, ask the front desk if they have any to lend. There may be a cash deposit required, or even a rental fee. Once you are connected, it may also be necessary to adjust some settings in your computer to get online. If you have having difficulty, look for information in the guest book that should be in the room. This is the booklet that tells you what the business center's hours are, and, sometimes, how much you will be charged if you steal a towel or the mattress. As with anything, if all else fails, contact the front desk.

When you check out, you usually need to do so in person. Some hotels have absentee express checkout like American hotels, but this is the exception and not the rule. Most often, you need to check out in order to return your key, to wait until the cleaning staff has confirmed that you didn't drink one of the for-fee beverages or steal the mattress, and to settle the difference between your "deposit" and the bill. Even though the hotel staff kept a copy of your deposit receipt, it is hard to say where it goes once you leave the counter, so be prepared for the front-desk staff to depend on your copy of the receipt for checkout. Be sure to check the hotel's calculations of how much your total bill is. You should do this everywhere in China when your bill is calculated manually. Few people will calculate it wrong on purpose, but mistakes can happen.

If you are staying long-term in a hotel, be aware that the cleaning staff may or may not knock before coming in to clean your room. Well-trained staff will always announce their arrival, but the cheaper the lodgings, the less training the staff will have had. So, either lock your door from the inside with the bar or chain lock, or don't run around in your skivvies (or less) before the cleaning has been done.

Campus Living

The vast majority of study abroad students in China live in a dormitory. There are a few types of dorms to be found on Chinese college campuses, though not all colleges will have all kinds. They are, in order of the likelihood of your staying there:

1) Foreign students dormitory
2) Foreign students apartments
3) Chinese graduate student housing
4) Chinese undergraduate housing

Many Americans use more toilet paper per bathroom visit than the Chinese (the difference is in technique, not level of hygiene), so your room may have only one small roll of toilet paper. Do not be afraid to ask the cleaning staff or the front desk for more. On a similar topic, some old motels have old plumbing that was not designed for flushing toilet paper. In these places, a wastebasket for the soiled paper will be found immediately next to the toilet, sometimes with a sign indicating its use. If you deposit the paper in the toilet, it may clog, but you can try the toilet once as you normally would at home to test it. If it doesn't clog, continue carefully. If it does, call for the cleaning staff, who may explain the role of the wastebasket as if to a three-year-old.

Foreign students dormitory at China Ocean University Yushan Campus

■ Foreign Students Dormitory

Foreign student dormitory housing is the most common living arrangement for Americans studying in China. The quality of such accommodation varies greatly from university to university, but is always better than the housing provided to Chinese students on the same campus. One of the reasons Chinese universities rarely allow foreign students to stay in Chinese dorms is that they would consider it to be the mark of a bad host to make guests stay in anything other than the best rooms available, even when an authentic Chinese university experience is what the foreign student desires.

Foreign student dorms are generally run like motels, and will even rent rooms to individuals not currently studying at the institution as long as they have some university connection. Thus, dorm life for foreign students in China is somewhere between motel living and dorm living. As with a motel, rooms are generally double occupancy, have a private bathroom with shower, are air-conditioned, and have one or two desks. Also as with a motel, the beds come with pillows, sheets, and blankets. As with a dormitory, the front desk staff become familiar with the residents and their lives and monitor who comes and goes, which increases the security of the building while reducing the liability for the university. Also as with a dormitory, cleaning of the room is the responsibility of its residents and not cleaning staff. The cleaning staff in a foreign student dormitory may clean the university-provided sheets on a monthly or even weekly basis, but they will rarely do more than that. You will also be on your own for toiletries and towels, though toilet paper will probably be provided.

When you check into your dorm room, you may need to pay a

Foreign student housing at Qingdao University

deposit, depending on the arrangement between your host university and study abroad program. The deposit is required so that residents do their best to take care of the items in the room, and so the university is not responsible for any damages incurred. It is very common for foreign students to knock over the glass-lined hot water thermos that comes with the room; if this happens, simply buy a replacement lining at an on-campus store (Chinese students knock over thermoses, too!), clean out the broken glass, and replace the bottle yourself. It's only a few RMB this way.

When you check in, make an inventory of the condition of the furniture and other items. If something is broken or inoperative, tell the front desk and your resident director on day one. The front desk may fix it, but it is more likely that they will merely make a note of it and not charge you for the damage when you leave. If the offending items really need to be fixed (e.g., an inoperative electrical socket), ask what the process is for asking for repairs and keep on it. Let your resident director know, too, but it is ultimately your responsibility to follow up on the issue and ask for the resident director's intervention if you run into a roadblock.

Your room should be wired for Internet service, though getting online can be a trying process. At some universities, getting online may simply be a matter of plugging your computer into a wall-mounted Ethernet socket. More commonly, though, getting online in your dorm room will take more work. At Qingdao University, for example, new residents must rent a modem from the Foreign Affairs Office, providing a deposit for the equipment (again, keep your receipt!) and a monthly rental fee. The student then needs to change the TCP settings on his or her laptop in order to connect with the university network. Every year, it takes a small group of students working together to figure out how to get online. At Ocean University of China's old Yushan campus, new residents must apply for Ocean University network accounts, which involves filling out a form that then goes through the Foreign Affairs Office to the IT office, which then activates the student's account with the university. For this, there is also a monthly Internet access fee. Once the account has been approved and set up, the university network recognizes the student's laptop's IP address, allowing the student to get online from any Internet connection on campus. Theoretically. The monthly Internet access fee at Ocean University was not prorated, so if you move in on the 29th of the month and want to get online imme-

Chinese thermoses of the kind found on college campuses

Hopefully you like fresh oranges with your coffee.

diately, you must pay a full month's access fee just for the last few days of the month… and it takes about two days just for the application to be processed. The staff at Ocean University recommend that students simply get online off-campus at an Internet café or coffee shop until the first of the month, but these present challenges of their own.

Another utility that may be treated differently in the foreign students dorm is electricity. Hotels build into their room rates excess use of electricity. University dorms, on the other hand, serve student populations who are much more price-sensitive than adult travelers. The relatively cheap per-night rates at university foreign student dormitories includes a certain amount of electrical use, but not the kind of round-the-clock air-conditioning to which many Americans are accustomed. Many universities allow foreign students a certain quota of electricity usage and then charge for use beyond that quota. The dorm will not give you a warning when you are about to go over the limit—you will have to be proactive in asking how close you are to exceeding it.

Though the foreign student dormitory may also house Koreans, Japanese, Russians, South Asians, and a smattering of students from other countries, your roommate in the double-occupancy room will mostly likely be another student in your program. Regardless of who you live with, remember to be courteous to one another when it comes to keeping the room tidy and the bathroom clean. The stress and excitement of living and studying abroad frequently results in new couples forming within a given study abroad program and sometimes between study abroad programs. It is up to you and your roommate to figure out how much privacy will be expected in the room and when. Your program director and the front desk staff will mostly likely put the kibosh on relationships between program participants and Chinese locals, so that should not be an issue. If a student already has a Chinese girlfriend or boyfriend, however, it is necessary to introduce him or her to the front desk as soon as possible. The dorm staff will likely feel uncomfortable with allowing locals unfettered access to the dorm, as it would be considered an invitation to future trouble. Many Chinese assume that foreign strangers are trustworthy and at the same time treat other Chinese as untrustworthy unless they become friends.

Your dorm may have rules regarding guests spending the night in your room. Ask about these rules as soon as you know you want to have a guest stay with you, even if it is after the program is over and before you have to move out. You may think that having a guest stay in an empty bed in a double room adds no costs, but it does mean another round of laundry and the increased risk that comes from having someone not associated with one of the university's partner programs staying in the dorm. It is very possible that the student or his or her guest will be charged for staying overnight in a room that already has an unused bed in it, so be prepared. Also be prepared to be told that a guest may not stay overnight. The dorm belongs to the university, and they have the right to manage it as they see fit.

Which brings us to our next piece of advice: while you are living at a Chinese university, keep in mind that you are a guest there, and—especially in Chinese culture—guests do as the host wishes (**kè suí zhǔ biàn 客随主便**). Unlike U.S. universities, where students are sometimes treated like customers and where "the customer is always right," Chinese universities are the parent figures in the parent-child Confucian dyad described in Chapter 1. The parent knows what is right for the child, guides the child into and through opportunities to flourish, and, in return, the child gives the parent [at least the appear-

Let the door guard know if you'll be late coming home Friday night and bring him a snack so he won't be too grumpy when you wake him up to let you in.

ance of] loyalty and deference. On a Chinese college campus, foreign students must play by Chinese rules. This is good advice to heed off-campus, too, but most study abroad programs have limited off-campus experiences. If the university says the dorms lock-up at 11 p.m. and to be inside by then, make sure you're back before 11 p.m. If it's Friday night and you know your gang will be back at midnight, let the dorm gate guard know on your way out and ask if it's okay for you to come back at midnight. The guard will appreciate your checking with him. Be sure to bring him a little snack, drink, or something when you come back the first time you're out late.

Some university dorms limit the kinds of cooking appliances that can be used on site, especially if they are fire hazards. Instead of sneaking things in, find out how people cook *and* adhere to the rules. Don't worry, your Chinese peers must adhere to the same rules.

■ Foreign Students Apartment

At one time, some universities with long traditions of hosting foreign students offered foreign student "apartments." As foreign student dormitory conditions have improved, these studio apartments have ceased to be much different from the dorm environment. If you do find yourself on a campus that differentiates between apartments and dorms for foreign students, the differences are: the furniture is a little nicer, the rooms a little cleaner, and the air

Living room and bedroom in China Ocean University Yushan Campus foreigner apartment

conditioning should be a little better in the apartment. These rooms also cost more per night than foreign student dormitory rooms. Staying at such a location does not really do a student any favors, as you sacrifice authentic living for comfort, and if comfort is what you seek, you should sign up for a hotel-based short-term study tour instead of a university-based study abroad experience.

Bathroom in Foreign Expert Apartment at Guizhou Normal University Old Campus

Chinese Graduate Student Dormitory

Chinese graduate student housing is a step up from undergrad housing. Graduate rooms usually house no more than four students each, and some universities offer complete apartments to PhD students. These are essentially the same as apartments found off-campus, except that you must be affiliated with the university to get in. Before you get your hopes up, these apartments are still not cozy by American standards, only more spacious and private than the undergraduate dormitory alternative. Like off-campus housing, the rooms will be made from poured concrete, the floors will not be carpeted, and the light fixtures will probably be very basic.

Doctoral Student Apartment at Qingdao University Laoshan Campus

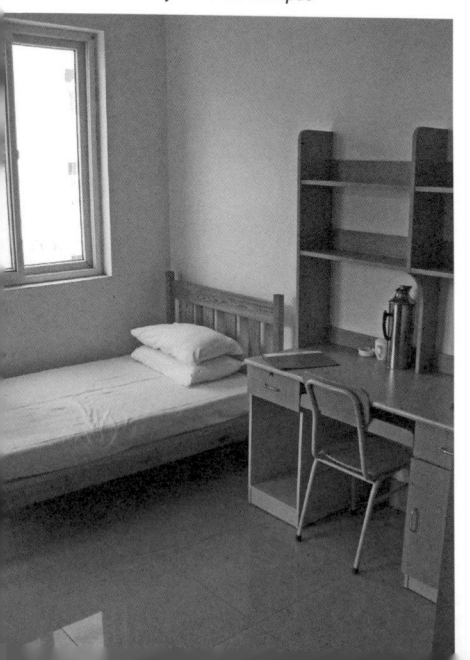

As Chinese universities continue to develop suburban campuses, the number of new-built graduate apartments available for foreign students will, at least initially, grow. As these suburban campuses fill up with Chinese students, however, these units will become more scarce. At the same time, units in universities' old downtown campuses may begin to open up. It is not common for foreign students to stay in Chinese graduate student housing, but it is possible. As with the undergraduate dormitories, if your program is able to arrange for you to stay in Chinese graduate student housing, either the single master's student rooms or the doctoral student apartments, try to appreciate the fact that you are experiencing an aspect of Chinese student life that some Chinese people actually experience themselves.

Chinese Undergraduate Dormitory

Most Chinese undergraduates live packed in rooms of six to eight people in two- or three-level bunk beds. These rooms may have a table or two and a sink for brushing your teeth. In northern China, undergraduate students often must take a shower caddy to a separate communal bathhouse to shower; in southern China, undergrads generally have a hall bathroom in which to shower. These dorms are not always equipped for Internet access, so there are numerous Internet cafes outside of college campuses. As you can imagine, there is little comfort and even less privacy in a normal Chinese undergraduate student's dormitory. Most dorms are divided by gender, and each dorm has one or more elderly dorm mothers who keep tabs on who comes and goes. It is very difficult for a foreign student to have a chance to experience dorm life as Chinese people do, so if your program has arranged for you to stay in a regular Chinese undergraduate student dormitory, you should treasure the experience. The first time you say to yourself, "This stinks! Why did my program do this to me?" remind yourself that most college-educated Chinese lived in the same conditions—or worse—for four years. Having even a little bit of this experience yourself will help you relate to the Chinese people with whom you will interact professionally and socially.

Chinese and American roommates celebrating the Fourth of July

Chinese Roommates

It has become popular for study abroad programs to arrange for Chinese roommates to live in the dorm with American program participants. There are many obvious benefits to living with a Chinese roommate, including:

- An easy "in" to a local person's social network.
- Ready opportunities for language exchange.
- Live-in cultural mentor.
- An opportunity to find out about differences in customs and behavior that you would not even have thought to ask about.

As with roommates anywhere, you may like your own roommate a lot, or you may simply get along well enough to share a room. If everyone in your program has a Chinese roommate, you will probably find you get along well with *someone's* roommate, if not your own. Then, it is up to you to develop a relationship of mutually beneficial reciprocity with that person.

Each Chinese person who agrees to be a roommate for a foreign student hopes to get something out of the experience, otherwise she or he would not do it. The sooner you recognize what it is your roommate would like to get out of the experience, the sooner you will be able to begin helping her or him achieve it, and in return, the roommate will help you with what you want. Usually, Chinese roommates are motivated by several things at once.

The most common motivation for a Chinese student to become a foreign student's roommate is to practice English. Studies have shown that there is a direct correlation between English proficiency and salary in China, so this motivation makes perfect sense. If you deny or ignore it, you may be sending the message, "I don't care about what you want, I only care about what I want," which is counterproductive in any culture. This motivation is easy for a foreign student to satisfy; the challenge is balancing it so that the foreigner has chances to practice Chinese, as well.

Another common motivation is a desire to share Chinese culture with foreigners. There is often an unconscious or unspoken missionary aspect to this motivation, a belief that Chinese culture is superior to others: if members of other cultures could only understand Chinese culture well enough, they would recognize its superiority. Before you scoff at this perspective, reflect on your beliefs regarding what you think is good about Western culture and see if it is such a foreign idea after all. And, crass as it may sound, this is a motivation that benefits foreign students well, provided that they are willing to play along with the idea. The foreign student can have many cultural experiences and additional language practice that the culture-missionary roommate offers as long as he or she does not kill the mood by trying to argue that the Chinese language is *not* more rich than others, or that Chinese food is *not* the best in the world. If there are elements of your culture of which you are proud, let them speak for themselves and let your Chinese friends decide whether or not they enrich their lives the way they do yours.

I personally like General Tso's Chicken (an American dish), but I have yet to convince anyone my own age in China that a tiny piece of chicken deep fried in a lot of batter and covered in a sugary sauce is delicious....

Some Chinese students become roommates to expand their own cultural horizons. They have seen the outside world on TV and in movies and want to know more about what Westerners "are really like." Chinese people are socially conditioned to assign prestige to European-American culture, something like the way Americans tend to think the English are classier than Americans are. Nonetheless, if you are not of European descent, your simple presence in China will create interest in your non-European cultural heritage, and your Chinese peers will soon learn that people of all ethnicities can make good friends. This is your turn to show what diversity means in your home country.

During the summer, your Chinese roommate may move in some time after your arrival because the Chinese school year ends in July, and your roommate-to-be has to concentrate on finals before moving in. When he or she does move in, keep in mind that "your" room now belongs to you both, equally. You may have paid a program fee that covers the cost of the room, but your roommate is paying with his or her time and patience with you, and may be paying a program fee of their own. You may have gotten used to a certain schedule or to using items in the room a certain

Outdoor air is considered preferable to machine drying in China.

way before the roommate showed up, but some of these things may need to be open to negotiation and compromise... which is one of the benefits of having a roommate to begin with. How can you learn the diplomatic arts without ever having had a conflict with someone from another culture?

Some differences of custom take weeks to appear, while others show up in the first few days. Some common examples of the latter include:

- What is considered a comfortable room temperature?
- Where and when to dry laundry?
- In what condition the bathroom should left after a shower
- What constitutes shared-use property?
- What to do if one person is a night-owl and the other is a morning person?
- How to share the cost and use of what may be the only Internet connection in the room?
- How to take meals together if the American's budget or tastes mean going to restaurants beyond the Chinese student's financial or culinary abilities?

If living in China is starting to sound like a lot of work, it can be. And that is one of the things you are going over to learn. If you have any intention of including China in your professional future, the more you learn about how things really work—when they have not all been taken care of for you by a travel agent or a resident director—the better informed you will be.

One of the skills you should be learning in China is how to accomplish short- and long-term goals in ways that make sense to Chinese people, and that make them feel comfortable. This is not to say that if you see an old peasant spit on the sidewalk you should throw out your hygiene standards. Instead, it means learning how a Chinese person would try to stop people from spitting on the sidewalk... which may not even involve talking to someone who just spat.

The way to accomplish many things in China is to develop personal relationships with the people whose support you will need. These relationships, called **guānxi** 关系 in Chinese, are based on the trust that comes from performing acts of reciprocity. Building up reciprocal relationships with the Chinese people with whom you come into contact is how you will achieve your goals in China. Here are some examples that are appropriate for this chapter.

We already listed some potential areas of friction between an American student and his/her Chinese roommate, such as room temperature, laundry, shared-use property, and so on. Many of these issues become much easier to bring up, let alone work out, if both roommates have already begun building a relationship of trust. Since trust in a Chinese relationship grows with reciprocity, there are many things a foreigner can do to demonstrate his or her willingness to build a relationship. The first thing many Chinese people do to indicate an interest in starting a friendly cycle of reciprocity is to invite the person of interest to a meal, with the assumption that the person who was invited will someday return the favor, either with an invitation to another meal, or with something more practical. If the foreigner has been on campus for some time already when the roommate moves in, the foreigner can invite the

Next time, let's go to the school cafeteria.

roommate to lunch at a nearby restaurant. The meal should be within the Chinese student's capacity to pay, however. This is because the Chinese student will feel bound to return the favor in equal or greater amount. If the foreigner "treats" the Chinese to dinner at the Hilton, the foreigner is really creating a debt that most Chinese students would be unable to repay, which then just creates discomfort instead of trust.

Another way to build trust and maintain the friendship cycle of reciprocity is to give a gift to the roommate on the day she or he moves in. This gift should be representative of the foreigner's home town or home university, and something that the Chinese roommate can display, indicating to her or his relationship network the existence of the relationship with *you*, a foreigner.

Finally, but perhaps most importantly, find out quickly why your roommate chose to become a roommate with a foreigner. If the reason was to practice English, imagine how much slack your roommate will give you if you willingly offer your time to improve his or her English. If you have already proofread your roommate's term paper, he may be willing to study at the library instead of in the room, thus allowing you to run the air conditioner at full-blast (which makes him sick).

If you live on campus, your roommate isn't the only person in whose good graces you want to get as soon as possible. Others include (in order of the Chinese social hierarchy): the Office of Foreign Affairs staff, the dorm front desk staff, the old men who watch the dorm door at night, the cleaning staff, the repair staff (if separate from the previous staff), and the university gate guards. Well before you need anything from these people, you should indicate that you want to have a friendly relationship with them by initiating the cycle of reciprocity. Again, an expensive gift would just make everyone feel uncomfortable. Think about what each person likes or wants, and try to provide that. Most of the older fellows drink and/or smoke—you can get them some beer or a couple packs of cigarettes that are a step or two above what they might normally smoke (which is probably the cheapies). Younger folks may also want to practice English or be invited to your classmates' Friday night foreign movie viewing. When you give a gift, say thank you for looking out for your class (which they would have already begun doing, so it is true). If you speak Chinese, you can say, **xièxiè zhàogu wǒmen** 谢谢照顾我们. It is modest to say you are thanking them for taking care of "us," even though it is understood that you mean "me." Do not say, "on behalf of my class, I would like to thank you for..." unless you are really giving the class's gift, as might happen at the end of your program. Otherwise, the recipient will a) assume the whole class paid for it and not just you, and b) be less likely to associate that gift with taking care of *you individually* when you need it.

Year after year, the American students who leave the best impression on Chinese university staff are those who recognize the importance of building personal relationships with the people responsible for their program's operations. It is not that these students never get into trouble, but rather, they know how to leave a good impression *despite* periodically waking up the night watchman to open the dorm doors at 1:00 a.m. on a Friday night. These students reflect well on themselves, making them welcome for future visits and interaction in that city, and reflect well on their programs, which will probably return to the same dorm and university the following year.

If you become exasperated by your living environment in a foreign student dormitory, remind yourself that you still have it better than your Chinese peers ever did. If you have a Chinese roommate, avoid complaining about the conditions, as it will only reflect poorly on you. What you can do, however, is use your *guanxi* and a positive attitude to try to improve the things you can and accept the things you cannot.

Host Families

When you are living in a dorm, the dorm exists because your money pays for it to be there. When you live with a host family—even though you are paying for it, too—it is truly your privilege to join their home for a period of time. Out of graciousness, the host family will probably make some adjustments in their lives to accommodate you, but they are under no real obligation to do so, since you are there to learn what life is nor-

In China, Joe Average does not live in an apartment so spacious that it can comfortably accommodate a foreign homestay guest, like this one could.

mally like in a Chinese home … and Chinese homes normally do not have foreigners living in them. This is your great opportunity to be forced to adapt to Chinese culture, and to learn about Chinese daily life long before your dorm-living peers do.

Chinese host families are generally middle- or upper-middle-class households who want to give their child more exposure to English-speaking Western culture. The fact that host families have sufficient space in their homes to house an extra person indicates that they have a fairly comfortable income and are not living hand-to-mouth. Many host families are paid to host, but it is uncommon to find Chinese host families who do it for the money, *per se*; the money is primarily given to cover the expenses associated with housing an extra person and the activities that the host family is expected to engage in on behalf of the student guest. Host families arranged by a program will usually have been well vetted as "positive" representatives of China, thus eliminating families who need to skim from hosting fees to get by. Now you know that your average Chinese host family is not a statistically average Chinese family. Foreigners in China very rarely have extended interactions with the kind of Chinese people that make up the bulk of China's population: working-class folks with very limited incomes and little or no exposure to foreign culture or languages. A learner's experience with a Chinese host family may be representative of a certain economically comfortable portion of Chinese society but will rarely be representative of the "average" Chinese person's life experience.

Making friends

When your host family picks you up at the airport or train station, it will probably consist of mom, dad, and their child.[1] If the parents do not speak English well, they may have their child initiate conversation with you in English, even if you already speak enough Chinese to hold a conversation. It will be in your long-term language-learning interest to go with the flow and allow the child to practice his or her English, even though you may be there to practice Chinese. If you let the child practice English with

---

1 Two cultural notes here: In Chinese, "dad" is said before "mom" so Chinese people would say "Dad and Mom." Though most Chinese families adhere to the one-child policy, ethnic minorities, the very poor and the very rich often do not. Minorities are not held to the rule; the poor have nothing to lose by breaking the law, and the rich can afford the fees associated with exceeding the one-child quota.

you, the parents will be glad they signed up to be hosts and then you can practice your Chinese with two happy Chinese adults. Odds are that they will create many opportunities for you to speak Chinese by introducing you to monolingual friends and taking you to places where the locals speak only Chinese.

If a member of the host family offers to take your luggage, you may make a polite refusal, but if the one offering is stronger than you let him or her carry it. It is considered the job of a good host to carry luggage for arriving guests, so it is okay to permit this and not insist on doing it yourself. Onlookers will think "that host is doing the right thing." If you are stronger than your host family members, though, it's okay to make sure you end up being the one carrying your luggage. You can let one of the host family members carry a small carry-on instead–that way everyone looks good.

The luggage-carrying dance is a good indicator of what kind of relationship you and your host family will start out with. The default relationship most Chinese will assume exists is that of host and guest, a highly ritualized set of behavioral expectations that have been passed down and developed for literally thousands of years. In Chinese culture, good hosts do not make guests do anything, from carrying luggage to washing dishes. Good hosts anticipate guests' needs and wishes and fulfill them without being asked, like always making sure the guest has hot tea to drink (what civilized human being *doesn't* want hot tea, right?), or providing sandwich bread to the foreign guest at dinner (foreigners all eat bread instead of rice, right?). Good hosts should also sacrifice their own interests for the needs of their guests, without ever letting on that they were inconvenienced. For example, when a host picks up a guest at the airport, a gracious guest will thank the host for taking time out of the busy day to make the pick-up; a gracious host will say that it was no trouble at all... even if the host had to call in a favor in order to get out of work that day.

The rituals governing the host-guest relationship are very commonly encountered in China because this is the default pattern for new relationships. For foreigners in China, it is especially common because visitors to a strange place (even if the visitor is also Chinese) are automatically "guests"

You don't have to let a 4-year-old carry your luggage, though.

and locals are automatically "hosts." Because the host is doing all the work and not letting on how much work it is, being a guest in China is pretty comfortable. However, the guest-host relationship is not the only one possible, nor is it a sustainable one. In the host-guest relationship, the host is always giving and the guest is always taking. Furthermore, the guest-host relationship is marked by a high level of politeness. In Chinese culture, polite = distant. Hosts treat guests with generosity in time and resources, but not in information. Information is reserved for people who have earned the Chinese person's trust. Such information includes materially useful items like connections to people of influence as well as "simple" things like honest feedback on your language ability.

Eventually, you need to move out of host-guest and into the reciprocity-based "pseudo-family," "friends," or "professional colleagues" types of relationships to have a long-term relationship in China. You know you have earned your host family's trust when they start to "tell it like it is." Foreigners in China all start off on that Cloud 9 where Chinese people say the foreigner's Chinese language skills are great because she or he can say "*ni hao*." Once you have earned someone's trust, they may point out all your incorrect tones or dress you down for eating out of turn at a banquet. Viscerally, going from pampered guest to being reminded that you are an imperfect human with a lot to learn about Chinese culture can be tough, but it is a healthy and necessary transition.

As a guest, a foreign learner will probably be given a private bedroom. This may be a spare bedroom, but frequently it is a room that a member of the family has given up for the guest. That member of the family—in the case of one of the author's friends, it was Grandma who was kicked out of her room—will then sleep in someone else's room or on the living room couch. If the learner is sleeping in someone else's room, it is a good physical metaphor for the blurred line between "private" and "public" in Chinese culture, a line that becomes blurrier as the guest-host relationship evolves into a more intimate (e.g., "family") one. Whereas American hosts are taught that guestrooms become the private space of the guest living in it, Chinese host families may continue to regard the guest student's room as belonging to the family. As

I'm telling you this as a friend. You just said something about the chairman's mother.

Yeah, I used your computer. Thanks!

the relationship becomes closer, host family members may feel it is okay to use the learner's personal property (like an iPad or shampoo) because close friends and family members in China can do so without asking permission. In fact, the act of asking permission can be perceived as an indicator of social distance and a low level of trust. Be prepared to share as much of your time, space, and possessions as possible, as this is an indicator of closeness. Trying to maintain the distinction between public and private that exists in Western culture can alienate host families who are not accustomed to it.

There are significant generation gaps in China that relate to the concept of personal property and private space. Many Chinese feel that Chinese children born after 1990 have a highly developed sense of "mine" versus "yours." Some even go so far to say that a great many of these "Post-1990" kids only understand "mine" because, as only children, they grew up being given everything they wanted by doting grandparents who raised them for the parents. Of course, this is a huge generalization, but it is worth knowing merely because so many Chinese people believe it. It is also good to know that many Chinese believe that this selfish behavior is an import from Western culture.

After you have had a chance to put your luggage in "your" room, it is time to give your hosts the gifts you brought for them from the U.S. If your program connected you with your host family before you left the States, you may have had the opportunity to find out what sorts of gifts would be appropriate for them. If not, no worries—the old standbys of hometown and alma mater merchandise still work. The exchange

The word is still out on the Post-2000 Generation....

You might need an extra suitcase just to bring back all the tea you could be gifted.

of gifts is part of the ritualized interaction between guests and hosts. Over time, the nature of the gifts will change to indicate changes in the nature of the relationship. At first, gifts are impersonal and come from the Chinese mental category of "gift": tea, small handicrafts, and local specialty foods. By the time you leave your host family, you will be exchanging gifts with sentimental significance, like framed photos of group activities, mementos from places you visited together, etc. If you keep in touch for years, you may eventually become so close that the gifts are entirely practical, like electronics or baby toys that are cheaper in the United States.

In Chinese culture, hosts are obligated to treat guests to a welcome meal that is fancier and more bountiful than a normal meal. This meal will most probably be the first meal that comes after your host family picks you up. If you arrive just before or at meal time, you may not even go home first before going to a restaurant. Alternatively, Mom or Dad may have stayed at home to cook while you were being picked up at the airport or train station.

This welcome meal will probably not be a financial burden to most host families. If you spend some time in the countryside, however, peasant homes may sacrifice a significant portion of their discretionary income in order to put on a respectable welcome (or going away) meal. Regardless of the financial sacrifice, the welcome meal is almost always out of the ordinary, so it is courteous to treat it as such.

Nearly every Chinese meal is served "family style." That is, a number of cold and cooked dishes will be placed at the center of a table and everyone at the table gets from those dishes. Fancy restaurants provide common-use spoons and chopsticks for use in transporting food from the center to one's own dish; cozier restaurants and many families simply expect the eaters to use their own chopsticks to get food from the common plates. If this sounds unhygienic, it kind of is. At a restaurant, it is socially acceptable to request common-use utensils for the dishes by asking, "Are there any public chopsticks?" (**yǒu méi yǒu gōng kuài? 有没有公筷?**). In a private home, it is a little more awkward to ask this question but not unacceptable. During your stay in China, pay attention to how people use their chopsticks–not only how they hold them, which is a popular mealtime conversation topic, but also how they eat with them. In public situations, most Chinese will not lick or suck their chopsticks, and instead will pluck food off of the chopsticks with their teeth, barely brushing the chopsticks with their

Family style dining

lips. This minimizes the unhygienic aspect of using one's own chopsticks to get food from common dishes of food.

A good guest will at least try every dish that is served. To do otherwise is to imply that the host inaccurately anticipated the guest's desires and, thus, failed to be a good host. If you do not like something, leave a little on your plate. A good host is obligated to put food on the guest's plate, and the host will continue doing so unless the previously served portion of a given dish is still there. The host's job at a meal is to make sure that the guests are sated.

That was great. No, I'm good. Really. Seriously. Oh, no, more?

An empty plate is a signal to the host that the guest is still hungry, so an empty plate will get refilled. So, fight the temptation to be a good *Western* guest who cleans your plate.

It is appropriate to compliment the food served. If at a restaurant, complimenting the food is interpreted as praise for the host's skill in ordering (ordering a Chinese meal really does require skill). If at home, complimenting the food compliments the chef's skill in cooking. As is the case anywhere, the guest's eager partaking of the food provided by the host is most obvious form of praise. With the host obligated to make sure the guest is sated, the host will repeatedly attempt to serve more food, even when the guest is apparently full. This is part of the ritual. The guest's role in this ritual is to insist that she or he is satisfied (not "full," as that implies you see the banquet as a refueling event rather than a social event) and to stop eating when there is almost no more food.[2]

When the host asks his or her guests if they are satisfied with the meal, the answer is always "yes," even if the meal seemed to be all fried insects that killed your appetite for the dishes that you would normally be able to eat. This is one of the obligations of a guest—to give the host face by appearing satisfied even if you are not. Making requests

---

2 Never eat the last bite of a dish served family-style, as this is considered selfish. The host may serve a guest the last bite, and then the guest may eat it, but the guest may not actively take the last bite or piece.

at a meal is one common trap into which foreign guests fall. In the U.S., guests are expected to make selections from a range of choices provided by the host; in China, the host is expected to make the right selection before the guest arrives. If a guest asks a waiter for a soda when everyone else is drinking tea, it means the host failed; if a guest tries to compliment the meal by saying "it's too bad there weren't more of those dumplings," it means the host failed. On the way home, even if you are dying for desert, just hold onto that craving until you have some free time. If you ask for ice cream after your first meal, you may just find yourself faced with an uninterrupted supply of post-meal ice cream for the duration of your stay!

It is Chinese custom to bathe before going to bed, so your host family may ask you if you want to take your shower first at night. Here is another chance to negotiate cultural behaviors with your host family. Chinese feel it is dirty to sleep on clean sheets with a day's worth of grime and oil on your body, while many North Americans feel dirty facing the world without having bathed in the morning. You can see how your host family reacts to a request to shower in the morning—which would eliminate your adding to the nighttime rush—or you can follow your hosts and shower at night and then maybe only wash your face or hair in the morning if you need to.

When you do go to take your first shower, be sure to ask how to use the hot water if your hosts do not volunteer this information. Many Chinese homes use wall-mounted water heaters that are much more energy efficient than the large cylinders found in American homes. American-style water heaters keep a certain amount of water hot all the time, ready for use at the turn of a faucet; wall-mounted water heaters are normally turned off when not in use, and when turned on, they heat the water as it comes in from the city lines. These units are fairly self-explanatory, but as they usually use flames of burning natural gas, it is better to be shown how to use the unit than to inadvertently fill the bathroom with gas while you figure out the dials.

Sometime during the beginning of your stay, the host family will very probably take you on sightseeing tours. Good hosts are expected to take out-of-town guests to all the major local sights and are expected to pay for it. It is nearly impossible and actually rude for a guest to pay for his or her own welcome activities; even if you found a way to secretly foot the welcome meal bill, you will probably just make the host feel that he or she failed at hosting, forcing them to find another activity with you to pay for. Instead of trying to pay for things that the host is supposed to pay for, it would be more suitable to start moving the relationship in the direction of "family" or "friends" by buying things for the family on your own initiative. For example, buy popsicles for the whole family during an outing, especially if you really have a yen for a popsicle but the host doesn't seem to think

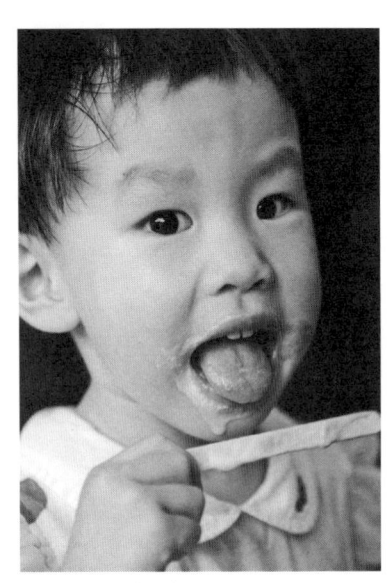

He will appreciate it.

about eating sweets. Buy a popsicle for each person in the group.

This is another important etiquette lesson: if you want something, make sure others around you have some before you partake. If you want a bottle of water, get waters for everyone; if you want to chew gum, offer everyone else a stick before you eat yours. You need to make sure you have enough of the item to offer it to everyone before you partake in order for it to be a genuine offer. Chinese people will instantly calculate whether there is enough of what you are offering for everyone, and if there isn't, most will decline the offer. If you ask before you even buy the water/gum/etc., the *polite* (socially distant) answer in Chinese culture is no, no matter how much the person you asked really wants that stick of gum, because that would mean selfishly requesting something. So, instead of asking if they want some first–which may cause someone to run and buy it for you–get enough to share with everyone in your group and start handing it out, leaving yourself until last. If this seems complicated, it really isn't. Just remember: if you want to consume something in the company of an in-group (water, gum, tea, your bag lunch, a chocolate bar you brought from home), make sure you can give some to everyone else first; if you cannot, then forget about it or wait until you are alone to enjoy it.

Living with a host family will reveal many areas in which Western culture and Chinese culture differ, and you will learn much from negotiating how members of the two cultures are going to get along in the face of these differences. Some differences are purely personal or familial and would be encountered by any two or more people living together, but they still need to be resolved in ways that are culturally informed. You will learn to protect your hosts' *face* as well as your own when communicating needs and desires; you will learn that sometimes you just need to suck it up and keep your mouth shut in order to be a good guest. Someday, you may get to be a host and enjoy the apparent satisfaction of good Chinese guests! There is no guarantee that you will like your host family, that they will like you, or that you will be able to acclimate yourself to daily Chinese life. However, you are most certainly guaranteed a learning experience that will leave a deep impression.

Key Hotel Words/Phrases:

Characters	Pinyin	English equivalent
房间	Fángjiān	Room
标间	Biāojiān	Standard double room
套间	Tàojiān	Suite
护照	Hùzhào	Passport
填表	Tián biǎo	Fill out a form
登记表	Dēngjì biǎo	Registration form
住	Zhù	Live in, stay
押金	Yājīn	"Deposit" (pre-payment)
刷卡	Shuā kǎ	Swipe a card (credit/debit/transit)
付现金	Fù xiànjīn	Pay cash
早餐票	Zǎocānpiào	Breakfast ticket
房卡	Fángkǎ	Room keycard
商务中心	Shāngwù zhōngxīn	Business center

Chapter 6
Being a Foreign Student in China

One important educational aspect of studying overseas is learning the local social "rules of the game." What kinds of behaviors and language are produced by people who know how to play the game? What behavior is expected of people in that environment? In the United States, it is commonly understood that if a piece of information is not found on the syllabus or in the textbook, and is only mentioned in one lecture, it is not considered fair game for an exam question. Is it the same in China?

In addition to expectations regarding all teacher-student interactions, there is another set of expectations regarding the role of a foreign student or visitor to China, and unless you are of Asian descent, you will be held to these expectations whether you like it or not.

This chapter is about who Chinese culture allows you to be when in their territory. When you are on the Chinese playing field, you are playing by Chinese rules, so you might as well know what some of these rules are before you unwittingly break them. After reading this chapter, if you choose to ignore some of the rules or be offended by them, at least you do so knowingly!

General Expectations About Student Behavior

Many native Chinese see foreign students as being capable of playing a limited number of social roles or identities. These identities come with certain behavioral expectations. For example, the "helpless foreigner" identity can lead to natives assuming that a foreign student is incapable of accomplishing even simple daily tasks. This can be frustrating for foreigners who feel infantilized, and tiring for locals who, trying to be good hosts, spend a lot of time doing things for their foreigner. This can be problematic in homestay and internship situations. The "student" role also comes with a set of culturally-defined expectations, as well. These expectations do not always overlap with what is expected of students in the student's home country. Thus, for those who want to leave a good impression on the Chinese people around them, it is useful to know how they expect you to act, and what actions they perceive as being the mark of a well-

Ma Zhiyuan listens to Zeng laoshi ("Teacher Zeng").

socialized, well-educated member of [Chinese] society.

First and foremost, a student in Chinese culture is lower than teachers and administrators in the academic hierarchy. This means that students either do what they are told by faculty and staff, or at the very least, do not say "no" to them (there are ways of nonverbally indicating disagreement). If a teacher tells a student to stay late, then the student will try his or her best to stay late, and change any plans she or he had previously made.[1] If the teacher tells a student that his or her exam answer was wrong but the student does not think so, the student would need to find an indirect way to indicate that there may be another correct answer to the question (not that the *teacher* was wrong!).

Unlike in many Western cultures in which students are considered almost socially equal to their instructors, and allowed—even encouraged—to disagree with received knowledge, the Chinese education system rewards students for remembering information exactly as it is delivered to them. This is how you achieve a good grade on the high school and then college entrance exams. Students who stray too far from what was taught to them do poorly on these exams and end up disappointing their families. This is not to say that Chinese students do not have their own opinions, only that the academic examination system that

---

1 This example is based on American expectations regarding student responsibilities, though. Chinese students normally stay late after school for extra study; students who have social plans on a school night are often those who are considered "bad" students. That is, they intend to go into the workforce after high school instead of testing into a good university.

Don't step out of line....

decides their fates does not allow them to formally express alternative opinions and viewpoints until they are already in college or graduate school, by which time, many have already learned that non-mainstream points of view are best kept out of public conversation.

Does this mean that foreign students in China cannot express alternative points of view? Of course not. It does mean, however, that foreign students who wish to establish and maintain the image of a "good student" (which will be important for establishing *guanxi*) need to learn how do so in such a way that reinforces the student-as-learner identity with which Chinese are familiar. For example, if a foreign student wishes to challenge his or her teacher on a point given in a lecture, the student could make the challenge in the form of a question: "I once heard someone say [an alternative opinion]. Teacher Wang, what do you think of that viewpoint?" This way, the student preserves the

I'll erase the board, Teacher Zhao.

teacher's giver-of-knowledge role while suggesting the possibility of an alternative viewpoint. In this context, trying to stump the teacher does no good for anyone.

Another student behavior that creates positive feelings among Chinese observers is voluntarily fulfilling needs of the teacher without being asked. For example, if a teacher is struggling with setting up an LCD projector, "good" students will step up and take over so that the teacher can concentrate on more teacher-like work than setting up the A/V equipment. Does every Chinese student do this kind of thing? Of course not! But the ones who catch their teachers' eyes do so, and benefit later when the teachers think of them for special opportunities or positions of responsibility.

In American classroom culture, these might be considered behaviors of a toady or a teacher's pet, and in China, they are too … the difference is that being a teacher's pet is a *good* thing, when done artfully. In Chinese society, those who want to get ahead get in good with their superiors. This starts in school and continues for the rest of professional life in China.

Some Pigs Are More Equal Than Others

Now that you know that Chinese schools are just as hierarchical as the rest of Chinese society, it is useful to know that there is a pecking order among the students, as well. This hierarchy is defined by the school when teachers name the student leaders in each class. These student leaders must earn the respect of their classmates, and sometimes even their votes, but positions such as "class monitor," "class representative," "class hygiene monitor," and so on are validated by the authority of the school. It is rare for Chinese teachers of foreign students to name a class monitor (**bānzhǎng 班长**), but when it does happen, it is good to know that this is a normal part of Chinese student life. Class monitors serve as intermediaries between classes and their teachers, a sort of sergeant for the teacher-officer. Another important thing is that even when the teacher does not name a 班长 or a 课代表 for a class, she or he may often ask the most capable student to handle more tasks, take more responsibility, and assume more authority. Instead of asking for

As you wish, boss.

volunteers, some Chinese teachers will use phrases such as **nǐ jiāojiāo tā** 你教教他 ("show him how to do it"), **nǐ bāng tā yíxià** 你帮他一下 ("give him a hand"), or **nǐ guǎn yíxià zhè jiàn shì** 你管一下这件事 ("take care of this task") to identify the students he or she believes are more capable and assign tasks to them. American students may feel uncomfortable with the idea that one of their own serves the authority, but it is a good lesson in the gray area between those who manage and those who are managed.

Teachers of classes for foreign students are often conditioned to expect less cooperation from the students than he or she would those in an all-Chinese classroom. This works in the favor of foreign students who have difficulty adapting to Chinese student expectations… until they try to do something in the real Chinese world, where few people are specifically trained to put up with foreigners who do not understand the social hierarchy.

Don't sit like this in the presence of a Chinese person whose respect you want.

Will This Be On the Test?

How much a foreign student needs to pay attention to Chinese student standards will depend on how "Chinese" the class is. Many foreigners in China take classes created exclusively for foreigners, taught by teachers trained in teaching foreign students (and trained in English and Western culture). More and more foreign students are taking classes in China with Chinese students (called "direct enrollment"), and in these classes, the behavioral (if not the performance) expectations are the same for the non-Chinese students as they are for the Chinese students. Even in classes for foreign students, if the teacher has little experience teaching foreigners, his or her expectations regarding the students may be very much informed by his or her own *Chinese* educational experience.

For foreigners in classes governed by Chinese expectations regarding student behavior, one of the most important questions that needs answering is, "what performance is required to get an A?" For now, the answer is often "show up." Foreigners taking college classes in China are often held to the same standard as American junior high school students in gym class: if you show up and stay awake, you'll get a decent grade. These halcyon days for foreign students in China will not last forever, though, so you might

Hey, where is everybody?

as well find out what it takes to get a good grade in a system that requires more than just dressing out.

Perhaps the most representative difference between Chinese and Western classes is that many Chinese classes do not have syllabi. In this high-context culture, the students are expected to know what is expected of them, and if they are unclear, the responsibility for finding out rests not on the teacher—as it does in the U.S.—but on the student. The reading list, the assignments, grading rubric; all these things may be undefined and may actually be decided as the term moves along. Frequently, there are only one or two things that decide a student's grade for the term: a midterm exam and a final exam. Anything from readings and lectures are fair game for these exams.

Skilled students—and especially skilled class monitors—will ask their teachers to hold a test review session before the exams. If they play their cards right, the students will be able to get the teacher to share most of the content of the test during these sessions.

The lack of a syllabus can be taken as a metaphor for the lack of a codified framework defining interaction between the school and the student. The dates of each school year, as well as the dates of holidays taken during the year are often unknown until very shortly before the dates in question. Even then, these dates may not be found on the school website; it is up to the students and parents to find out what these dates are by their own means. When a teacher is going to be absent and class canceled, the teacher may only tell the class monitor. That class monitor will do his or her best to inform all the students in the class, but if a foreigner is only auditing a class, or otherwise not an official member, the monitor may accidentally overlook that student. In Chinese culture, where *guanxi* is everything, maintaining positive relations with the class monitor can mean the difference between showing up for a class that has already been canceled and sleeping in.

Preparing for Class

For foreign students directly enrolled in classes for Chinese students, the best course of action is to keep in touch with the class monitor, and make a point of regularly asking what is expected of the class. Because students are expected to know this already, the foreign student may need to spend a little personal time in order to earn the reciprocal flow of information from the class monitor: helping the monitor with English homework, sharing snacks with him or her, etc.

In classes designed for foreign students, finding out what the teacher expects will be a lot easier: the teacher will probably tell the students what chapter is being covered, and which parts of the chapter will be tested when, e.g., vocabulary quiz on day two of the new chapter; grammar quiz on day three, etc. It is safe to assume that, unless otherwise notified, all vocabulary in a chapter may be tested, including "supplemental vocabulary." In the U.S., "supplemental" often means "not on the test," but many Chinese teachers do not differentiate.

Preparing for Chinese classes for foreigners is generally a straightforward affair consisting of memorizing a lot of vocabulary items and sentences that use the target grammar patterns in the current chapter. If you can write each new word in characters and use it appropriately in a sentence, you should do fine on the vocabulary quiz. If you can use the grammar patterns in grammatically and socially-appropriate sentences, you should do fine on the grammar quizzes. If asked to write a short essay on a theme found in the chapter, the safest thing to do is to sew together sentences from that and previous chapters, substituting some key vocabulary here and there. Until your language skills have reached the point where you can differentiate between creative writing and simply ungrammatical sentences, it is more instructive to model your writing after the examples in your texts.

The Pros and Cons of Being a Foreign Student in China

The good news is that foreign students in China are almost always held to different standards from Chinese students. The bad news is that these standards are much lower, making it less likely that the classroom experience will prepare foreign learners for real life in China. Chinese students are expected to memorize tremendous amounts of information and reproduce it at exam time; in high school, students spend all of daylight hours (and many nighttime hours) at school studying, and even though college life is much easier, the expectation that a student can be asked to sacrifice a great deal of "personal" time to studying remains. Foreign students, on the other hand, are often treated with kid gloves, creating a kind of velvet bubble in which the foreigners feel that life is pretty good… except that the velvet bubble is a kind of cultural fence keeping the foreigners from truly participating in Chinese society on Chinese terms. When the author was a student at a famous university in Beijing in the late 1990s, we shamelessly negotiated with our teachers for less homework because the teachers did not realize that we did not have this kind of power in the U.S. At another famous university in Beijing, foreign students in a fledgling English-language master's degree program were recently allowed to cheat on exams so that they could get passing grades. The skills learned in these two examples are not well-adapted to life outside of the special environment of foreign students studying in China, and would need to be unlearned in order to earn respect in the local culture. Remember, even if you do not plan to return to China after your study abroad experience, your program directors will, and your behavior will affect how the Chinese host institution treats your program in the future.

Do's and Don'ts of Being a Successful Student in China

Do:

- **Pay attention in class**
  Even if you are tired/bored/hungry/hung over, your teacher will notice whether or not you are paying attention. You never know how earning your teacher's respect will benefit you, but you can be sure that losing your teacher's respect will result in nothing good.

Teacher is not going to be pleased.

- **Help the teacher before he or she has to ask for it**
 This is the mark of a well-brought-up individual in Chinese society. Make sure there is chalk/markers in the classroom; help the teacher set up classroom equipment if you know how; move chairs and tables into the arrangement your teacher prefers, etc.

- **Be proactive in finding out what you need to do in order to meet the class requirements**

- **Wait until a pause to raise your hand to ask a question**
 Let the teacher finish his or her thought before raising your hand, as some teachers may feel obligated to cut themselves off to answer your question. Though they are happy to help you, it is thoughtful to not make them lose their train of thought.

- **Be cautious in how you offer your own ideas and opinions**
 Many teachers of Chinese as a foreign language expect their foreign students to be more expressive and contentious than Chinese students would be, but that does not mean that they have come prepared to be contradicted, especially during class.

  If you are taking a regular Chinese course with Chinese classmates, offering an opposing opinion in class could very well be asking for trouble. Keep in mind that your professors in China give you readings about ideas they agree with and want you to agree with, as well. If you criticize or disagree with the assignment, it is very possible that the instructor will construe it as a criticism of his/her own views and legitimacy as an authority on the subject. Some cultures encourage students to publicly criticize canonical interpretations, but Chinese culture is not one of them.

  If you disagree with something in the course, bring it up with the teacher in private and couch your disagreement in humble terms: you are asking because you do not understand, or lack enough experience to interpret the facts accurate, etc. It is unlikely that a student will be able to convince an instructor–who is presumably an authority on the subject–that the student knows best, so arguing your point like a lawyer may result in more hard feelings than changed minds.

  Unless the teacher makes a point of saying that he or she purposefully chose a certain article in order to invite criticism, you should be very cautious about expressing disagreement even if the article was not written by your teacher.

- **Be seated and ready to learn before the start of class.**
 Chinese teachers are not expected to be in the room until class begins. So, do not take

your queue from the teacher, but from the Chinese expectation that students should be in class first.

Do not:

- **Interrupt the teacher**

- **Start packing up to leave when class time is up**
  The class is over when the teacher dismisses it, period. All Chinese teachers understand this, so your responsibility is to the teacher in front of you, not the teacher in your next class.

- **Eat or drink in the classroom. If you need a drink or snack, wait until break time and leave the classroom.**
  It is considered disrespectful to the teacher to eat or drink in class. Drinking is less inappropriate than eating, though, and the rules relax a little for college students. However, because many foreigners speak Chinese like Chinese elementary school students, their Chinese teachers may unconsciously expect their foreign students to adhere to child-like classroom expectations more than college student ones.

- **Say that the teacher is wrong in front of other students or teachers.**
  A little common sense goes a long way. In some cultures, students score brownie points by pointing out holes in a teacher's argument or calculation. This is not the case in Chinese classrooms. If a teacher makes an error, wait until after class and politely point it out in private so that the teacher does not lose credibility or face. For example, if the teacher says that Manchester is the capital of England, after class, you can approach him or her and say you think London might be the capital of England. A conscientious teacher will go and look it up, so that lets the Internet be the one to tell the teacher he or she really was wrong. You only said the teacher might be wrong....

A Note About Teachers' Expectations for Foreign Students

So few foreign students have bothered to understand or adapt to the expectations of their host country that the bar is often quite low for impressing Chinese teachers. Many foreigners go to China on a lark, or because they could not get into a decent university in their home country, and so many foreigners have little intention of establishing a positive image for themselves in China. Certain countries have even earned a reputation for sending uncouth students to China, students who are loud at night, sleep through classes, and are disrespectful of those around them. They have made it easy for the rest of us to look good by just adhering to some basic rules of adult behavior.

Even if you only intend to go to China once or twice in your lifetime, you lose nothing by acting under the assumption that the Chinese people with whom you have regular contact might someday be willing to help you out in a time of need … if they like you.

Social Expectations Outside the Classroom

Understanding how Chinese teachers expect students to act in their classrooms is helpful for establishing positive adult relationships with people in positions of authority. It is also useful to know how other Chinese students—and their parents—expect foreigners to behave. In cases where you already meet these expectations, you have little work to do. In cases where you do not, knowing what the default expectation was will help you to politely manage the Chinese side's expectations and positively manage your image.

First of all, to Chinese who have few interactions with foreigners (and this is most Chinese people), "a foreigner is a foreigner is a foreigner," with only a few major distinctions based mostly on skin color. Chinese people tend to imagine humans existing in a hierarchy of cultural evolution with Chinese at the top, Caucasians in second, South Asians in third, and Africans coming in last. Latin Americans rarely factor into Chinese racial cosmology, possibly because there are relatively few Latin Americans in China. It may be a small comfort to know that the average Chinese city person is an equal-opportunity discriminator: prejudice against darker skin color applies to Chinese people, as well, with dark skin implying a peasant background.

When a Chinese person with little experience with foreigners meets a foreigner, he or she may begin with some pre-programmed assumptions about what kind of animal a foreigner is. Some of these assumptions include:

- Foreign males play basketball.
- Foreign women are more licentious than their Chinese counterparts.
- Foreign women who smoke are counter-culture rebels (because Chinese girls who smoke often are).
- Foreigners all speak English.
- Foreigners are hairy and/or smelly.
- Foreigners have poor math skills.
- Foreigners are abrupt and selfish (but that's okay, "that's just the way they are").
- Caucasian foreigners are rich.
- Americans are kicked out of their homes at the age of 18 because American parents do not love their children as much as Chinese parents do.

Statue in the burial grounds of Confucius and his descendants in Qufu, Shandong.

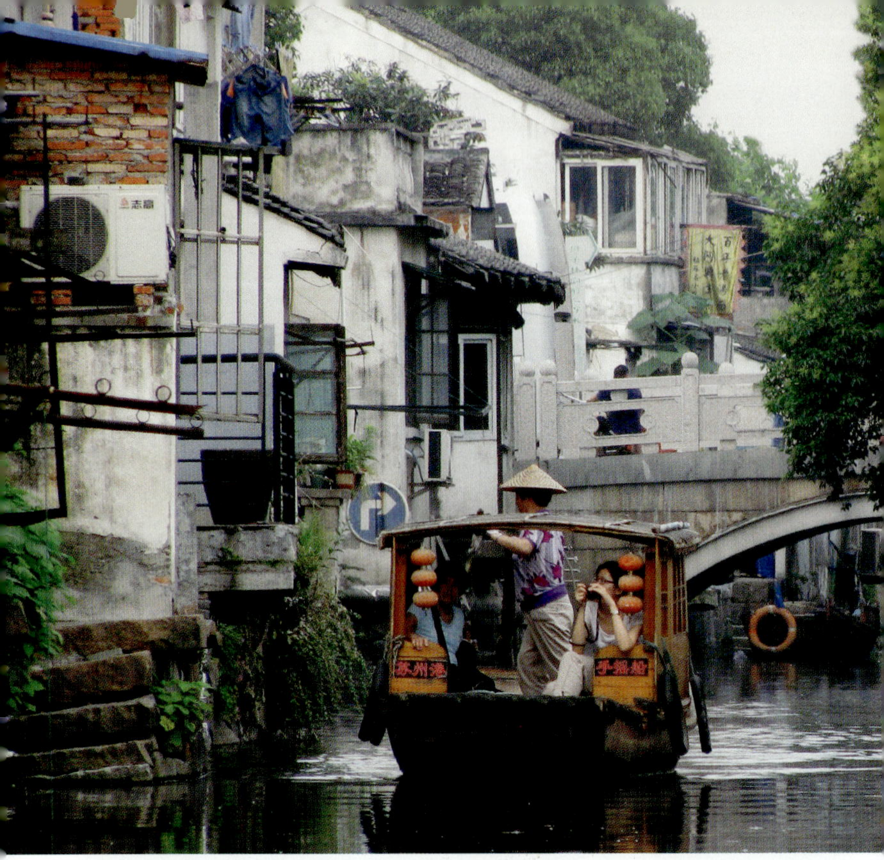

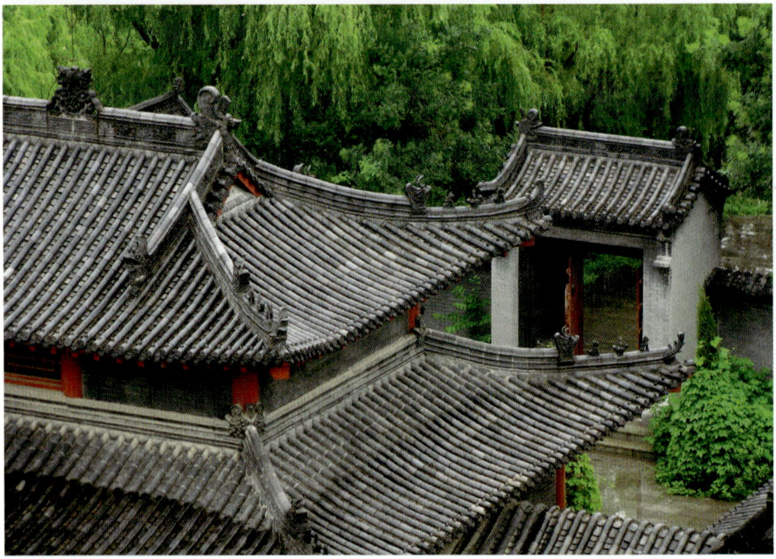

Left: *A tourist gondola in Suzhou.*
Bottom: *Part of the Mu Family Estate in Qixia, Shandong.*
Opposite Bottom: *Classic roof tiling outside Zibo, Shandong.*

Top: *Photos like this one—captured in Canlongshan, Linzhou, Henan—will captivate viewers back home.*

Above: *The picturesque falls at Huangguoshu.*

Opposite: *Early morning on Mt. Tai., Tai'an, Shandong.*

Huang Long Park, Sichuan.

Strikingly beautiful water lilies, Zibo, Shandong.

Qingdao's Laoshan Mountain offers breathtaking views.

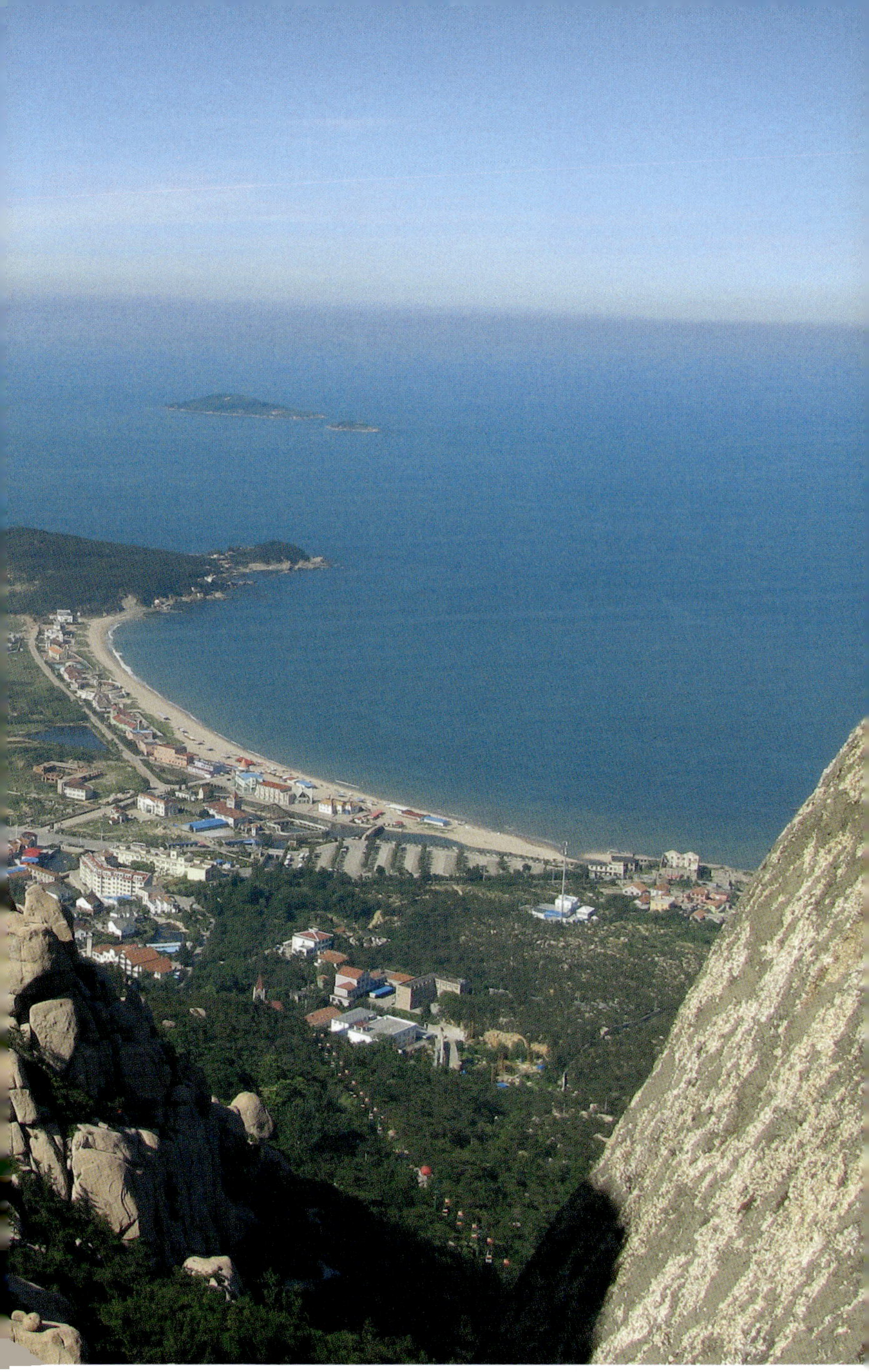

Above: Qi State Wall, Laiwu, Shandong.
Opposite Top: The Summer Palace (颐和园), in northwest Beijing.
Right: City scene in Harbin.

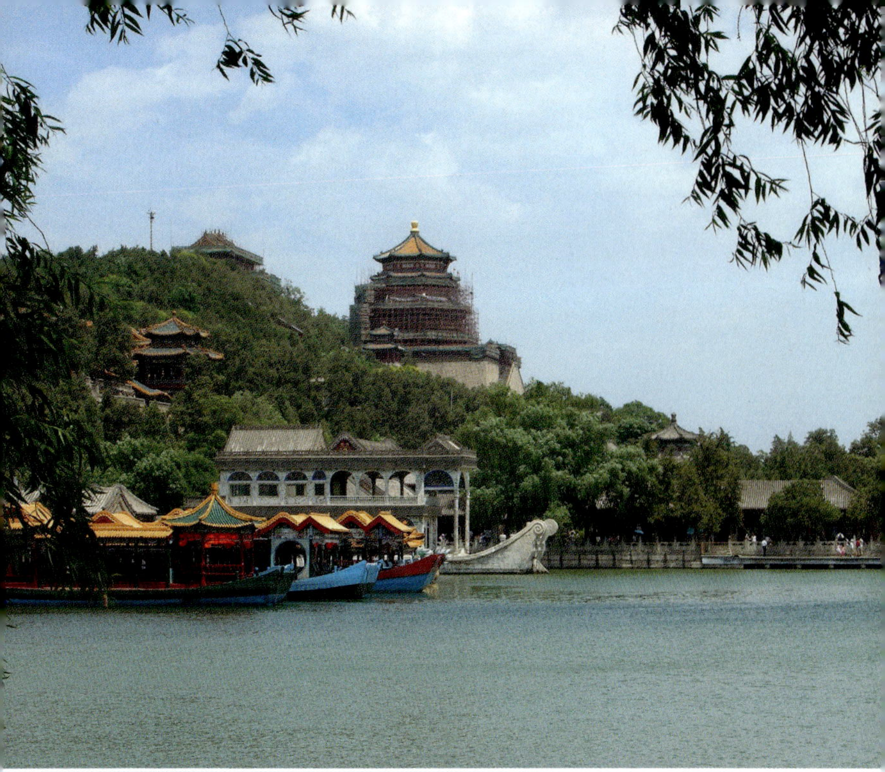

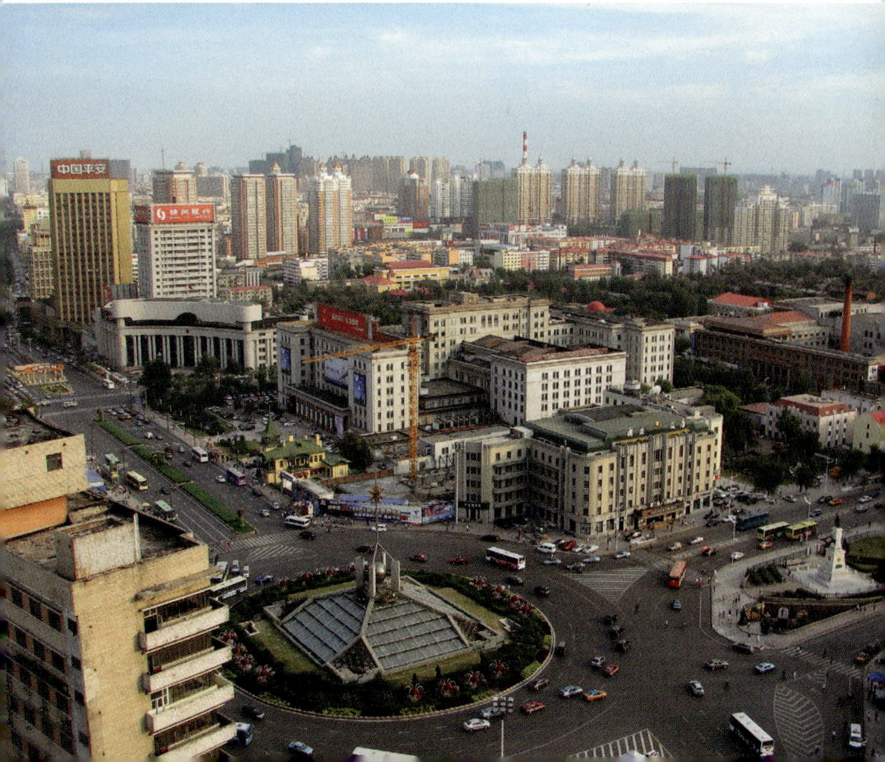
中国平安

Top: A basic banquet setting, Qingdao, Shandong.
Above: Chopsticks make a fun souvenir and are easy to pack.

Top: *It can't be that bad....Zibo, Shandong.*
Above: *A spicy home-style dish outside Kaili, Guizhou.*

Top: *Patrons outside a local restaurant in Jiading, Shanghai.*
Above*: Diners enjoying noodles in Ji'an, Jiangxi.*

Top: *Toasting cements social bonds, Qingdao, Shandong.*
Above: *Enjoying a feast, family-style, in Qingzhou, Shandong.*

Top: *An elementary school class in Shenzhen, Guangdong.*
Above: *Students celebrate as a program draws to a close in Qingdao, Shandong.*

Top: *The "class monitor" (banzhang) leads the class in giving Teacher Xie a toast of thanks—using tea instead of alcohol— in Qingzhou, Shandong.*

Above: *Students interview a local in Qufu, Shandong.*

Top: A student assists an artisan with silkscreening in Weifang, Shandong.
Above: Tibetan prayer wheels, Jiuzhaigou National Park, Sichuan.

Young ethnic Miao women in the annual Sisters Festival parade in Taijiang, Guizhou.

Top: A student enjoys participating in a performance in Qingdao, Shandong.
Above: A teacher practices the fine art of bargaining for a souvenir in Taijiang, Guizhou.
Opposite: American students conduct an interview assignment with villagers while an old resident enjoys the commotion outside Mengyin, Shandong.

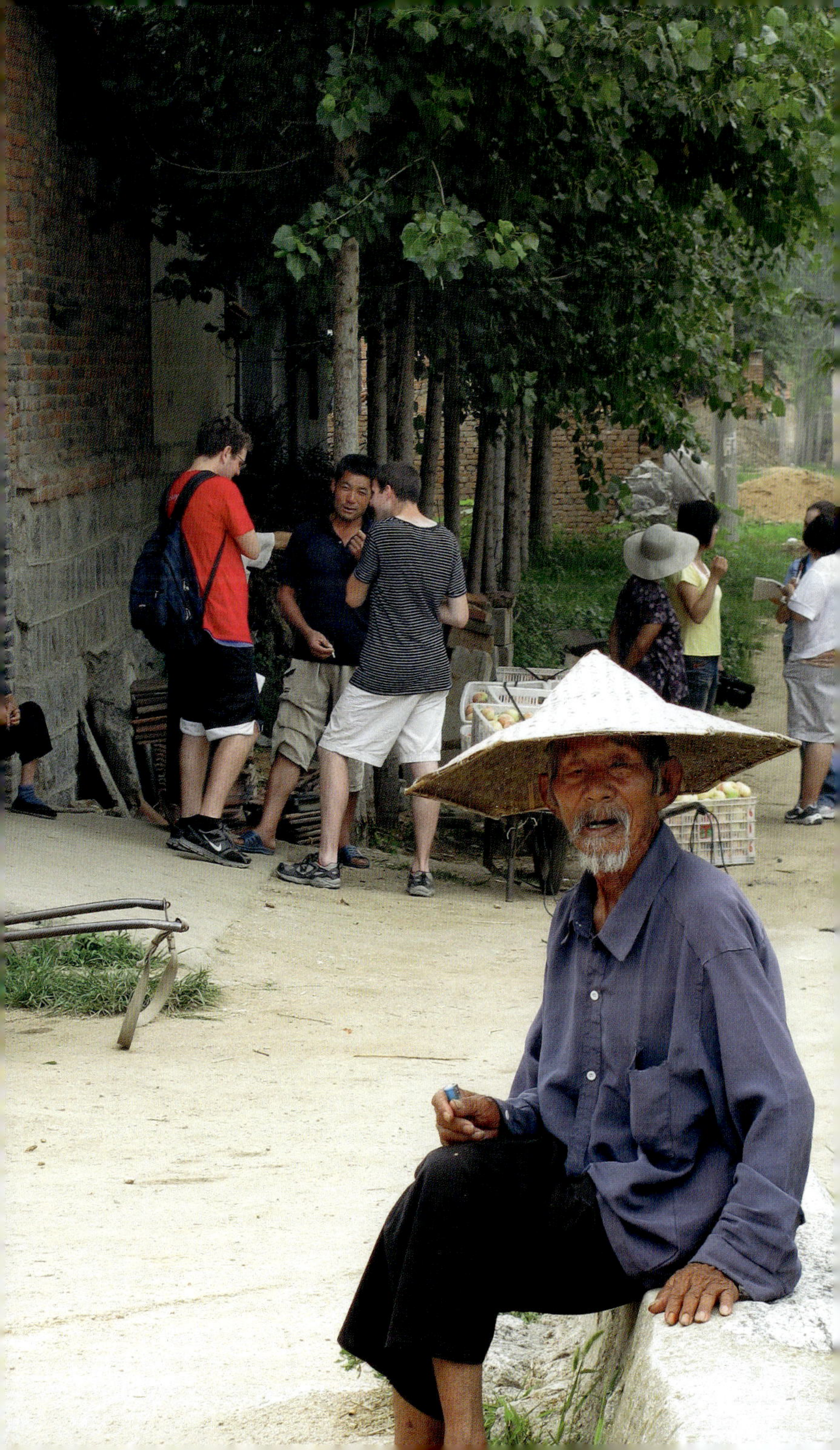

Changhaizi Lake in Jiuzhaigou National Park, Sichuan.

A pool in Jiuzhaigou National Park.

The Great Wall at Badaling, Beijing.

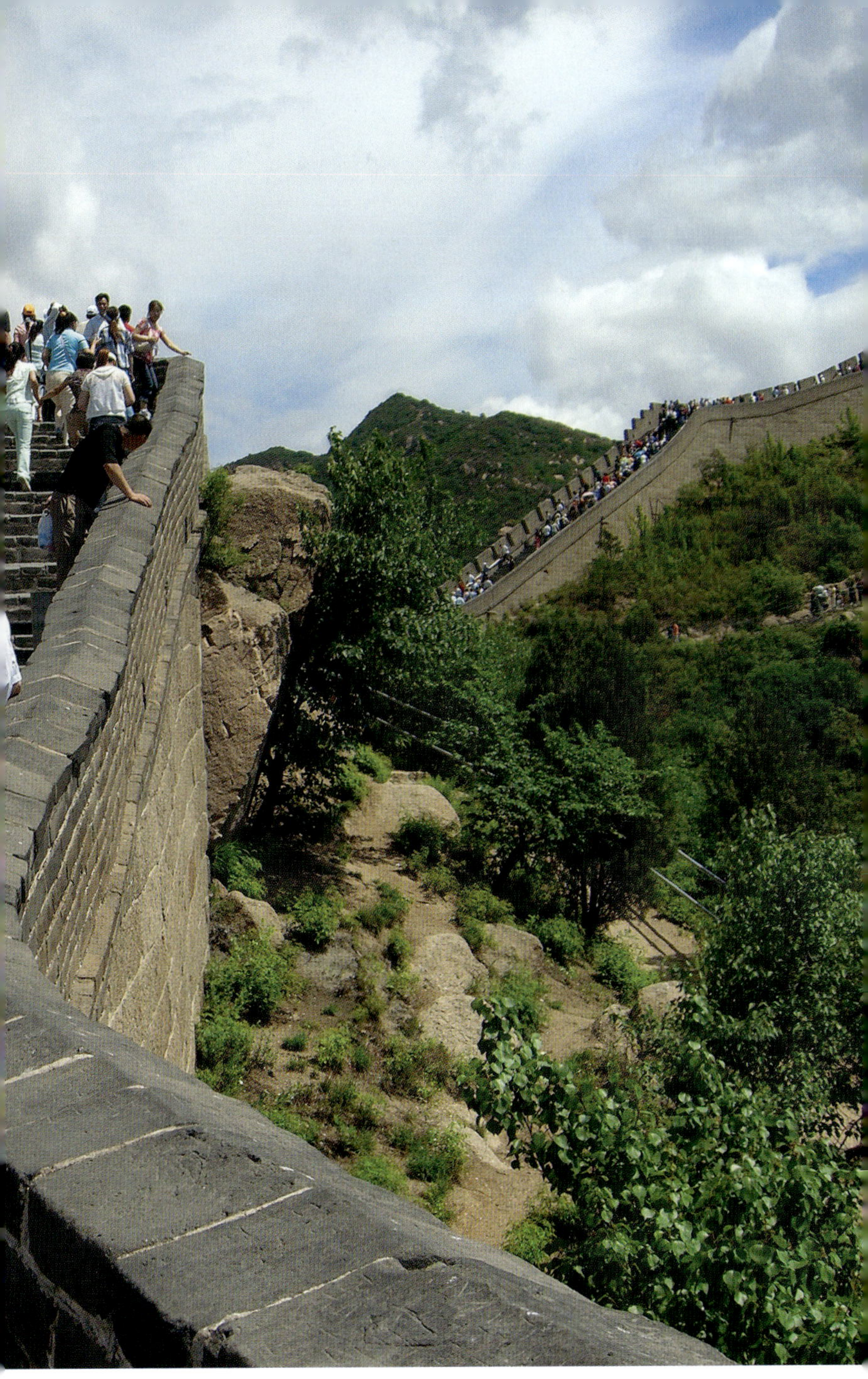

Top: A freighter goes downstream along the Bund in Shanghai.
Above: The slowest trains are called "green skin trains" (lǜpí chē 绿皮车).

Top: *A typical rural inter-village bus. This one runs between Zhenyuan and Taijiang in Guizhou Province. Stickers on the windshield indicate both terminal and intermediate stops, though anyone at the side of the road can flag it down, too.*

Above: *A train platform in Shanghai.*

上島 咖啡

Top: A bullet train shoots into Beijing above the catenaries for slower trains on the ground.
Above: A Shanghai subway platform at an off-peak time.
Opposite: One of many light rail lines in Shanghai.

Top: Taking the bus in Beijing.
Above: By Chinese standards, this public bus in Qingdao is not crowded!

Bicycle parking lot on Qingyuan Rd., South Beijing.

Most major Chinese airports are nearly brand new; this one is in Zhengzhou, Henan.

I am here to party.

- What you know about your own cultural tradition includes everything they know about it.[2]
- Chinese-Americans are not foreigners. They are Chinese who were born/grew up overseas.

When you meet a Chinese person outside of class for the first time, he or she may begin the conversation with some or all of these assumptions about who you are. Some assumptions are fairly easy to confirm or deny: just give me a basketball and I can prove that not all foreign men can play with it. Other assumptions are a little trickier: an American does not need to be rich to afford a trip to China, but the vast majority of Chinese people cannot afford such an intercontinental trip, even if many of the Chinese people you meet can. By the standards of most Chinese, any foreigner who can afford the plane ride she or he took to be standing in China is pretty well-off.

Many of these assumptions are quite innocent, and if a Chinese child is curious about a foreigner's hirsuteness, it really is just curiosity, even if it may be coupled with a laughing comment about being less evolved than the less-hairy Chinese. Like being stared at by people unused to seeing foreigners, this is just one of those things you either take with a grain of salt or you get out of the China business.

Other assumptions may require some work and/or adaptation on the part of the foreigner–and willingness on the part of the Chinese counterpart–to overcome in order to build a healthy relationship. The relationship between what a woman wears and how she expects that to reflect on her is a good example. Modern urban fashion allows professional young Chinese women to go to the office in clothes that the average American would consider more appropriate for go-go dancers. A young American woman wearing short-shorts in China, on the other hand, might be targeted by aggressive young men because they see that fashion choice as reconfirming their assumptions about foreign women.

---

2 This author has been stumped more than once by references to European philosophers who appear to be part of the canon of Western philosophy taught in China.

You can find people to play basketball with everywhere.

Of course, foreign women do not need to wear shawls in China, but knowing how behavioral decisions we make as foreigners confirm or clash with pre-conceived notions many Chinese have about us can help us to create the kind of persona we wish to have in China. The persona that is created by a certain set of casual clothing in the U.S. might create an entirely different persona in China, and vice-versa. At the same time, if you do fit the stereotype and like to play basketball, that's fantastic. You can make friends quickly on the courts, and you can meet many new friends through your "ball friends" (**qiú yǒu**, 球友, people with whom you play ball). If you can play basketball or badminton, you will never be lonely in China.

What a "Student" is in Chinese Culture

One of the roles foreigners studying in China play is "student." What a student is to a Chinese person can be slightly different from what a student is to a Westerner. For one, Westerners expect many students to have some work experience, and to have participated in extracurricular civic activities such as volunteering and political campaign work. Thus, an American college or graduate student is considered by many Americans to be a relatively mature individual with experience in society. Chinese college students, on the other hand, have been intentionally isolated from the "distractions" of the non-academic world all the way through twelfth grade, and it has only been in the past 5-10 years that college students have begun taking temporary jobs during breaks. As a result, many Chinese people perceive "students" as kids who have little or no knowledge of the real world, and, therefore, have little to offer to working professionals.

The discrepancy between Western and Chinese student identities is particularly problematic for foreigners interning in China during the course of their academic careers. If they introduce themselves as students, they will be activating in their listeners' minds those assumptions about what a "foreign student" can and cannot offer an employer. It is in Western interns' best interests to introduce themselves as interns from abroad as their primary identity, follow it up with a description of relevant work experience and then relate their school affiliation. Many Chinese people believe that foreign education systems, while being strong in developing creativity, are weak in terms of being able to produce students who remember and process data well. Even if your credentials indicate that you were a "good student" in your home country's system, it may not indicate to an internship host that you are capable of handling the tasks that a Chinese student can do. Furthermore, as a *foreign* student, your lack of experience in a Chinese environment may make the internship host hesitate to assign tasks with high people skills content because they are highly defined by cultural expectations. The best way to learn is by doing, so it will be up to you to prove that you will not embarrass your internship host while you learn to perform tasks they assume foreign students are incapable of completing.

Whether you are interning in China or simply want to be regarded as the broadly-skilled, value-adding individual you have worked hard to become, here are some ways to avoid being perceived as a wet-behind-the-ears foreign student:

- When interacting with professionals, dress in business casual clothing. Shorts and flip-flops say "student on vacation" wherever you go.
- Leave your backpack or satchel behind
- Avoid wearing a hat on days you might interact with professionals, as you should take your hat off in their presence and you don't want to show them bed-head (or unwashed hair).
- If you carry a notebook for recording new language items, make notes discretely afterward, when you are no longer a member of the conversation. See the next point.
- If you are learning Chinese, try to avoid asking a lot of language questions when engaged in a professional conversation (e.g., with a guest speaker). The Chinese speaker will consider someone who engages the content of his or her speech as a peer while considering someone who focuses on the foreign language aspects as a student (and therefore not a player in the game).

- Maintain straight posture in the presence of authority and peers you want to impress with your maturity/professionalism. Slouching is for kids and counter-cultural people.
- Before going into a conversation situation with a Chinese professional (e.g., a banquet or a guest speaker engagement), think of 2-3 questions about the anticipated topics that you can use for conversation starters. They will show that you are engaging the content and make you part of the interaction.
- If you are giving a professional presentation and need your audience of non-teachers to see you to be a professional rather than as a student practicing to give professional presentations in Chinese, consider using your native language if your language skills are not yet professional-grade. When you give a professional presentation to a Chinese audience, your goal is to convince your audience of the value of your pitch, not that you are a foreigner speaking Chinese.

Your Role as a Representative of Your Nation

Many North Americans are raised to see themselves as individuals first and members of a group second. East Asians, on the other hand, are raised to see themselves as members of groups[3] first. As a result, when Chinese people are in the presence of a foreigner, many of them consciously believe they are representing their country/ethnicity. Even though few North Americans feel the same way, most Chinese will take each foreigner as a representative sample of the foreign country's culture and opinions.

Your behaviors and even your opinions may be interpreted as being representative of all your countrymen and women. Each time you impress people with your maturity, each time you get sloppy drunk, each time you spit on the sidewalk like a peasant, each time you give up your seat on the bus for an old person, you are creating an image against everyone else who looks like you will be judged.

It is not up to you whether or not you represent your culture. It is up to the people who observe your behavior, and most of them do think you represent your culture. This is a large responsibility: uphold it and you will help create a positive image for everyone; fail to meet it and you create an uphill climb for each successive foreigner who has to prove that those of us studying in China are not just there to throw up in the bushes and pick up Asian women.

---

3 Many Chinese believe that people born after 1990 are more like Americans in this regard, however.

Your Role as an English Speaker

When you show up with your foreign face and assumed fluency in English, it is only natural that some people will see you as their English Angel, sent to help them improve their language skills (or their child's). Regardless of your other skills, many Chinese will see a foreigner as a potential English teacher, first and foremost. Just like study abroad programs whose language pledges imply that the Chinese exist only to teach us Chinese, many Chinese have a hard time imagining a useful role for foreigners in China other than teaching them English. And, like Chinese who are patient with language-pledge-bound foreigners, it behooves us to be patient with Chinese who wish to practice English with us.

Language exchange outside Mengyin, Shandong

A little judicious use of English will satisfy the needs of many Chinese who hope to practice their English with you. Often, these mini-lessons will earn you a free meal, or, even better, a new friend. Sometimes, all you get in return is the pleasure of having helped someone, but that's okay—after 150 years of bullying the Chinese, foreigners can stand to build up some good karma.

Where you might need to be careful is when someone wants more of your English-language help than your kind heart is willing to give. It may be a parent who wants to buy you lunch every Saturday after a morning of tutoring (which is worth up to ¥200/hour), or it may be someone who noticed that you like to study Chinese in the park at a certain time each day, and they begin to innocently stalk you for English help every day. Then, you need to be careful with how you negotiate less or no English instruction. After all, to them, it costs you nothing to help them with their English and you may even be getting regular meals out of the deal, so a refusal to do so can be interpreted as unfriendly or ungrateful.

One of the most appropriate ways to get out of these situations is to appeal to their own sense of kindness and say that you would love to help them with their English, but that your program has given you several new assignments that you need to concentrate on. They will very probably offer to help you complete these assignments, so be ready with a reason that would preclude that (e.g., you

Odds are ancestors of your countrymen had something to do with the second destruction of the Yuan Ming Yuan palace in 1900.

have to work with your teacher or classmates). The best reasons are ones that are true, but if the only reason you do not want to tutor someone is because you want that time for yourself, a white lie is infinitely better than the truth, and Chinese people expect white lies instead of the truth in such cases. That is, if you give someone a reason for not doing something, they assume that it could be a made-up reason designed to protect their face. When both the speaker and the listener know that something said is a white lie, is it a lie? In China, white lies are mutually-understood code for "I don't want to do what you want me to do, but we both know it is more hurtful if I actually say that." So, before you tell someone you can't tutor them in English anymore because you would rather be reading a book on the beach, remember that the person would rather you tell them you have too much homework now. If you truly do not want to interact with someone at all, they should understand after a couple indirect rejections in a row.

Especially if your Chinese ability is not great enough to carry on conversations on a variety of topics, helping people with their English is a good way to start conversations with the locals. Depending on how much you like each of these people, you can choose whether or not to develop these conversations in to deeper relationships and interaction. If your reasons for going to China include developing a better understanding of Chinese people and their culture, English tutoring and advice can be a convenient avenue to accomplishing this outside of class.

Standing Out in a Crowd

On Sesame Street, there used to be a segment in which they showed a number of objects and the viewing audience was invited to point out which one was different. If you are not of Asian descent, when you walk around China it can be one big game of "one of these things is not like the others" for the locals.

One of these things is not like the others.

Outside of the central business districts of tier-one cities, it is common to hear kids and the less-refined blurt out, "**wàiguó rén**" (foreigner), when they see a foreigner. Alternatives include, **lǎo wài** (a more colloquial way of saying "foreigner"), and, in Cantonese-speaking areas, *gway low* (foreign devil). When the author's parents lived in Taiwan in the 1970s, little kids would point to them and yell, "**dà bízi**," which means "big nose."

If it feels like being an animal in the zoo, it may be an accurate analogy: for people who only see foreigners on TV and on the Internet, seeing a real live one can be a little exciting, causing the less-inhibited and less cosmopolitan to call out loud what they are seeing. If you saw a tiger in your neighborhood, you might yell "tiger!" out of surprise, and without a drop of animosity.

It can be uncomfortable to be pointed out as the different one over and over, but this comes with the territory of studying a culture in which only about 10 million citizens (less than 1%) do not look East or Southeast Asian. Just keep in mind that when people point you out as a foreigner, it is out of curiosity and not malice. Some foreigners in China never get used to this phenomenon and feel uncomfortable each time they are singled out. The rest of us, however, have some different ways of dealing with the situation, depending on the individual and the circumstance:

- Ignore it
  Though most monolingual foreigners learn within a couple days that lao wai and waiguoren refers to them, many of the Chinese who call us out do not expect us to realize that they are talking about us. Ignoring the comment does not surprise anyone and you can forget it quickly.

- **Smile and wave**
  Sometimes, foreigners take the opportunity of being pointed out to play out being the foreign celebrity. It can be as simple as turning to the person who said *lao wai* and giving a friendly wave of the hand, or it can be hammed up into a little meet-

and-greet with some little kids who are excited to talk to a foreigner. Kids all have to take English in school, but very rarely have an opportunity to speak with a living, breathing native speaker. If you are walking through a rural village on a trip and attract the attention of the local whipper-snappers, the brave ones will get a kick out of being able to practice their English with you. The shy ones will enjoy just being part of the fun.

- **Make a joke**
  Cross-cultural humor is generally a dangerous area because many jokes do not translate well, but even foreigners who are used to being pointed out as a curiosity crack a sarcastic joke in response once in a while, saying things like "where's the foreigner?" and

Pointing Out the Obvious: Just Saying Hello

One of the first things that foreigners in China have to get used to is the fact that in Chinese culture, pointing out the obvious is frequently used as a greeting. Just as Americans often ask each other "what's up," expecting no answer other than "not much," Chinese will say something like "you're back!" to someone who has just returned from a trip or just a day at work. The point isn't to convey any useful information, just to acknowledge the presence of someone you know.

Since this is a common greeting, avoid the temptation to give a sarcastic response like, "No, I'm not back. I'm his twin brother." It probably won't make any sense to the Chinese person who thought she or he was just saying "hello."

Other common situations include:

- Running into a friend at a store and saying, "you've come to buy things?"
  你来买东西? nǐ lái mǎi dōngxi?

- Seeing a friend leave their office/dorm/class building and saying, "[you're] going out?"
  出去? chūqù?

- Seeing a friend eating in an open-front restaurant and saying, "eating?"
  吃饭? chīfàn?

- Seeing a friend come out of a restaurant and saying, "you ate?"
  吃饭了? chī fàn le?

- Seeing a friend studying in an empty classroom and saying "you're studying?"
  你在学习? nǐ zài xuéxí?

looking around, or telling the intrigued Chinese person that she or his is really a Uyghur,[4] not a foreigner.

Making a joke in this situation can be problematic because if it is sarcastic ("is it really obvious that I'm a foreigner?"), it can come off making you appear oversensitive and uncomfortable, which may be accurate, but it does you no good to advertise it. Sarcastic jokes in this situation often just don't make sense to the Chinese person: she or he may not understand why pointing out the obvious (which is a common Chinese rhetorical practice, anyway–see the box to the left) could elicit a sarcastic response.

Aww, look! He can pick up food!

■ Performing Monkey Syndrome

The dark side of being an ethnic celebrity in China–that is, a non-Asian–is that foreigners are sometimes asked to just be foreign for entertainment's sake. For example, a foreigner might find him or herself invited to a dinner banquet as foreign eye candy, to give face to the banquet attendee who brought the foreigner. In that situation, the foreigner may not be expected to do much other than sit there and participate in toasts. When a foreigner is applauded for doing something a Chinese person would normally be expected to do anyway, it is sometimes called the "Performing Monkey Syndrome." When a human being rides a bicycle, it is nothing special, but when a monkey rides a bicycle, it's cute, because bicycle-riding is for people.

Some foreigners love being performing monkeys because it is an easy way to garner attention and frequently results in praise and positive reinforcement. Other foreigners find the role to be insulting, as it can imply that, as foreigners, we are not on the same level of humanity as the Chinese who are entertained by watching us.

---

4 The Uyghurs are a Central Asian people who live in Western China. Like "foreigners," they have large eyes and noses and many of them have a thick "foreign" accent when they speak Chinese because their native language is closely related to Turkish and Mandarin Chinese is nearly as foreign to them as it is to you.

Whether or not an activity is monkey-like depends less on what the activity is and more on the context in which it is performed. Taking the monkey-on-a-bicycle analogy again, a monkey riding a child's bike in a circus ring for an audience whose entertainment is derived from the monkey doing "people things" is definitely a performing monkey. A monkey that breaks a world record for cycling endurance is interesting because it is doing something that takes anyone work and skill to accomplish. Thus, a mature foreigner repeatedly asked to sing a children's song like "Two Tigers" (**liǎng zhī láohǔ 两只老虎**) for Chinese audiences could be seen as a performing monkey, while the same foreigner singing with friends in a karaoke parlor would just be socializing.

One of the gray performance areas in which many foreigners in China find themselves (especially those who speak Chinese and so are more plugged into society than others) is the Chinese television industry. On TV, there is a very blurry line between being a performing monkey and just performing. A few foreigners are able to mold their on-air images to their liking, but for the vast majority of foreigners on TV, the producers mold them to the audience's liking. This often involves playing the role of "The Foreigner," a role that may require doing one or more of the following, depending on the program:

- Speaking Chinese with inaccurate tones
- Playing a missionary in dramas set in pre-Revolution China, a role that usually is simply background for the Chinese drama going on in the foreground
- Singing Chinese songs that make the Chinese audience feel like foreigners love China. One of the author's former students was asked to perform a song called "I want to marry a Chinese man" for a nationally-broadcast television program. Other foreigners sing revolutionary Chinese songs, which may be kitschy for them, but may imply a very complicated political subtext regarding legitimization of the Chinese Communist Party's policies since 1949.
- Being brash or selfish in a fictional role
- Being a foil for a Chinese male character who eventually "gets the [Chinese] girl"

All television performances are designed to please the viewing audience, so if the viewing audience wants foreigners who reaffirm their assumptions about who foreigners are or how much they should be enamored with Chinese culture, even the most enlightened director will be hard-pressed to deliver anything else. This is not to say that the entertainment industry outside of China is any different, but your chances of getting on Chinese TV are probably greater than your chances of getting on TV at home, so you may actually have to make some decisions about what

Fifteen minutes of fame in Huangdao, Shandong

persona you want to have in the China media.

Like speaking English in China, there are times when being a performing monkey can be strategically useful. Perhaps it can be a way to get into a banquet with important people, or a way to get one's foot in the door of the entertainment industry. In any case, if you are going to play the role of a performing monkey, at least do so because you have already calculated that it will benefit you somehow. It can be very difficult to say "no" to a Chinese person asking you to be a performing monkey, and even harder if that person thinks the request is actually giving you a great opportunity and not demeaning in any way. Just remember, if you agree to the performance, do your best to maintain control of your image. If you use an invitation to be foreign eye candy at a banquet in order to meet the important people in attendance, be sure to balance the "look-at-the-foreigner-do-cute-things" routine with mature conversation. Otherwise, you run the risk of remaining the monkey instead of becoming a peer.

Wrapping Up

So far, we have mostly been talking about when you are the center of attention. A common trap into which new arrivals in China fall is making the inaccurate assumption that all the Chinese that is being spoken around them is being spoken about them. It is only natural for people with limited skill in the host country language to worry that everyone is whispering about the funny-looking foreigners. When your language skills reach the point at which you can tell what everyone around you is saying, you discover that—like anywhere in the world—people are talking about their own lives. For every Chinese tourist in Beijing who gawks at foreigners there are 10,000 Beijingers who wouldn't look twice at a foreign face.

To some extent, foreigners studying and working in China are the people who the Chinese can imagine us being. Foreigners are English teachers, NBA fans, people who throw stones and live in glass houses, like to invade other countries in the name of freedom, and people who go to China because, well, who wouldn't want to go to China? China's where it's at! Going along with a certain number of assumptions can make for an easier ride—you just have to judge who you are talking to. If a random stranger in a park strikes up a conversation with you and asks if you like China—the assumption is often that you must love China in order to have chosen to study there—the easy answer is to say, "yes." Oftentimes, the real answer is much more complicated. If you think your interlocutor really wants to know what makes you tick (some do, many don't), go ahead and tell your story. If you would rather wrap up the conversation and get back to sunbathing, you can just say, "I love learning about Chinese culture" and move on. No one is hurt or confused and, hopefully, you are telling the truth.

Maybe you are a China-loving, English-teaching basketball star. In that case, you've got it made, professionally and socially. If you do not fit that mold, be patient and let it be known at a pace that your audience can handle. If you can do that, you will make more sense to your Chinese peers; people who make sense are considered more reliable, and if you are considered reliable, you are friend material.

Chapter 7
Daily Life

Much of your learning in China will take place outside of class. Not only does the excitement of being there help you remember what you see and hear, but mathematically, the time you spend in a classroom will only be a fraction of the time you spend in China, regardless of the program in which you participate. In this chapter, you will learn how to get around and take care of the things that get us through life, from laundry to leisure. If any of the activities covered in this chapter are handled for you by your program, you can at least find out what they are insulating you from so that you know why they have to charge you a program fee!

Local Transportation

Public transit systems in Chinese cities are convenient, reliable, and far-reaching. In large cities like Beijing and Shanghai, the public trans-

Beijing Subway Station

portation network now extends into distant suburbs where apartment buildings are sprouting up between fields of crops. In such megalopolises, buses, subways and light rail lines carry the still mostly carless Chinese population to and from work and to meetings with friends, relatives and colleagues. Learning how to navigate the public transit system wherever you are will greatly expand your geographical reach and give you access to a wider variety of activities and services—and without breaking the bank.

The easiest form of public transit for foreigners in China is the subway. China's tier-one cities—Beijing, Shanghai, Guangzhou, and Shenzhen—all have subway systems, and the tier-two cities (provincial capitals, for the most part) are building them with support from the central and provincial governments. About ten have already completed lines, and more are on the way. The main advantages of taking the subway are that it is fast and the process of buying a ticket and reaching your destination can be done in Chinese and English.

Chinese subway ticket machines have bilingual touch screens and the signage in stations and along the platforms are bilingual as well. As long as you know the name of your destination station, you will be able to get there. Since TIC ("This Is China," a favorite phrase of expats when frustrated), it can't be *that* easy, can it? As usual, the answer is, "it depends." If you are in Shanghai, it really is that easy. The following is an outline of how an ideal trip on the subway goes:

1. Enter the station
2. Look around for the ticket vending machines (if the signage is poor, you might have to hunt a little).

Shanghai Subway ticket machine

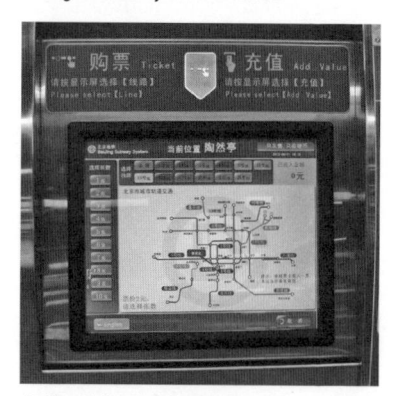

Beijing Subway ticket machine

3. Differentiate between the new ticket and add-value machines (for those with long-term passes). Usually the machines with no one using them are the add-value machines.

4. Use the touch screen to touch your destination station.
5. Change the number of tickets if you are buying for more than one person.
6. Enter the requested amount of money in change or cash.
7. Retrieve your ticket and change (if any).

Shanghai subway ticket

Beijing Subway trackside line map

8. Use your ticket to get through the turnstile (the specifics of this step vary by city).
9. Follow signage to the line and direction of travel you need. If you are unsure, just go down to the platform and look for the station-by-station maps that indicate which track leads to where.

Shanghai Subway trackside line map

10. Wait by the track in the area so designated by lines on the floor.
11. A small number of stations serve two lines on the same track; if this is the case at your station, look for signage indicating what line the next train serves. This sign may be next to the track, indicating how many minutes until the next two or three trains arrive and where they are going, or the sign may be on the front of the lead subway car.
12. Get on and go! Listen to the public address system and get ready to get off when your station is announced. If the car is crowded, people usually start jostling their way off when the door opens, as that is when you find out how many people in front of you were going to get off at the same stop.
13. Remember to give up your seat for elderly, infirm, and pregnant passengers, as well as to those who are carrying young children.

If you have ever ridden a subway before anywhere, the process is essentially the same. Several major Chinese cities have light rail systems that are integrated into their subway systems to varying degrees. After you take just one trip in a given city, the second trip will be easy. Here are some things to look out for that could be a source of frustration, though:

- Each city's system is slightly different. This owes to the date of original construction, date of most recent updating, system builder, and the foresight of whoever oversaw design and construction. Do not get frustrated by each system being slightly different—it is like that all over the world.
- Different systems use different tickets. For example, Beijing and Shanghai use thin plastic cards the size of credit cards that are electronically programmed with the fare you purchased; Guangzhou and Shenzhen use green plastic tokens that are electronically programmed with your fare, as well, so you only get one token regardless of the fare. Be prepared for anything.
- Different systems dispense tickets differently.
  - In Beijing and Shanghai, touch-screen-operated machines dispense plastic card tickets.
  - In Shenzhen, the green token vending machines only take ¥1 coins and ¥5 bills. If you have neither, you can get change at the service window.
- The Shenzhen subway lines are named by their terminal stations as well as numbers. For instance, Line 1 is also called the Luobao Line, after Luohu in the East and Bao'an in the West. Make sure you know both names of the lines you need, as they are not always labeled with both names on station signage.
- On some ticket machines' touch screens, only major stations are labeled; if you need to touch a minor station to get your fare, you may need to touch the number of the line on which it is located in order to get a screen that shows all of its stations.
- If you can, avoid taking the subway during rush hour or when it is raining. At these times, the stations and trains are jam-packed. However, if you just want to know what it feels like to be in a mass of people denser than anything you have experienced in the U.S., go for it.

Subway maps are available online, so you can do your research before you set out. Also, Google Maps' public transportation directions tool can tell you what subway (and bus) lines to take to get from point A to point B. Back in the day, we had to buy a paper transit map from a street side newspaper vender (which you can still do, if you want to).

A cheaper alternative to the subway is the public bus system. This is also your only public transit option in smaller cities and cities where the subway is still under construction. Chinese buses reach more places than the subway does and can often put you practically at the front door of wherever you are going. Furthermore, unlike most bus systems in the U.S., each bus stop has a sign that lists all the stops reached by buses that stop there. With a little research before you set out, you can get wherever you want to go for as little as ¥1, and usually for no more than ¥3. The rub is that Chinese bus information is almost entirely in Chinese.

The preparation you need to do before taking a bus ride in China is find out which lines you need to take, where those stops and transfers are, and if you need exact change. Below is a step-by-step procedure for taking the bus.

1. Using a printed city map, Google Maps, or BBS postings in Chinese by people asking other Netizens how to get from point A to point B, figure out where to get on the bus, where to change buses if necessary, and where to get off. Chinese bus lines are referred to by number in the format "#路车" (# lù chē)
2. Bring at least ¥3 in singles (coins or cash) and go to your departure stop.
3. At the stop, check the sign for your target bus line to see if it is exact change only (无人售票 wú rén shòu piào "No one sells tickets"). Such buses cost one fare for the whole trip. Usually, only buses that go a long way across the city have variable

Signs from minor bus stops in Southwest Beijing

rates and a human ticket vendor on board.
4. Also at the stop, make sure you are at the stop for the bus going in the right direction. If not, you may have to cross the street and walk a little bit to get to the corresponding stop for the other direction of travel. In cases where the bus travels on one-way streets, the same stop for the other direction may be a block away.

5. Finally, check the sign at the bus stop to see what time the first and last buses on your intended lines are. This is indicated by the terms 首车 shǒuchē "first bus" and 末车 mò chē "last bus." The times listed represent the time when the first bus leaves the first stop and the time when the last bus leaves the first stop. Most first buses leave before you even get up, but some last buses leave at the end of rush hour. Don't get stuck!

6. Get on the bus and drop your money in the money slot next to the driver if there is one (a no vender bus). The slot will often be labeled in Chinese with the price, but not always. If there is a ticket vendor, you can either seek him/her out or sit down first–both are acceptable, as the vendor will come through the bus selling the tickets by asking passengers their destinations.

7. If you get your ticket from a vendor, hold on to it until you get off the bus. Sometimes the vendors forget to whom they have already sold tickets, so you may need to show your ticket. Some PA announcements tell riders to show their ticket as they get off, but no one pays attention to this.

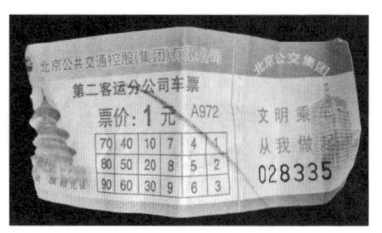

Ticket for a regular Beijing bus

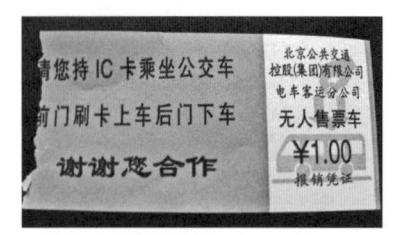

Ticket for a Beijing electric trolley bus

8. Some buses have announcements that say what the next stop is so that you can get ready to get off; others do not and you have to ask the driver to give you a heads-up, or keep your eyes glued to the bus stop signs that go by the window. Often, simply asking the driver or ticket vendor if the bus you are getting on goes to [your destination] will often result in their telling you when you get there.

9. Unless the bus is too crowded to move to the back, passengers are expected to board at the front door and alight at the back door. If the bus is only moderately packed, start shouldering your way to the back as soon as the bus leaves the stop immediately before your destination.

There is a variety of buses in service in China, and trying them out is part of the fun of getting around. You can find buses that run on power from overhead lines, buses that run on liquefied natural gas, large buses without air conditioning, large buses with air conditioning (sometimes that run the same line, but for ¥1-2 more), double-decker buses,[1] and also 20-passenger mini-buses. The latter are more common in small cities where the population is not large enough to warrant a fleet of large buses.

If you plan to take the bus to an appointment you must reach on time (or early!), take a practice ride at least one day ahead, and, preferably, at the same hour that you plan to leave on "D-day." It may be a breeze catching your bus at 11am, but you may have to skip one, two or even three jam-packed buses with no room for more human beings if you leave during rush hour. A practice trip will teach you a lot while you are not under the pressure of keeping an appointment.

A final note about public transit in Mainland China—in major cities, many locals use smart cards that can be loaded with money and swiped to get on subways, buses, and, in some places, taxis. These cards require providing a deposit and are sold only at certain major stations. If your stay in China is short, or if you will not need to commute by public transit on a regular basis (e.g., you live on campus and most of your scheduled activities are on campus), it may not be worth the trouble to get such a card.

---

1 Seats on the second floor are easier to find, probably because it's a pain to go up and down, and because sunshine-hating Chinese prefer the shade of the first floor.

Taxis

Chinese public transportation is great... and so are the taxis. Chinese cities have fleets of taxis roaming the streets looking for fares at all hours of the day. Even seemingly minor side streets will eventually have a taxi come along (though it is easier to try flagging cabs from the side of main streets). Taxis cost much more than public transportation, and in return, you get door-to-door service and the ability to haul luggage, groceries, gifts, etc., and to pile up to four people in one car. Depending on where you're going, using a taxi for a small group can cost the same as taking a nice bus to the same place.

Taxis in Shenyang

Another advantage of taking a taxi is that you do not need to do nearly as much research before you set out. If you are going somewhere famous, like a train station or a landmark hotel, you need only say the place name and off you go.

If your destination is not famous, or if you do not know, bring the written name, address and phone number of your destination and give it to the driver when you get in the car. As long as you provide an accurate address, it is the driver's responsibility to figure out how to get you to your destination, not yours. Below is a typical taxi trip, step-by-step:

1. Stand next to a street with a fair amount of traffic, including taxis. If you rarely see a taxi and/or the taxis you do see are always full, go to a more trafficked street.
2. Taxis with no passengers have a small plastic sign on the dash or suspended from the ceiling in behind the windshield that says "for hire" and 空车 (kōng chē "empty car"). This sign is flipped down when there is a passenger in the car and the meter is running.
3. To flag a taxi, extend your arm out at 90 degrees or less and wave your hand from your wrist as if you are calling a pet to your side. In parts of some cities, taxies can only stop at places where they will not block traffic, e.g., intersections, curb cuts, taxi stands, etc. Keep this in mind if several empty cabs pass you and they obviously saw you. Another common reason for being passed by empty cabs is that it is shift change time for the drivers and they are heading somewhere to hand off the car to their partner who will drive for the next 12 hours. Unfortunately, shift changes often occur during rush hour.
4. Once you have hailed a cab, you can get in the front seat or the back, even if you are travelling alone—the driver will not be offended.
5. In major cities, taxi drivers assume that foreigners know the few phrases needed for a cab ride and will usually ask "where to?" in Chinese. This may be said in many ways:

   - **Qù nǎr?**
     去哪儿？
   - **Dào nǎr?**
     到哪儿？
   - **Dào shénme dìfāng?**
     到什么地方？
   - **Qù shénme dìfāng?**
     去什么地方？
   - **Shàng nǎr qù?**
     上哪儿去？

In smaller cities, the drivers may simply not know any other way to interact with people than in Chinese and thus default to these phrases that they would ask any fare. In cities with 2008 Olympic venues (Beijing, Qingdao) and the 2010 World Expo (Shanghai), a good number of cabbies can ask "where?", but you should still provide the destination in Chinese, spoken or written.

6. After you tell or show the driver where you're going, the car will start moving (if it hasn't already), and within a few sec-

Taxis | **165**

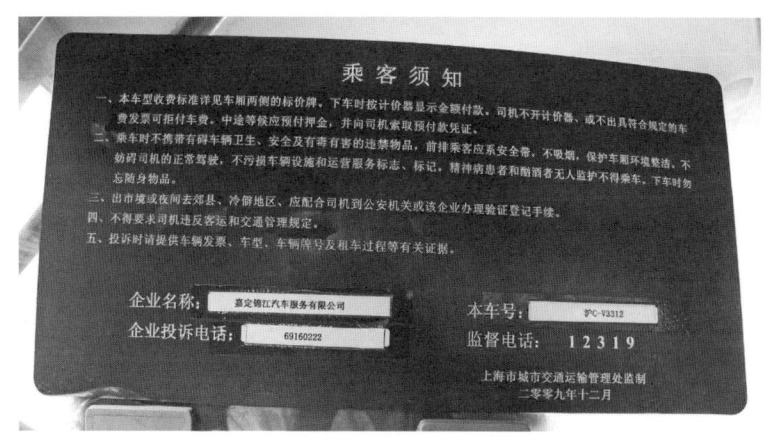

Behind the driver's head, this sign lists the company complaint hotline (bottom left) and the taxi's license plate number (2nd from bottom on right).

onds, the driver will flip down the "for hire" sign and start the meter going. If the driver does not start the meter within 15 seconds or so, and there are no extenuating circumstances (e.g., a complicated traffic pattern, pedestrians, etc.), you can politely ask the driver to start the meter: 现在可以打表吗? **Xiànzài kéyǐ dábiǎo ma?** ("Can you start the meter now?"). Rare is the driver who will try to take you for a ride–their name and license information is clearly visible in the car and can be written down for later report and complaint. Furthermore, passengers who are not provided a receipt at the end of a ride–which happens automatically when the meter is used–can refuse to pay the fare! If you have any reason to doubt your cabbie, write down the driver's name and license number from information found on the dashboard or Plexiglas screen around the driver.

7. These days, most cabs in any given location have the same starting fare, though some cabs in some cities are more luxurious than others. This is reflected in a higher base fare and a higher per-kilometer charge. When the meter is flipped on, it will usually start at the number that should be shown on a sticker in a back side window. The more developed the city, the higher the number. As of mid-2012, ¥13 was the highest base fare encountered. This amount will get you a few blocks before it starts to rise with the distance traveled. The meter will also advance when stopped for long periods of time.

8. Many students of Chinese love to practice speaking and listen-

ing with taxi drivers. They are a captive audience, most love to talk, and many are disgruntled about "The Man," which plays very well to Americans who are predisposed to thinking the Chinese system is seriously flawed. If you are learning Chinese, feel free to let the driver know you speak some by asking about his or her family or job. Often, that is enough to open the floodgates and the driver will talk at you for the rest of your ride.

9. Upon reaching your destination, the driver will flip the "for hire" sign back on and the meter will automatically start printing your receipt. In most places, a fuel surcharge of ¥1 or ¥2 is added to the fare on the meter, and an additional receipt for this surcharge is provided if asked for; in Shanghai, the fuel surcharge is included in the base charge, which is ¥1 higher on the meter than in the window sticker.

10. It is unnecessary to tip taxi drivers in China. You can take your receipt if you want it; if not, the driver can throw it away for you.

Now that you know how to take wheeled transit[2] in China, we will cover how to take the cheapest form of transportation of all, what the Chinese jokingly refer to as the "Number 2 Bus" (二路车 èr lù chē): walking. Chinese cities are fairly dense, so a lot of ground can be covered by walking. All the necessities of daily life can be found within a 20-minute walk of most schools and hotels in China.

The first "step" in getting to know your neighborhood on foot is to just head out the door and start walking around. As it said on my room key at the Marriott Courtyard Inn in Jiading (suburban Shanghai), "wandering is encouraged." If your sense of direction is poor, pick up a map from a streetside newspaper vendor and mark where your home base is. To reduce the possibility of getting lost, pick a street, walk as far as you feel comfortable, then turn around and go back. Variations on this strategy include walking out, cutting over a block, and then walking back on a parallel route. This way, if the new route is blocked or curves, you can still get back to the street that goes by your home base.

While you are exploring, be aware of the stores and buildings along the way. Once you have a pretty good grasp of what is in your neighborhood, make a list of what you've found and what you have yet to find. The following is the list I keep in my head when exploring, including Chinese terms for many

---

2 There is also the Maglev, the train from Shanghai Pudong International Airport to a subway stop on the edge of development in Pudong District, which runs on a track made of magnets that repels the train so that it travels on a sliver of air. As this is the only train of its kind in China and it only goes to the airport from a subway station in the suburbs, it is not treated in detail here.

of them that you can use when asking for directions, which we'll cover in a moment:

- Were there any restaurants? If exploring during meal time, which restaurants had a lot of customers and which ones were empty? 饭馆 fànguǎn "restaurant"
- Were there any laundries? 洗衣店 xǐyī diàn "laundry," 干洗店 gānxǐ diàn "dry cleaner"
- Barbershops? 理发店 lǐfà diàn
- Pharmacies? 药店 yào diàn 药房 yào fáng
- Were there any side streets or alleys worth further exploration?
- Were there any public restrooms that may come in handy after an evening of fun? 公厕 gōngcè
- Where do the buses that run on other streets go? Do any of them go places I want to go that my closest bus line does not serve?
- Any convenience stores? 便利店 biànlì diàn (a chain store) 小卖部 xiǎo mài bù (mom-and-pop)
- Shoe/leather repair? 修鞋的 xiū xié de "[places] that fix shoes"
- Travel agency or airplane/train ticket vendor? 旅行社 lǚxíng shè "travel agency;" 飞机/火车售票处 fēijī/huǒchē shòu piào chù "plane or train ticket office"
- Western restaurants? 西餐厅 xīcān tīng
- Shopping malls? 百货店 bǎihuò diàn "department store," 商场 shāng chǎng "mall," or 商城 shāng chéng "mall"
- Parks? 公园 gōngyuán
- Health care clinics? 门诊 ménzhěn
- Post office? 邮局 yóujú
- Cell phone service providers? 电讯公司 diànxùn gōngsī
- Internet café? 网吧 wǎngba
- Printing/faxing/scanning/ID photo-taking shop? 打印店 dǎyìn diàn "print shop," 复印店 fùyìn diàn "copy shop." There may be one FedEx office in your city, but there will be hundreds of little independent shops.

You can think of it as a scavenger hunt. In fact, I have my students do such a scavenger hunt as their first in-country assignment for our study abroad program. It is easier to remember the location of useful places when you discover them on your own than when a teacher tells you where they are.

After you have made a first pass of your neighborhood, see what's on your list that you have not yet found and start asking for directions. Many of the business owners in your neighborhood will also be residents, so you can ask people who work in your neighborhood where things are; chances are, they go to the same places themselves.

If you have not taken any Chinese courses, here are some useful phrases for asking directions. Be sure to find relevant audio files on the Internet so that you know how to pronounce them accurately.

Say this when you are fairly certain there is a [certain kind of store] in the neighborhood, but don't know where it is:

请问, _____ 在哪儿?
Qǐngwèn, _____ zài nǎr?
"May I ask where the _____ is?"

When you already know that there is a [certain kind of store] nearby, but do not know how to get there:

请问, 到 _____ 怎么走?
Qǐngwèn, dào _____ zěnme zǒu?
"May I ask how to get to _____?"

When you aren't even sure there is a [certain kind of store] in the neighborhood, e.g., a Western-style restaurant:

请问, 附近有没有 _____?
Qǐngwèn, fùjìn yǒu méi yǒu _____?
"May I ask if there is a _____ nearby?"

This may not be within walking distance.

Of course, the easy part of asking for directions is the asking; understanding the answer is the real challenge! It takes formal training to learn how to follow directions in Chinese to a target location; if you have not had that yet, you can use gestures to indicate that you need the answer in the form of pointing or a written map. At least with pointing, you can ask for directions at a number of waypoints, eventually reaching your destination. With the exception of a Western restaurant, the places on the list above should all be found within walking distance of your home base, as they are basic neighborhood services.

When you walk or jog around China, you need to relearn how to cross the street. When you were little, your parents probably taught you to look left, look right, and then continue to look left and right as you cross when there is no traffic. If you went to college in an American college town, you may have learned to let your guard down a little because local drivers knew that pedestrians in a crosswalk have the right of way as soon as their foot touches the asphalt. In China, while walking, as with driving, everyone has to look out for themselves.

The easiest and safest way to cross a street on foot is to do so using a pedestrian overpass. You may have to walk to the end of a block in order to reach one, but it is a safe way to go, especially if the city has erected fences in the median and next to the sidewalk specifically to prevent people from crossing the street at level and/or jaywalking.

Not all cities have pedestrian overpasses, and those that do don't have them on all streets, so sooner or later you will have to learn how to cross the street in China. In some cities, locals actually do wait for the crosswalk light to give them the okay, even when there is no traffic guard there telling everyone to keep on the sidewalk until the light turns; Shanghai is a good example of this. However, most intersections in China are not protected by human guards, nor do the locals pay much attention to the crosswalk light…and with good reason–drivers do not pay attention to the crosswalk light, either. If they did, they would never get to go!

So, how do you cross? First, if there is a crosswalk light, it is safer to cross when it gives you the go-ahead because most cars in motion are going parallel to your path instead of across it. Second, as you cross, continually look both ways. Cars may come from anywhere at any time, and cars do not stop before turning, regardless of the color of their traffic light. Third, if there are other people crossing in the same direction as you, cross with them, but try to keep at least one other pedestrian between you and the direction of traffic. You might as well let someone who knows what they are doing set the pace. Finally, crossing the street, especially in small cities, is basically a slow game of Frogger, with everyone going whenever they see an opening. Always assume that a motor vehicle will not stop for you, even if that vehicle has a red light. And, never, ever, play chicken with a truck or bus.

If it sounds scary to cross the street in China, at first, it is! Eventually, you get used to it and either enjoy the challenge, or just put up with it.

As you walk in China, always be aware of the ground ahead of you and keep your eyes open for things that could trip you up, soil your shoes, or both. At the most innocent end of this spectrum, there are bumps and ridges built into many sidewalks to help the blind know where to go. These textured tiles can be felt through the shoes and through the rod that blind people carry to feel out the ground. If it is the thought that counts, the Chinese are way ahead of Americans in considering the needs of the blind when building sidewalks. That said, the textured tiles often lead right to holes and vegetation that were installed after the sidewalk was initially made. Other times, the tiles lead to a tall curb, with no indication that a curb is coming. The seeing also need to look out for steep curbs, uneven pavement, open manhole covers with no cordoning off, active construction areas, dog excrement, and, depending on where you are walking, human excrement. Also; a word to the wise, try not to step on the grates that cover holes for rain drainage: all manner of things are

He cannot stop for you, even if you are standing in front of him.

Share the road.

deposited there, some of which you would not want on the bottom of your shoe. Split pants (baby pants with a hole for the crotch) were designed for these grates and the base of trees and bushes planted along sidewalks.

Finally, you will see many people walking in the street when there is a perfectly good sidewalk right there. Though you may prefer to avoid the dirty dangers of sidewalk walking to the motorized dangers of walking on the street, keep in mind that walking on the side of a street is socially acceptable in many places and may be the best way to get around sidewalk congestion caused by parked cars, parked bicycles, street vendors, sidewalk cafes, construction, and crowds.

Riding a Bicycle

Bicycle-riding was once the primary form of wheeled transport for Chinese people. As long as you could afford the bike, there were few subsequent expenses incurred other than occasional repairs (which were very inexpensively provided by sidewalk-based repair people). Today, bicycle-riding has been replaced by scooter riding as the inexpensive form of personal transportation. If you will be in China for an academic year or less, it may not be worth buying two-wheeled transportation of any kind unless you are an avid cyclist, as the dangers of joining the fray may not offset the convenience of not having to wait 5-20 minutes for the next bus.

In the old days (over 10 years ago), Chinese cities had bicycle plus pedestrian lanes that were usually separated from motorized traffic by a median. These theoretically dedicated lanes are gone in most cities, leaving bicycle riders to use automobile lanes; there are too many obstructions and pedestrians on the sidewalk to safely ride there. Bicycle usage is barely regulated at all: no license is required, and riders are basically expected to ride however they want when no traffic police are present. If you choose to buy and ride a bicycle, here are some tips:

- Buy a second-hand bicycle if you plan to lock it outside, as bike theft is quite common.
- Some bikes come with a lock that prevents the rear wheel from moving when in the locked position. Invest in another lock that you can use to lock the bike to an immovable object.
- Consider buying a bell to put on your handlebars. There is no Chinese equivalent for "passing on your left/right" used by the public, only bells (and only sometimes).
- No one except bicycle enthusiasts wear helmets in China, but feel free to do so if you wish.
- Be extra careful when crossing traffic. The cost of repainting a scratched car may be greater than the value of your bicycle!
- You will probably be the fastest non-motorized thing on the road. Be responsible and avoid weaving in and out of pedestrians.

Scooters and Motorcycles

Public transportation is so convenient in most places in China that you might find that the danger of driving a scooter does not outweigh the benefits. Five years ago, before Chinese cities built subways and light rail out to the suburbs, there might have been a good case for a long-term foreign student investing in a scooter, but probably not anymore.

Most scooters on the road these days are e-bikes that can be plugged into any regular socket to be recharged. They are quiet and some pedestrians fear them, but many Chinese cities encourage the use of e-bikes for the sake of the atmosphere. Gas-powered scooters have more oomph, and avoid the trouble of recharging, but they are heavier and seem to be a dying breed. Be forewarned, many e-bike owners sell their used scooter when the battery is about to die, so consider the price of a new battery when negotiating.

Scooter and motorcycle owners must register their vehicle and obtain a license plate. This can be done at the point of purchase if bought new; if bought used, the license remains with the bike, and needs to be signed over to you at the local Transportation Bureau.

Electric scooters in Shanghai

Driving a motorcycle with an engine over 50cc in size requires a motorcycle driver's license as well as a license plate. Regulations change all the time, so ask your local scooter/motorcycle store what are the relevant regulations for owning and riding the kind of vehicle you wish to purchase, new or used. In Beijing, for example, there are two kinds of scooter/motorcycle license plates: Jing A 京 A and Jing B 京 B. Jing A plates allow the vehicle to be ridden anywhere outside of the 2nd Ring Road, and are no longer issued. The only way to get one is to buy a bike that already has one. Having a Jing A license plate considerably raises the price of the vehicle. Jing B plates, which are still being issued, can only be legally used for driving outside the 4th Ring Road.

Driving a Car

Road traffic in China is a dog-eat-dog jumble of every imaginable form of transportation—sometimes even donkey carts—and the only observed rule of the road is Never Yield. Yielding the right of way is literally a foreign concept on Chinese roads.

For most who read this, there are few reasons to drive a car in China that trump the related safety concerns. People who drive in China do so because it gives them freedom of movement beyond taxi service, their social status is such that they feel they should be able to pick up guests, or because their professional image requires them to have a car as a status symbol. For the average student studying in China–

Keep your eyes peeled.

and the average resident director, for that matter—these are not relevant reasons to take the risk of driving a car.

If you are a little nutty and/or wealthy, the "easiest" way to get a temporary driver's license is to go through an international rental car company such as Hertz or Avis. For several thousands of RMB, you can obtain a temporary driver's license based on your U.S. license and then rent a car for use only in the city where you will be living. This may only be possible in Beijing and Shanghai. If you embark on this quest, be prepared for conflicting advice, unanticipated fees, running around to get forms, copies of documents and photographs, and being limited to certain kinds of car models for new drivers.

I have ridden in cars in China since 1998 and am still hesitant to get behind the wheel there. I no longer fear riding in any cars except those driven by individuals who bought their licenses (really) and a few individuals who simply lack awareness of the implications of their driving decisions. Professional drivers in China—like most taxi drivers—are like a roller coaster: they may take you on a scary ride, but you are never really in danger. I have foreign friends who have driven, and have even owned cars in China, and they love the freedom that comes with driving. They were also long-term expatriates with well-paying jobs.

To most readers of this book, I implore you to put off considering driving in China until you have accrued many more years of experience.

Satisfying the Needs of Daily Life

Sun Yat-sen conveniently provided us with a Chinese phrase describing the necessities of life: 衣食住行 yī shí zhù xíng, which means clothing, food, shelter and transportation. We have covered shelter and transportation; now, we move on to food, clothing and other things that are important for getting by on a daily basis, including money, communications, and hygiene.

A traditional Chinese meal includes the entire food pyramid.

■ Food

From the art of preparing it to the role its consumption has as a medium for cementing relationships, food is an essential element of Chinese culture. The Chinese are so invested in their food traditions that many of them cannot imagine a rational human being who would not be completely won over by Chinese cuisine. For some visitors to China, Chinese food indeed enchants and entices from the get-go; others need some time to adjust and a select few never really get used to the flavors, textures, and sources of Chinese food. In this section, we will briefly look at the role of food in Chinese life, discuss how to maintain a nutritionally-balanced diet while studying abroad, and how to avoid food-caused illness as well as possible.

A traditional Chinese meal is an expression of Chinese philosophy, a social event, and a marker of one's identity. Ingredients are balanced without being measured, dishes are prepared with a minimum of kitchen tools, flavors are played off of each other, nutrients are provided without an excess of one type or another, and each dish should be served ready to eat with only a pair of chopsticks and a spoon for soup. Once on the table, meals are generally eaten "family-style," with shared plates of food placed in the center of the table, on a lazy Susan if necessary. The flavors of the dishes vary from region to region in such a way that many individuals prefer to eat the flavors of their youth for the rest of their lives. So that you know what kind of food your home-base-to-be is known for, the following is one version of the "Eight Main Cuisines of China:"

- **Shandong Cuisine (鲁菜 Lǔ cài)**–known for heavy, salty flavors, and a primary influence on Beijing cuisine.
- **Guangdong Cuisine (粤菜 Yuè cài)**–known for *dim sum* and dishes cooked to preserve the original flavor of their ingredients. Cantonese people are

also famed for eating anything; one saying goes, "if it flies, crawls, or swims, a Cantonese person will eat it," and another, "the only thing with legs that a Cantonese person will not eat is a stool." It is customary for Cantonese people to first wash their restaurant-provided chopsticks, cups, and bowls with hot tea and dump the used tea in a bowl provided for this purpose.

- **Sichuan Cuisine (川菜 Chuān cài)**–defined by bold flavors created by use of garlic, hot peppers and the husk of the seed of a kind of citrus plant that is usually called "Sichuan Pepper" in English. Food at Chinese-American restaurants called "Szechuan" style usually has little or no relationship to true Sichuan flavor.
- **Hunan Cuisine (湘菜 Xiāng cài)**–defined by overwhelming use of fresh hot peppers, resulting in spicy food.
- **Jiangsu Cuisine (苏菜 Sū cài or 淮扬菜 Huáiyáng cài)**–often delivers meat that is soft and sauces that are white; not as widely found outside of its home region as Sichuan and Hunan cuisine.
- **Zhejiang Cuisine (浙菜 Zhè cài)**–typically light, less oily, and somewhat sweet.
- **Fujian Cuisine (闽菜 Mǐn cài)**–characterized by heavy use of fungi and seafood.
- **Anhui Cuisine (徽菜 Huī cài)**–uses stewing and braising much more than the stir-frying found in other regional cuisines.

Nearly every region of China has some distinctive flavors or dishes, even those that fall outside of the traditional "Eight." Examples of other commonly-found regional cuisines include, Northeastern (dōngběi 东北), Xinjiang (xīnjiāng 新疆), Yunnan and Guizhou (Yúnnán 云南 and Guìzhōu 贵州), Shanghai (Shànghǎi 上海), and Northwestern (xīběi 西北).

There is another style of food that is simply called "homestyle" (jiācháng cài 家常菜). These are dishes that are not complicated to make (by Chinese standards), and that can be made by any adult who knows how to cook. There is no representative flavor or mode of preparation for this cuisine, but old standbys such as twice-cooked pork, stir-fried kidney and any quick-fried leafy green vegetables count.

Most Chinese neighborhoods will have a few home-style restaurants, a Sichuan or Hunan restaurant, and a noodle and/or dumpling restaurant, with the possible addition of some locally-popular regional cuisine. For example, Guilin-style rice noodles are popular in many Southern Chinese cities, and Fujian's Sha County (Shā Xiàn 沙县) style is popular in eastern China.

There are a few main types of restaurants that are differentiated primarily on the cost and quality of service, though not necessarily on the quality of flavor. At the top are grand restaurants with numerous private banquet rooms, each decorated like a wealthy person's home, with their own restroom and their own TV/karaoke set up, in addition

Lunch with a private room and private service

to couches and chairs for pre-meal entertaining. Usually, each private room at a restaurant such as this has one to three waitstaff assigned to it. There may be an open dining area on the first floor of such restaurants where customers can order the same food, but without the privacy of the individual rooms. These restaurants frequently have elaborate dishes that are difficult to prepare and priced to match. Many dishes at such restaurants cost ¥50 or more; some seafood dishes with individual portions (e.g., one crab/abalone/sea urchin/etc. per guest) can cost ¥200 or more per person.

Below this are nicely-finished restaurants that are smaller in scale and only slightly cheaper in price. If you have a private room, you may need to share your waitstaff with other rooms in your hallway.

The next step down are modestly-decorated restaurants in which the open area seating greatly outnumbers the private rooms available, and the prices are in the $$$ rather than $$$$ range. An average meat dish at such an establishment now might cost ¥35. A number of chains also operate in this market space, including Ajisen Ramen 味千拉面, which serves Japanese food, **Xiǎo Féi Yáng** 小肥羊 (now owned by Yum! brands of KFC and Pizza Hut fame), which serves Mongolian-

Nicely-furnished private dining with bathroom, but no private staff

Satisfying the Needs of Daily Life | 177

Enjoying hotpot at Haidilao

style hotpot, and **Hǎidǐ Lāo** 海底捞, a Sichuan-style hotpot restaurant.

Somewhere between these mid-range restaurants and the basic establishments that follow are Chinese fast food restaurants. Such restaurants are standardized to offer similar flavors across franchise locations. Because they maintain a certain level of hygiene, service and brand image, their prices are higher than small individually-owned restaurants, but lower than casual dining restaurants and usually lower than foreign fast food.

Near the bottom of the spectrum are mom-and-pop establishments

Dim sum at Bifeng Tang, a national chain

in which décor is minimal, service is minimal, and hygiene is minimal, but price is also minimal and

Food served at a local joint in Jiading, Shanghai

flavor can match and often exceed that of expensive restaurants. In fact, because the meals taken in expensive restaurants often consist of more talking than eating, guests in the swanky establishments do not seem to mind that the food prepared there is often much greasier and heavier than dishes in cheap little restaurants. These small restaurants are sometimes called **dàpāi dàng**, after a style of roadside restaurant that sprang up in Hong Kong after World War II.

One of the best things about these small restaurants is that many of them offer lunch specials called **gàijiāo fàn** 盖浇饭, which consists of a smaller-than-family-size portion of your dish of choice,

Kungpao chicken on rice

served with white rice. Normally, these lunch specials are limited to home-style cooking menu items. These specials are sized for the individual lunch diner, and at ¥8–15 each, very affordable.

At the very bottom of the meal provider scale are street vendors. For very little money, you get flavor, convenience, and mystery ingredients. Street vendors often sell from mobile carts that have a glass enclosure on top to protect their cooking implements and ingredients from the weather. Street vendors are perfect for breakfast, snacks, and what Taco Bell euphemistically calls "Fourth Meal" in the U.S., but has an actual name in Chinese: 夜宵 **yèxiāo**. Common street foods include: savory pancake (**jiānbíng guǒzi** 煎饼果子), miniature steamed dumplings (**xiǎolóngbāo** 小笼包), cold starch jelly (**liáng fěn** 凉粉), cold wheat noodles or rice flour dumplings (**liángpí** 凉皮), skewers of meat and tofu pieces cooked in a spicy broth (**málà tang** 麻辣烫), cold noodles (**liáng miàn** 凉面), fritters (**yóu tiáo** 油条), stewed pork sandwich (**ròu jiā mó** 肉夹馍), "stinky tofu" (**chòu dòufu** 臭豆腐), and kabobs (**ròu chuan** 肉串).

Most Chinese people who go to the West want to go back to eating Chinese food after a couple meals. Americans going to China can usually make it for a couple weeks before they hanker for some good old-fashioned non-stir-fried food. In tier-one cities, there are many options for Western dining; in tier-two cities, you will find franchises of major fast food chains; in tier-three cities, you may find one or two Chinese-owned restaurants that cater to locals who want to experience Western culture every once in a while by eating a fried cube steak with a side of potato salad. As of this writing, the following U.S. restaurant chains could be found in major cities: Kentucky Fried Chicken, McDonald's, Pizza Hut, Subway, Burger King (only a few so far), Häagen-Dazs, Domino's, Papa John's, TGI Friday's, Hard Rock Café, and Hooters. For the coffee drinkers, there are Starbucks in all major cities and Dunkin' Donuts in some. KFC has a corporate strategy of localizing menus to suit customers' tastes, while McDonald's tends to maintain the same basic menu all over the world, give or take places that do not eat beef. American fast food tends to be more fresh and succulent in China, but since it is about the same price in China as it is in the U.S., it makes for a more expensive one-person meal than eating a Chinese lunch special.

If you absolutely must eat at a Western restaurant, but cannot find the KFC or McDonald's, your nearest four and five star hotels will offer Western dishes, if not have complete Western menus—at corporate expense account prices. If you find yourself living in a tiny county-level city (maybe you stayed in China as an EFL teacher after your study abroad program ended) with a meager population of a million people or less, you may tire of the cube steak and potato salad. In this case, you will have to make your own Western food using ingredients from the supermarket. I ate a lot of PB&Js when I lived in Yantai in the late 90s (there are more choices there now).

Next, we will walk through the casual dining process, from finding a restaurant to leaving with your leftovers. In this section, we will cover casual dining alone or with friends, where there is little ritual formality regarding who sits where, who orders for whom, who drinks what and when, etc. Here, we are talking about the kinds of non-business-related daily meals that students and teachers frequently have in China.

As mentioned before, try to be aware of which restaurants are busy at meal time and which are not. The ones with few people are probably not very good, since millions and millions of Chinese vote with their feet at lunch and dinner time. Places with a lot of people probably have tasty food, but flavor and hygiene are often completely unrelated in China. Many Chinese people half-joke that their favorite mom-and-pop style restaurants cook with so-called "ditch oil" (**地沟油 dìgōu yóu**), named after cooking oil that was scooped out of ditches and trash cans and reused, a phenomenon that was reported in the Chinese media a couple years ago. No one wants to believe that their favorite restaurant is unhygienic, but few really want to find out, either. Don't expect the official inspection system to look after you, either. The avoid-an-empty-restaurant rule works just as well, if not better, than a government inspection.

Chinese fast food, like American fast food, is ordered at a counter and then taken on a tray to a table. If it is lunch or dinner time, you may have to wait for a seat to open up. At hole-in-the-wall restaurants of the kind that have a limited menu (perhaps variations on a theme of soup noodles or dumplings), customers often seat themselves and tell the owner what they want. In such restaurants, everyone there is practically within hugging distance, let alone speaking distance. In sit-down restaurants larger than a walk-in closet, you will usually be shown to a table. Sometimes, you need to get the attention of a harried waitress in order for this to happen. Do not expect to be asked "smoking or non-smoking." There is no distinction. If you are seated near a smoker and it makes you uncomfortable, move to another table without giving the smoker(s) a nasty look. If you are seated at a position that has cold air conditioner air constantly blowing on it, feel free to change tables or to move the slats on the air conditioner vent so that the wind goes elsewhere.

At small restaurants, the menu is sometimes written on the wall; at restaurants with about six or more tables, there will be a menu booklet. At nice restaurants, the menu will be professionally printed and sometimes have color photos of all the dishes. Few menus will be bilingual, and restaurants that do have English menus are usually more expensive. An important exception is that some restaurants found just outside the gates of university campuses will have an English menu specifically to attract study abroad students. The English menu may not be as extensive as the Chinese one, but it should help you to learn new dishes.

Most Chinese menu items are listed in the following categories, even if they are sometimes lumped together under only a couple headings (e.g., 炒菜 chǎo cài stir-fried dishes):

- **Lunch specials on rice** (if the restaurant is low-key enough to serve them) 盖浇饭 gàijiāo fàn
- **Cold dish appetizers** 凉菜 liáng cài
- **Soups** 汤 tāng
- **Pork dishes** 肉类 ròu lèi (Without any modifiers, the word for meat means "pork" by default.)
- **Poultry dishes** 鸡肉 jī ròu
- **Beef dishes** 牛肉 niú ròu
- **Mutton dishes** 羊肉 yang ròu
- **Seafood dishes** 海鲜 hǎixiān
- **Vegetable dishes** 蔬菜 shùcài or 素食 sùshí (Being in the vegetable section of the menu only means vegetable matter is

Chinese fast food in a Shenzhen mall

the main ingredient—there may still be meat in it.)
  - **Green vegetables** 青菜 qīng cài
  - **Tofu** 豆腐 dòufu
- **Starches** (rice/noodles/dumplings, etc.) 主食 zhǔshí
- **Beverages** 饮料 yǐnliào and alcohol 酒水 jiǔshuǐ
- In many small restaurants, the beverage menu is the glass-doored refrigerator. It is not considered rude to bring your own drinks to Chinese restaurants, though the higher-class the restaurant, the higher-class the BYOB should be: e.g., wine they do not serve; special tea you prefer, etc. There is rarely a corking fee for bringing your own liquids.

There's our drink menu.

A good rule of thumb when ordering family style for an informal meal among friends is to order one dish per person for groups of four or less and n-1 dishes for groups of five or more. Three people might order three dishes while six people can order five. The more important the occasion, however, the more food will be ordered, to make sure that there are no empty plates. For example, if a Chinese friend you made in the U.S. takes you out to dinner in China, he or she may order more food than you could possibly eat—especially if there are other Chinese guests there who would expect a host to be generous to the point of wastefulness.

Your waitress will more than likely stand next to your table while you look over the menu and only leave when you are done ordering. Don't feel pressured to make up your mind(s) quickly. If the waitress needs to leave and come back, she will let you know. Some earthy places will just leave the pencil and paper on the table for the customer to write down the order. If not there already, a pot or pitcher of tea will show up at your table soon after you sit down; this is the Chinese equivalent of the free ice water we get in the U.S. If the waitress asks what kind of tea you want with your meal, it means you have to pay for it. If you want a free beverage, you can ask for boiled water (白开水 **bái kāi shuǐ**), which will be served in a teapot. If you are like me, stingy and drink a lot with your meals, you can pour the boiled water/tea into both your teacup and your beer/beverage glass so that there is always one container cooling off while you sip from the other one.

There is a system to ordering that Chinese people use to maximize flavor and nutrition. If you follow this system, the wait staff will consider you to be a normal adult. If you do not, you will still get what you order, but they may try to convince you to change your order to match their expectations. An analogy might be if you went to McDonald's and said you wanted a chocolate shake with four French fries inserted at the end. Sure, they can do it for you, but they would wonder why.

The main rule in ordering is to have a balance of meat, vegetable and starchy dishes. Thus, a normal three-dish meal for three people might be:

- Cashew chicken **yāoguǒ jīdīng** 腰果鸡丁
- Stir-fried bok choy **xiǎo bái cài** 小白菜
- Steamed rice **bái mǐfàn** 白米饭 (in the south) or noodles **miàntiáo** 面条 (in the north)

Note that fried rice is considered fulfilling the starchy food category, and not a member of the meat or vegetable category. Many Chinese restaurateurs are perplexed by Americans who order fried rice and another starch (such as dumplings) for a small group; they wonder, "Well, which is it, do you want the rice as your starch or the dumplings?" If you want steamed white rice, tell the waitress how many bowls your table wants; it will not come automatically because there are other starches you might want instead. Furthermore, rice is the staple starch south of the Huai River; north of the Huai, wheat flour noodles and dumplings are the staple starch. Some restaurants will give you a large bowl of rice for everyone to share. Hunanese restaurants often serve rice in a small brick-like bowl in which the rice is a little dry but often costs more than regular soft steamed rice. If you want to eat steamed white rice along with your dishes, ask the waitress to bring out the rice when she comes out with the first dish: 现在可以上米饭吗? **Xiànzài kěyǐ shàng mǐfàn ma?** ("Can you serve the rice now?") This is especially important in northern China, as their wheat-based starches are normally brought out at the end of the meal as a separate course.[3]

Many meat dishes include vegetables such as green peppers, onions, and shredded carrots. It is okay to substitute a meat dish with a high ratio of vegetable matter for a purely vegetable dish. It could be considered overdoing it at a three-person meal to order two meat-only dishes such as sweet and sour tenderloin and dry-fried intestine, especially if the meat is from the same animal.

The great part about most Chinese menus is that the name of the dish tells you what is in it and how it was made; you do not have to guess what is in a Happy Family is or how Princess Shrimp is cooked, like at many Chinese restaurants in the U.S. When you see 椒盐虾 **jiāoyán xiā**, you know that it

---

3 The wheat-based starches—noodles, dumplings, pancakes, etc.—usually have meat and/or vegetables in them, so they can serve as an independent course much better than a bowl of white rice.

Satisfying the Needs of Daily Life | 183

Bamboo shoots and preserved ham

is shrimp (**xiā**) fried in salt (**yán**) and Sichuan peppers (**jiāo**, here). After you order it once, you know that *jiaoyan* dishes come to the table dry and crispy.

The following are some dishes that Americans tend to like and that most restaurants tend to have. You can start with these as old stand-bys and branch out from there. One group of four students I once had in Qingdao would each lunch together every day, ordering three dishes they knew they liked and one dish they had never had before. This way, they quickly expanded their repertoire.

- Sweet and sour tenderloin 糖醋里脊 **tángcù lǐjí**
- Not to be confused with sweet and sour pork 糖醋肉 **tángcù ròu** and 古老肉 **gúlǎo ròu**, which are usually very fatty
- Twice-cooked pork 回锅肉 **huíguō ròu**
- Kungpao chicken 宫保鸡丁 **gōngbǎo jīdīng**
- Cashew chicken 腰果鸡丁 **yāoguǒ jīdīng**
- Beef on a sizzling platter 铁板牛柳 **tiěbǎn niúliú**
- "Three fresh items from the ground" 地三鲜 **dìsānxiān**
- Tomato fried with eggs 西红柿炒鸡蛋 **xīhóngshì chǎo jīdàn** (tomatoes are called **xīhóngshì** in northern China, lit. "red Western persimmon") or 番茄炒鸡蛋 **fānqié chǎo jīdàn** (tomatoes are called **fānqié** in southern China, lit. "foreign eggplant")
- Lettuce fried in oyster sauce 耗油生菜 **háoyòu shēngcài**
- Caramel-covered apple, banana or potatoes 拔丝苹果、香蕉、土豆 **bāsī píngguǒ, xiāngjiāo, tǔdòu**. This is mostly found in northern China.

Many foods you may have come to love at Chinese restaurants in the U.S. are hard or impossible to find in China. These include: General Tso's chicken; orange chicken; lemon chicken; Happy Family; water chestnuts; broccoli; those peppers that look like pointy miniature corn cobs; the brown sauce made from cornstarch and soy sauce; the white sauce made from cornstarch; large blistered deep-fried egg rolls; duck sauce; the wasabi-flavored yellow mustard sauce; egg foo young (as eaten in the U.S.); chop suey; anything with "Szechuan" or "Hunan" in the name, like Szechuan Beef or Hunan Shrimp.

As you order, here are some warnings:

- The following meats are served with the bones:

  - Chicken, except for in dishes with "diced" (丁 dīng) in the name
  - Pigeon
  - Fish, even when the fish meat is filleted (鱼片 yúpiàn), you must be careful
  - Rabbit
  - Frog

- Seafood is generally served with the head. Head meat and juices are considered especially good.

Head-on goodness

- Outside of vegetarian restaurants that cater to the Buddhist crowd, "vegetable dish" does not mean "vegetarian." Many vegetable dishes add ground pork for flavor. If you are vegetarian, it is important to tell the waitress that you do not eat meat:

  > 我吃素，我点的菜请不要放肉。
  > Wǒ chī sù, wǒ diǎn de cài qǐng búyào fàng ròu.

  "I eat vegetarian, please do not put meat in the dishes I order."

- Most cooks (including people at home) add MSG to their dishes. If you do not want MSG, you can say 请不要放味精 Qǐng búyào fàng wèijīng. "Please do not add MSG."

- Foods that Americans consider to be bizarre are often considered to be delicacies in China. The good news is that they rarely have euphemistic names like Rocky Mountain Oysters. As long as you can translate the name of the dish, you know what you are getting, like silkworm pupae, cicada nymphs, pig intestines, drunken shrimp,[4] etc. Chicken feet are sometimes called "Phoenix Feet," but you still know what you're getting.

Duck feet

It has become popular in the past few years for mid-range restaurants

---

4 Drunken shrimp are shrimp that are put in a pan of strong liquor instead of water, inebriating them before you consume them raw.

to give dinnerware to customers in a shrink-wrapped package delivered by a disinfecting service, as shown in the photo below.

Because it costs money to have these items collected and sent to the disinfecting service, as soon as you open the package, you are agreeing to the roughly ¥1/set charge. The same goes for packs of tissue that may be found on your table. If there is a plastic package of tissue, it costs money; if the tissue is a toilet paper roll in a plastic cozy, or if the waitress puts a pile of napkins on your table, there is no extra charge.

When eating family style with friends and family, it is normal to use your own chopsticks to get food from the dishes in the center of the table to your individual saucer or bowl. You will know if this is the standard at your meal if there are no common-use chopsticks or spoons provided for each dish. Even at business meals, many people will dispense with using the common-use chopsticks. Because everyone is poking their own chopsticks into the common dishes, it is considered rude to suck food off of your chopsticks if something is stuck. Along the same lines, it is polite to bring a bite of food from the main dish to your personal saucer and hover there momentarily before lifting it to your mouth. This gives drops time to drip on your plate instead of the table or your lap, and it reduces the impression that you are just shoveling food into your maw. Partly because of the chopsticks use and partly because it just looks selfish, diners in polite company (even if informal) should not dig out the ingredients they like most in a given dish. If you love eggs and eggs-and-tomatoes are served, it would be terribly gauche to eat all the eggs out of the dish.

Be considerate of the other diners and balance the amount of eggs and tomatoes you pluck out.

Well-run restaurants try to bring your food out all at once, though this is not always possible. Especially in immature restaurants where the flavor brings in a large crowd, but the owners do not yet know how to handle it, dishes may come out slowly and be distributed unevenly among the guests with no regard for who ordered when. Particularly frustrated customers will tell the waitress to cancel the last dish if it arrives so late that the customers are already full from the first dishes that were served. Naturally, most waitresses and restaurateurs will say that your dish has already been started, even if it hasn't. You will know in five minutes if this is the case, since many dishes can be stir-fried in that amount of time.

Once all your food is on the table, your waitress will generally not come back to ask if you need anything. In nice restaurants, the waitress will stay in your private room and pour drinks and exchange plates full of bones and shells for clean ones without being asked (if she is good at her job). In other places, though, if you need something like a teapot refill, you will need to get the waitress's attention. Some Chinese will yell at the waitress to get her attention, almost angrily calling, "**fúwùyuán!**" Some Chinese and most foreigners are not comfortable doing this, even though it is often so loud in the restaurant that you need to shout in order to be heard. Alternatively, you can wait until the waitress is at most a couple tables away and then call her, or you can waive your hand in the air when she looks your way. If you need more tea or hot water, take the tea-

A boiled water thermos

pot lid partly off and hold it for her to see. This means "refill." Once in a while, you may find yourself at a busy restaurant where it is faster for you to find where they keep the boiled water thermoses and refill your teapot yourself.

You will also need to get the waitress's attention if you are ready to pay the bill. The two most-used phrases for "check please" in Chinese are **mǎi dān** 买单/埋单 and **jié zhàng** 结帐. The former comes from Cantonese and has gained nationwide usage. Even if your waitress is beyond earshot, if she sees you mouth the words **mǎi dān,** it is usually enough to get the process started. When she brings you the bill, look over it to make sure it is accurate. Mistakes are made, and often enough to warrant always checking your bill. This is also the time to tell the waitress if you want to pack up your leftovers, "**dǎ bāo**" 打包. Different regions handle doggy bags differently. In Qingdao, leftovers are dumped into thin clear plastic bags; in parts of Shanghai, they are put into clear plastic bags which are then put in Styrofoam bowls; in yet other places, you will get a clamshell-style Styrofoam box; the nicest places will give you microwave safe hard plastic boxes. The waitress will box up your food for you unless you tell her you will do it yourself. At a fast-food restaurant, you do not need to clear your table— there are staff who are supposed to do that. If you try to bus your own table at a fast-food restaurant, you may just be making the clean-up staff look bad in front of their manager, so don't feel bad about someone else clearing your table.

When your waitress returns with your change–most restaurants are cash-only–then you're ready to go. Restaurant staff are all paid minimum wage or above and do not expect tips. As you leave your table, be sure you have all your personal belongings. The staff may thank you on your way out. You can smile in response, or say, "*xièxie*," though foreigners are more likely than Chinese to thank the service providers back.

Many first-time visitors to China are intimidated by the restaurant experience: not only are there unfamiliar processes and expectations, but many menu items are illegible to beginning students. Too many students resolve the issue through pure avoidance, electing instead to eat processed food from the closest convenience store, leaning heavily on instant noodles and cookies. Now that you know what to expect at a Chinese restaurant, you have no excuse to eat an unhealthy diet. All that is left for you to pursue a balanced diet is to learn how to get fresh fruit.

During the summer, you can buy fresh fruit from vendors that park their carts or tractors next to the sidewalk at strategic locations (strategic for the amount of food traffic, as well as for ease of retreat when the municipal management officers show up to check for vendor licenses). Year-round, you can get fresh fruit at the supermarket, though for a somewhat higher price.

During the summer, fruit is easy to find on the streets of Chinese cities.

Buying supermarket fruit is easy— you just pick what you want and take it to the checkout, like at home. Buying fresh fruit is only slightly more challenging.

You start by asking how much the fruit in question costs by asking, 这个 [fruit], 怎么卖? zhège [fruit], zěnme mài? Literally, this is, "how is this [fruit] sold?", or "what is the price per unit or per unit of weight?" The answer will most likely be in *renminbi* per **jīn** 斤, a pre-metric Chinese unit of weight roughly equal to a pound. Vendors rarely try to gouge you, but if you want to be safe, ask the price when someone else is looking at the fruit, too. Or, listen to the answer when a local person asks the price. Few vendors are willing to give two prices to two people standing next to each other! Once you know the price, start picking the individual fruits you want. The vendor will use an electronic scale or an old-fashioned balance to weigh the fruit, multiply by the unit price and tell you how much it costs. If there is any communication breakdown, you can point to the calculator and look confused. This will result in the vendor putting the bill on the calculator screen for you.

If you bought fruit with skin that you eat, wash it before eating it. Chinese people tend to skin all their fruit, including grapes, but if you do not, so just wash it in the sink at the dorm before you eat it. Some people use produce detergent (available at supermarkets), and some people even use a drop of bleach mixed with about half a gallon of water to wash their fruits and veggies. How far you go in washing your fruits is a personal choice that has more to do with your level of risk aversion than the amount of pesticides on your fruit.

■ Laundry

When you are studying in China, you are at least 5,000 miles away from your parents' laundry room. Fortunately, you have a few options in terms of getting your clothes clean, and they run the gamut from super-economy cost for "good enough" results to super-expensive for "meeting with the mayor" results.

The cheapest way to wash clothes with no special care requirements is to pour some detergent in your plugged-up sink or bathtub and wash them by hand. As you will see from the color of the water when you rinse, you really are getting out the dirt. Rub the fabric together in the soapy water to loosen up the dirty particles; after doing this for a batch of clothes, drain the water out, put new water in and use the same movements to get the soap out of your clothes and into the new water. You may have to do this a couple times to get the soap out. When you are done, hang your clothes on hangers, drape them on a drying rack you can buy at a supermarket (buy it before you start washing!), or hang them from your dorm's drying lines (if you live in a dorm).

The best value method for washing your clothes is to use your school's dormitory washing

Satisfying the Needs of Daily Life | 189

Air-drying clothes is common and economical.

machines. They may be coin operated, which makes them a little more expensive than pouring detergent into your sink. At around ¥4 per load, it won't break the bank. The washing machines might be Asian/European sized, which is a lot smaller than what we use in the U.S., so keep this in mind when planning how often you do your laundry. The times that are most convenient for you to use the dorm washing machine are usually the same times that are more convenient for everyone else: afternoons and weekends. If you can avoid these rush hours by doing laundry early in the morning or late at night, you will not have to wait nearby for a machine to open up.

Very few places in China have dryers. They are electricity hogs, and Chinese people feel that sunshine is good for drying clothes. That many places in China rarely see the sun, and that the air in China itself is pretty dirty does not seem to bother them. Another advantage of avoiding washing machine rush hour is avoiding drying line rush hour, which immediately follows washing machine rush hour. This should be common sense, but check the weather before you do laundry, since you cannot hang your clothes out to dry when it is raining. For small amounts of clothing, like your underwear, you can hang things to dry in your dorm room, but unless you keep your air conditioner running all the time to keep the air dry, hanging wet laundry in your dorm room can create a musty environment, especially if you live in a damp climate to begin with (like Qingdao).

The next level up in laundry service includes drying, and it involves a trip to the neighborhood Laundromat. Chinese laundries are full-service establishments: you drop off your clothes, they wash them, fold them, and give them back to you in a couple days. It may cost about ¥8-10 per piece of clothing, which is pretty expensive, compared to a couple yuan for detergent and a few yuan for an entire load of laundry washed by yourself in the dorm washing machine. However, that price is pretty good compared to the last option.

Four- and five-star hotel laundry service is the peak of laundry service: for ¥20+ per piece of clothing, you get... the same thing as taking your clothes to the Laundromat, minus having to physically take your clothes to the Laundromat. This option is best for the monolingual executive who does not have time to find the laundry service, would not be able to ask for directions anyway, and whose company picks up the tab. If you are reading this, you probably do not fall into this category.

■ Money

In the early days of overseas study, students bought traveler's checks in the U.S., wrote down all the checks' serial numbers, found a local bank that could actually process traveler's checks, and then cashed them in over the course of the program, leaving the un-cashed ones in a locked suitcase. Today, we have it easy—a debit/ATM card will get you local currency from nearly any Chinese ATM. Yes, there is a fee for foreign transactions, but you pay that fee at some point in every method of converting currency, whether in the form of a fee to your bank, or a lower exchange rate that covers the cost of service.

ATMs can be found all over Chinese cities. If you are a Bank of America customer, you can even avoid foreign bank ATM fees by using Construction Bank of China ATMs because of an agreement between the two institutions. Chinese ATM's can be found standing alone, as well as collocated with bank branches. You use Chinese ATMs the same as you do American ones, and most even have English language instructions. If you need a large amount of cash, as resident directors sometimes do to cover group activity expenses, be aware that different ATMs have different withdrawal limits, both per day and per transaction. You may be able to withdraw up to ¥5,000/day from a given ATM, but if the per-transaction withdrawal limit is ¥1,000, then you will need to do five 1,000 yuan withdrawals in a row. Some ATMs are in a booth or room that requires swiping the card to gain access; your American card will be able to do this. In fact, I was once able to gain access by swiping the magnetic strip on my driver's license, too….

It is good to always have ¥100-200 on your person at all times. This is enough for a taxi ride from most points A to points B in your city, which is your most likely situation for needing cash at the last minute. I once had a student tell the taxi driver to take her back to campus from a club, only to discover after getting out of the cab that our university had a new main campus located far away from our own cam-

A suite of Chinese ATMs

pus. Having extra cash on hand is perfect for such times.

Credit cards are accepted at more and more locations in China, but they are still most commonly accepted at hotels, fancy restaurants, and chain supermarkets. Cash is still king in China. A word of warning about credit cards—getting a cash advance on a credit card is different from withdrawing cash with a debit card. It is often impossible to use a credit card to get a cash advance from a Chinese ATM, even if the credit card has a PIN.

A China Mobile service station in Zhuhai

■ **Communications**

The primary form of communication in China is the cell phone. If you will be in China for only a week or two, and you will be accompanied by a program director nearly all of the time, it is unnecessary to get your own cell phone since most of your time and activity will be pre-planned and communicated to you in person. For everyone else, get a cell phone as soon after you get settled in as possible.

The mobile network companies in China are China Mobile, with nearly 700 million subscribers, China Unicom, with about 200 million subscribers, and China Telecom, with 130 million subscribers. All three are state-owned. China Mobile has the best cell phone coverage, though the other two networks are, for all intents and purposes, just as good.

Chinese cell phone companies sell the little chips called SIM cards that go inside a phone and give it a phone number. You can get the actual phone from that store, from the Internet, from cell phone shops on the street, or even use your U.S. cell phone. The advantage of using your U.S. cell phone is that you already own it; the disadvantage is that you have to unlock it before you go, and, if it is not a smart phone, it probably cannot display Chinese characters, an important function when so much communication is done by text message.

The easiest service for a short-term visitor to get is a pay-as-you-go plan. Some of these plans even come with a basic phone as part of limited-time promotions. For only a couple hundred RMB, you can be up and running in a day. All you need to do is bring your passport, a few hundred RMB, and the phone you intend to use to the mobile network company's store and then choose which phone number you want. While it is essentially that simple, no cell phone plan is really *that* simple. If you want to know how much your roaming costs, how much it costs to send and receive text messages, if there is a monthly fee deducted from your balance during periods of disuse, etc., etc., and you don't think you would understand all that in Chinese, bring a bilingual friend. Otherwise, you can smile and nod and sign whatever they put in front of you and hand over your passport for copying when they ask for it. If you feel at all uncomfortable about the network having a copy of your passport, keep in mind that the amount of information they have about you is small potatoes compared to what American credit rating agencies and any stranger who pays $20 online for a background check know about you.

If you run low or out of minutes, you will receive a text message from your mobile network. Just go to a branch office of your network company (they are all over the place) and give them money to put more minutes on using some pass codes. They will often be happy to do it for you if you look like a clueless foreigner. Many mom-and-pop convenience stores and newspaper/magazine kiosks also sell cell phone minute recharges.

Once you have your cell phone, be sure to observe Chinese cell phone etiquette:

- Many people consider it rude not to answer your phone, but it is also considered face-giving if you turn off your phone during a meeting with someone. You will just have to measure the relative social status of who you are talking to, compared to who might call you at the same time.
- You have to pay for voice mail in China, and few people buy that service. If you don't answer a call, you'll only know the number it came from. This may be one reason people answer their phones wherever they are.
- You will see people answering phones—and loudly—in places Americans would consider it rude; there are some other Chinese who also find it rude, but many places in China are loud and the cell phone talking is just one part of the cacophony.
- Texting is common, and you can text superiors, but remember to use polite language.
- Your cell phone number is not considered private information; people may ask for it and they expect you to tell them.
- Friends in China can call each other whenever they need to, and you are available as long as your phone is on.

In the last year or so, WeChat or **Wēixìn** 微信 in Chinese, has practically replaced texting on cell phones. WeChat is an app for smart phones that allows the free exchange of text and audio messages on a one-to-one as well as a one-to-many basis. If you have a smart phone in China, you definitely want to download WeChat, as practically everyone you know will be communicating on it.

The other main form of communication among people who are

probably your peers is the Internet. We have already discussed how to get Internet service while you are settling in. Once you are online, it is a good idea to set up a Weibo.com account and a blog on Sina.com. Weibo is the Chinese version of Twitter, and it is just as hot as Twitter is. With a Sina blog, you can share your experiences with both Chinese and American friends, though you may have to teach your American friends and family how to navigate your blog. If you want a social networking page that your Chinese and American friends can access, then Renren.com is the most popular one; xiaonei.com is also popular, and it is for students in college. If you want to post or watch videos, Youku.com is the biggest site for this in China.

Why, you might ask, are they not using Twitter, Blogspot, Facebook and YouTube? Because those sites are blocked in Mainland China as being threats to national security. As websites owned by foreign companies and hosted on foreign servers, the Chinese authorities have difficulty controlling what is said on them; Chinese websites, on the other hand, are censored on a daily basis, to maintain "social harmony." Chinese people–and Netizens,[5] in particular–do not like being told what they can and cannot talk about. There is a long tradition of Chinese people talking about everything: the good and the bad, the true and the false, the secret and the no-longer-secret. Chinese Netizens find ways to circumvent the censors and continue to talk about whatever they want to.

Your emails are easier to monitor than your phone calls, so be a little more careful about writing anything threatening to Chinese social harmony or national security, including things about Tibetan independence, Uighur separatists, detained human rights activists, etc. As scary as this all sounds, you are much more likely to email your folks about seeing babies peeing in the gutter than to write about geopolitics. If you are a political junky and all you care about are the topics that make the Chinese government seethe, it is in your and your program's best interest if you hold off writing about the really incendiary stuff until you get back to the U.S. You can still talk about it, and find out what Chinese people think about these issues (when they think about them at all), but just don't put it on the Internet.

■ Hygiene

Bathe regularly, wear clean clothes, and brush your teeth. Now that you know how to do the laundry, you can do all these things with ease. Here, we will briefly touch upon a few aspects of health and hygiene that are different in China.

First, many Americans are much more interested in dental hygiene than most Chinese are. If you take good care of your teeth, bring your own dental floss and toothbrush. If your biannual tooth cleaning comes

---

5 "Netizen" is how the Chinese translate 网民 wǎngmín (online people) into English.

up while you are in China, feel free to get it done locally if you live in a tier-one or tier-two city—the equipment will be the same as what your dental hygienist uses at home. Mouthwash can also be a little challenging to find, though it is available in large cities. It is okay to rinse your mouth out with tap water after brushing your teeth. Ingesting that small an amount of tap water will not make you sick.

Second, you may need to get your hair cut in China. Once you learn the process, this can become a very pleasurable experience. First, print or put on your smart phone a picture of what your hair looks like when you like it the most. Bring that image to the barber/salon and show it to them. Even if you barely speak Chinese, they'll understand. Step 1 is washing your hair, which may take place in a back or upstairs room. Don't be afraid if you are led off to what appears to be a dark part of the building... unless there aren't any hair-washing stations where they lead you. This hair wash is included in the price of the haircut. You can tell them you don't need to wash your hair if you're in a hurry (**bú yòng xǐtóu, xièxie 不用洗头, 谢谢**). A massage from the shoulders up is often included in the hair washing stage, and at no extra cost, as well. If they have massage beds, they will probably offer you a full-back massage for a little extra. This may add 20 minutes or more to your stay, so keep an eye on the clock if you need to.

After you are massaged, washed and rinsed, the young lady (sometimes man) will take you to a barber's chair and call one of the hair cutters over. He (sometimes she) will do your hair as normal, and then send you back for another rinse. The barber will then blow-dry and comb your hair and then it's time for you to pay. All that usu-

Getting a haircut in Shenzhen

ally costs about ¥15-30. Not bad for US$3-5, right?

The tendency for students abroad to feel liberated from social constraints, combined with the ubiquity of prostitution in China, makes the sex industry a topic we should cover in this section. Engaging the services of a sex worker is tantamount to playing Russian roulette with your health and life. It is estimated that about 8% of Chinese prostitutes have gonorrhea, 15-20% have chlamydia and different populations of prostitutes were found to have between 30-70% infection rates for herpes simplex II. One study calculated the infection rate among prostitutes for syphilis to be about 6% nationwide. That is a downright mean disease. Remember that alcohol consumption and the impairment of judgment that comes with it often precedes solicitation of a prostitute, so the simple act of wearing protection may be ignored in the heat of passion and drunkenness. Make the decision to avoid the sex industry before you start drinking and agree among your friends that you will not let each other dabble.

Other than the general scarcity of deodorants, maintaining a healthy level of hygiene is easy to do with commonly-available products. Your convenience store and supermarket will stock a variety of shampoos, toothpastes, razors, facial creams and feminine products. Unless you are wedded to a particular brand, you can find all these daily necessities locally.

Leisure

Your daily needs are met now, so you can let your hair down and do some things for fun! And, while they are called leisure activities, they can be just as educational as your coursework and program-designed activities. It is normal for American students to seek English language pursuits in their off hours during a study abroad program, and a certain amount of recharging is necessary, but I hope that you will seek out Chinese leisure activities, as well, and take full advantage of being in the country in which you have invested so much time and money.

■ Shopping

When their program in China is about to end, many students find they need to buy an extra suitcase to bring home all the stuff they bought. These items generally fall into three categories: souvenir arts and crafts, clothing and accessories, and pirated goods. In this section, we will give you some tips for buying souvenirs and clothes; you're on your own for the copyright-infringing pirated goods!

One of the most important things you can learn about buying souvenirs is to differentiate between items that are specific to one tourist site versus items that are generally Chinese. For example, an "I climbed Mt. Tai" t-shirt is site-specific, while a polyurethane imitation lacquer

You can buy one of these guys anywhere.

laughing bodhisattva statuette is not. This is an important distinction because you will be tempted to buy generic Chinese souvenirs when you are at tourist sites, but the vendors there know that people in China on vacation are much more willing to part with their money than people there for some time.

Whether you are at the Great Wall, the Terra Cotta Warriors, or the old part of Suzhou, most of the souvenirs will be exactly the same things, made in factories outside of Shanghai and Guangzhou. These items include jade-like glass jewelry, high copper-content imitation silver Tibetan jewelry, lacquer-looking bodhisattvas, chirping plastic crickets in large plastic peanut shells (seriously), prints of Chinese artwork, and so on. Not only can you get these at the tourist sites, but you can often get them in a market in your home base city. Just ask someone at your campus or someone in a park near your home base where you can buy these things. If you don't know how to say it, download a picture of a laughing Buddha figurine or a jade pendant, show it to someone and say you want to find a cheap one.

At the market that sells the generic cheapie tourist goods, start by walking around listening to what prices are being quoted to other people. Sometimes you get good information and sometimes you just hear what people are paying for a bracelet you're not interested in. When you are ready to start buying, ask what a vendor is asking for a certain item and counter-offer with half that number. If they laugh you out of their booth, it is useful information that you can use at another booth that sells the same thing. If they laugh at you but give a counter-offer, you're on your way! For mass-produced tourist tchotchkes, you should never pay more than 75% of the vendor's opening price; if you buy a lot of one item, you may be able to get a price that is less than 50% of the vendor's opening price. Don't be afraid to walk away—this is an important bargaining tactic. Furthermore, since the market is in your home city, you can come back any time you want.

At a tourist site, when you are buying something that is specific to that location, the vendor knows that you are probably not coming back, and if you buy something, it is for sentimental/souvenir value. Usually, this means it is worth more to you than a generic souvenir. Fortunately for you, most of these site-specific souvenirs are

Snuff bottles with painted interiors are a popular souvenir.

also made in distant factories, so the vendor paid just as little for it as the generic items. Some vendors will tell you that your price is so low that they would prefer to hold onto the item and sell it to a tourist who is willing to pay more for the sentimental value. The best way to test the veracity of this claim is to walk away. There are going to be at least five other vendors of exactly the same item at any major tourist site. Having so many visitors creates a hyper-competitive market in which many vendors sell the exact same things, and you can hop from vendor to vendor seeking the lowest price. Play them off each other instead of letting the vendor play on your desire for a souvenir.

For most students studying abroad, the mass-produced items will be good enough for gifting back home, and even for your own use. There are finer versions of many of the things you see at tourist sites, as well: gold laughing Buddhas, real jade jewelry, a kind of colored glassware called **liúlí 琉璃**, watercolors on scrolls painted by professional artists instead of by art students, go sets crafted by artisans, etc. These nice items often cost over a hundred U.S. dollars, so few students buy them until after they graduate and return to China with a salary. If you are in a position to drop serious cash on such items, you can find them in upscale malls, where fashion-conscious locals buy them for home decoration and nice gifts. If you are in a tier-three city, you may need to travel to the nearest tier-two city to find such a mall and such stores.

The second type of item that many students like to buy in China is clothing. You can shop for clothes in upscale malls, low-end malls, from sidewalk vendors, in night markets, and at regular stores on the street. It is true that you can find clothing in China at a lower price than in the U.S., but you get what you pay for, so if you are looking for low prices, focus on items of clothing or accessories that you do not plan to wear too many times and just enjoy the novelty. You can find well-made clothing in upscale malls and sometimes in stores called "export clothing stores" (**wàimào fúzhuāng diàn 外贸服装店**). These stores sell clothes manufactured for the export market, but the factories had extras that could be sold domestically. Made for export does not necessarily mean top-quality, though–different country markets have different standards. Name brand clothing like Polo and Tommy Hilfiger actually cost more in China than in the U.S., so do not assume that just because something is available in China it is cheaper there. If you like shopping, be sure to know what the U.S. prices of items you like to buy are before you go.

Before you go to China, find out what your clothing and shoe measurements are in metric or European form. Many shoes today are labeled with their sizes in several markets; if your shoes do not have a European or Chinese size on it, just go to the shoe store and look at the boxes of shoes in your size until you find one that lists several countries' sizes. Clothing in the U.S. rarely has multi-country size labeling, so you may just have to try things on in China to know your size. And be sure to try things on–it is very difficult to return an item in China, even if you have a receipt. It is almost unheard of. I learned by trying shirts on that Chinese men's shirts have shorter sleeves than U.S. men's shirts... even Chinese shirts that are labeled for export to the U.S.! Often, men's shirts in China have a narrower shoulder, as well. Try things on!

■ Active Leisure

The larger the city in which you live in China, the more options you will have in terms of exercise and outdoor activities. The Chinese have been spending the last 30 years trying to create stable economic environments for their families, and that has meant spending most of their time working or in group leisure activities that contribute to the cementing of professional relationships (e.g., karaoke). Once the second generation of single children reached adulthood, however, the economic contributions of their parents have allowed them to pursue more "selfish" forms of leisure that consume more resources than they create for those engaging in them (e.g., camping). In tier-one cities, you will be able to find, with relative ease, any form of exercise or leisure that you enjoy in the U.S., and probably some that would be outside of your price range at home but not in China. In large cities, you can find fitness centers, paintball teams, ultimate Frisbee, bicycling, basketball, and even American football, in addition to the traditional Chinese activities of badminton, ping-pong and martial arts.

To find traditional Chinese activities, ask the foreign affairs office at your university, and they can connect you with instructors. To find Western-style activities, you can also ask the foreign affairs office, as well as search the local expat sites on the Internet. Other resources for finding non-traditional activities include the English department and the physical education department at the local university. Staff there may be able to guide you to what you are looking for. Students in your dorm who have been there for months or years are also a good resource for finding exercise facilities. As with everything, you get what you pay for. Tier-two cities have state-of-the-art fitness facilities as well as fitness centers that are not as glitzy and may not have the latest or most complete sets of equipment, but will get the job done. And, the less fancy ones are sometimes much closer to your university than the nice one, which will be located near the expensive real estate in town.

You never really know what you are going to find until you start looking for activities. The small city of Linzhou in Henan Province has a paragliding club that supports an annual international paragliding event on the top of one of the peaks of the Taihang Mountains there. You may even be able to organize a club for students on campus who are interested in doing whatever you do for exercise or outdoor fun. Keep in mind, though, that most outdoor activities that require gear are still expensive activities in China. If you like mountain climbing or camping, you will have to pay top dollar for international brands from the one or maybe two stores that sell such items. Also, for activities like camping or long-distance biking, there is limited infrastructure: there are few campgrounds in China, so you would have to okay the idea with the owners of your planned campsites, whether park officials or farmers. If you would like to do intercity biking, be prepared to rough it—between major cities, the only motels are really seedy establishments that serve long-distance truckers. The hygiene at their attached restaurants is also questionable. Finally, be aware that the air pollution in China has a greater affect on some people than others; before you engage in a strenuous outdoor activity that you would not find strenuous at home, just jog around for an hour or more and see how your breathing is. If necessary, you can limit your strenuous exercise to indoor urban facilities and to the countryside for outdoor activities.

■ Local Sightseeing

Each city in China has a list of places for which it is known, a mixture of temples, natural phenomena, Washington-slept-here-type buildings where famous revolutionaries spent time, and man-made landmarks. The validity of this list is reinforced by the social obligation to bring out-of-town guests to these spots, and by the fact that they are frequented by many visitors. It does not take much sleuthing to find out what your home base city's famous spots are—residents are inculcated with the list from an early

Qingdao's Laoshan offers scenic vistas.

age. Just ask the most convenient local what the top spots in your town to visit are, and you will likely get The List. Because this is a canonical list, it should be easy to reach each place on it via public transportation. Qingdao's Laoshan is far from downtown, but it is such an important local attraction that you can take a public bus all the way from old downtown to the base of the mountain. The Great Wall at Badaling is even farther from downtown Beijing, but you can likewise catch buses and tourist trains that can take you there.

Beyond the list of places that residents consider must-see locations may be places in which you are personally interested. For example, those in Qingdao interested in Chinese history might want to see the former residence (which is a minor tourist attraction) and grave (which is not) of Qing reformer Kang Youwei. If you are studying in Shanghai and seek sites of historical import, you can take the subway out to Jiading and then take a taxi or bus to downtown to walk around the old town, where, in 1645, locals resisted the rule of the new Manchurian Qing Dynasty—including the imposition of the Manchurian shaved forehead and long braided hairstyle—and as a result, the Qing army went through the city stealing and murdering three times in a month and a half. If you are interested in steam locomotives (there are still a few working in China), you can use the Internet to hunt down any local survivors of the steam era. Some of these sites may have historical significance in China that is largely unknown, while others may only be significant to enthusiasts of hobbies that hardly exist in China. Sometimes visiting these locations are

Way off the beaten path in South Beijing

the most rewarding because it takes work to get there, find what you are looking for, and then explain to the people there why you are interested in it at all! Hunting for trains in China has often taken me off the beaten path and introduced me to people I would not otherwise have met. On one trip to Beijing, I met a woman from Xi'an living in a hovel in a dirty little village southwest of the city. She showed me how to get through her village to get trackside, and also told me a little about her and her son's life there, selling clothes on the street in Beijing. You may see a woman like this selling clothes downtown, but would you get to chat with her if she is always looking out of the corner of her eye for the next sale or, worse, the municipal management officers kicking out unlicensed vendors?

■ Drinking and Nightlife

Night life is the highlight of the experience for many a student while studying abroad. It is unrealistic for any parent or resident director to expect that students studying in China—especially those of college age and above—will not go out drinking. There is no drinking age in China. I would like to impress upon readers of all backgrounds that responsible drinking can be part of an educational experience in China, especially because learning to drink responsibly will serve these students well when they enter the workforce and work in China. Drinking is an extremely important part of Chinese professional and social culture, so learning how to drink like an adult is a valid educational goal for an adult study abroad experience. Many behaviors in which foreign students engage while drinking are not considered adult behaviors in China. This section is a primer on what constitutes mature adult drinking in China rather than tips on how to find bars and discos. After many years of taking students to China, I have learned that students are better at the latter than their teachers, and they need no encouragement from an authority figure to go find them.

Toasting: greasing the social axles

Students don't need to be able to read this character for alcohol to know where to find it.

The most important difference between drinking in China and the West is that adult Chinese drink to form and cement social bonds. Alcohol in China is a medium of social exchange that is used for toasting. Toasts always indicate—through words or just a look—that there is a relationship between the people drinking. To drink alone would be a waste of alcohol. Few Chinese drink to get drunk; many do get drunk, but that drunkenness is an indicator of the depth of feeling and respect they have for the individuals whom they toasted. Furthermore, mature Chinese rarely drink to the point at which they engage in obnoxious behavior such as destroying public property or displays of public indecency. In fact, at business banquets attended by two or more "teams," attendees will monitor their alcohol intake so that they never lose self-control. This is because business deals are negotiated at the end of business banquets, after the toasting has been going on for some time already.

This leads us to another important difference: the drinking venue. Most drinking in China takes place at meals, which tempers the effect of the alcohol, and also means you are drinking with people you know or have been introduced to by a trusted third party. Not being plugged into Chinese society, it is difficult for foreign students to find themselves at professional or social meals at which alcohol flows, so they follow their native cultural assumptions and look for alcohol in bars and nightclubs. Every Chinese city has these establishments, as well, but their role in Chinese society is quite different from Western society. Bars, but especially nightclubs, are the haunts of many "bad seeds." Such places are usually too loud to hold a good conversation, so it is hard to build a real relationship there. Even the toasts can barely be heard. Sure, a lot of young people like to go dancing on the weekend, and that is fine, but students need to be aware that there are nightclubs and there are nightclubs. In Qingdao, for example, one night club is known informally as the "peasant migrant worker club." It is a place where girls and boys get involuntarily groped and personal belongings go missing. Another nightclub in Qindao is popular among the "rich second generation" (**fù èrdài** 富二代), the idle rich children of not-so-idle rich parents. A newly-arrived American student might not know how to say no if new "friends" from the club want to take them somewhere or do something that conflicts with the program's schedule or behavioral expectations. In short, some nightclubs are more innocent than others, but you always want to have your guard up when you go. That girl that seems really into you may not play for free, either.

A final word on drinking to students and resident directors alike: people who want to drink will find ways to do so, regardless of what obstacles are put in the way. Rules can be ignored, locked doors can be opened by people on the inside; gates can be climbed. If a program wants its rules ignored, or its students falling off of fences, it will enact draconian policies that only stop the innocent. If a program wants students to learn to drink responsibly, it can introduce them to local Chinese society so that they can learn to drink with responsible adults who may then invite the students to social events which take the place of bars and nightclubs. Second, instead of trying to establish no-drinking rules, adult-oriented programs can consider establishing policies regarding what happens to students whose extracurricular activities (of any kind) affect their and their classmates' experiences in the program.

You are now ready to explore your community and live there indefinitely…or at least until the program ends. In the next chapter, you will learn how to get out of your community to see what the rest of China looks like.

Get out there!

Chapter 8
Intercity Travel

As long as you live in a city, getting away for a weekend or longer is fairly easy. Even if you live in a village, once you get to the nearest county town, you can access China's vast intercity transportation network. Serving everyone from low-income peasants to globe-trotting business people, intercity transport comes in a variety of forms and prices. Naturally, the cheaper the option, the slower and dirtier it is, however, thanks to central government subsidies designed to keep mass transit an attractive option, fast and clean forms of transportation can still be relatively low-priced. In this chapter, we will look at each form of transportation available for intercity travel, introducing where you can go, how to get tickets, how to board, and what to expect once you are on your way.

The first step in deciding what form of transportation to take is to compare your options. There are so many variables and "it depends" factors that we will just provide as much information as possible so that you can sort it out in your head. You will find that many things in China are like this: better to learn the strategies for finding out what you do not know than to try to learn everything at the start, which is impossible.

You have many transportation options just leaving Shanghai Pudong International Airport.

Rail Travel

Traveling by train is still the most popular form of intercity transport in China. The state-owned national rail network connects all major cities and many minor ones, many destinations can be reached without even changing trains, and there are so many different classes of trains and accommodations that travelers on any kind of budget can usually find something they like.

To determine if you can reach your destination by rail, you can go to www.huochepiao.com. This website is only available in Chinese, but it is up-to-date and has train and ticket information for trains that do not show up on English-language websites run by travel agencies that cater to foreigners. If you or someone you know can use this website, this should be your first point of reference.

The areas around the tier-one cities are particularly suited to train travel, as there are numerous departures. Corridors in which rail travel is clearly preferable to air include:

- Beijing-Tianjin
- Shanghai-Suzhou-Nanjing
- Shanghai-Hangzhou
- Hong Kong-Shenzhen-Guangzhou

With the arrival of bullet train service on dedicated rights-of-way, rail travel has become the preferred mode of transport between even more distant cities, including:

- Shanghai-Beijing
- Changsha-Shenzhen/Hong Kong
- Wuhan-Shenzhen/Hong Kong
- Beijing-Qingdao

In the near future, most provincial capitals will be linked by bullet train lines.

Advantages of rail travel include: price, frequent departures, downtown stations, limited security delays, you get to see the countryside as you go and, you can often strike up conversations with interesting people; or, rather, they strike up conversations with you!

Depending on where you are going, there are several classes of train in which you can ride.

The more popular your start and end points are (e.g., major cities or tourist destinations), the more choices you have. Generally speaking, the higher the class, the higher the ticket price. With the higher price comes a shorter trip, better service, a higher level of sophistication among the passengers and, as a result, a more hygienic environment. Here are the classes of trains available today, from highest to lowest.

■ Bullet (G) trains gāotiě 高铁

China's bullet train system is still under construction, but is expected to be completed by 2020, when most of China's major cities will be connected by these trains. Indicated in schedules by having a "G" before the train number, *gaotie* trains run up to 350 km/h and really give air travel a run for its money. The government has made taking the *gaotie* between major cities convenient by offering numerous departures every day (they only run in the daytime). As of the time of this writing, there were over 40 *gaotie* trains making the 1,069 km trip from Guangzhou to Wuhan between 7:00 a.m. and 7:20 p.m. every day, one departure every 10-20 minutes; that is more frequent than most of the commuter buses in the American city where I live. Compare that $70 trip of about four hours by bullet train, downtown to downtown, to going by air: between Guangzhou and Wuhan, there are 9 departures per day, the flight takes 1.5 hours, plus an hour at the departure airport, plus at least an hour getting to and from the air-

A gaotie bullet train

port on either end, you cannot bring liquids in your carry-ons, and the ticket costs between $50 and $150, depending on the time of your flight. Many Chinese travelers are beginning to say, "Why bother?" when it comes to flying a route also served by bullet trains.

Because the *gaotie* trains run on their own tracks, they generally serve stations built only for them. The only exceptions are terminal stations in major cities that have been adapted to serve the new trains. Keep this in mind when planning your trip–the *gaotie* station may be some distance from the station(s) that serves all the other trains in town.

■ Multiple-unit electric (D) trains dòngchē 动车

Outwardly indistinguishable from the *gaotie*, *dongche* are built to run to a maximum speed of 250 km/h and are the fastest trains found on regular tracks in China. On schedules, their numbers are preceded by a "D." Though slightly slower than *gaotie* trains, *dongche* trains are a good deal, but they are being phased out in favor of the *gaotie* trains running on the parallel dedicated rights-of-way.

■ Intercity (C) chéngjì 城际 and Direct Express (Z) zhídá 直达 trains

These are trains that run between relatively close cities with few stops in between. C trains appear to be limited to the Beijing-Tianjin route, while Z trains appear to be in the process of being phased out in favor of faster and slower trains using the same line.

■ Special Fast (T) tèkuài 特快 and Fast (K) kuàisù 快速 trains

Today, the names appear euphemistic compared to G, D, Z trains, but once upon a time, the T and K trains were the vanguards of increasingly faster rail service for those who had benefitted first from the economic reforms under Deng Xiaoping. T trains stop at provincial tier-one and -two cities while K trains stop at tier-three cities. The quality of equipment can vary greatly, but most T and K trains are air conditioned.

■ Regular speed service pǔkuài 普快 and regular service pǔkè 普客

At the bottom of the speed totem pole are "regular speed service" and "regular service trains." Also called "slow trains" (**màn chē**), these trains are indicated in schedules by having no letters and only a four-digit number. These trains are really cheap because they are slow (they stop everywhere and have to wait for all other trains to pass), use old equipment, frequently do not have air conditioning, and the level of service is low. You can take a G *gaotie* from Beijing to Wuxi (an industrial city outside of Shanghai) for about $80

A K train that has just arrived in Shenzhen West Station, with a slow "Green Skin" train waiting in the background

and it will take only five hours to go the 1210 kilometers. By comparison, you can also take a slow train for as little as $23... but it takes 17.5 hours to get there.

These trains essentially serve poor people; foreigners are few and far between on these trains. Taking a slow train can make for a good story... but often one of those kinds of stories that you enjoy more the farther you are from the experience. Expats have reported seeing farm animals on these trains, and I once saw a young mother help her baby relieve itself on a piece of newspaper laid in the aisle for the job.

As recently as 20 years ago, these slow trains were extremely common. Many adults have fabulous stories of taking a "green skin train" (so named because the train cars back then were all copies of green Soviet equipment) to and from college during breaks, when everyone else in the country was taking the train and there were no seats to be had. It may be worth taking a slow train between two close stations just to get a taste of what so many people experienced in the 1980s and '90s.

■ Extras (L) 临客

The L stands for **línshí kèchē** 临时客车, translated literally as "temporary passenger train," and known in American railroading as an "extra section." These are trains that are added to the schedule at peak times to accommodate increased ridership. As L trains are added primarily to accommodate migrant workers going home for major holidays, they are cheap and slow.

If you can, try to avoid traveling during peak times such as Spring Festival, May Day and National Day. The number of Chinese who travel home for Chinese New Year makes it the largest human migration on earth, taking place at the start and end of the Spring Festival holiday every year. If you travel during the Spring Festival holidays, you may find yourself unable to buy a comfortable ticket on any form of transportation and get stuck on a green train while having a profound cultural experience.

Seating Class

If you are still operating under the belief that China is a classless communist proletarian paradise, the choice of rail seating class should quickly disabuse you of the notion. As indicated by the different levels of trains, there are different levels of accommodation aboard each train. Though the name of the seating class may be the same, the actual ride experience will vary, depending on the quality (speed) of the train itself. The basic seating classes are described as follows, in order of least to most comfortable.

■ Hard Seat yìngzuò 硬座

"Hard seat" gets its name from the seating on the old green trains, which were hard, bench-like affairs. With each step up in the speed of a train's schedule comes an upgrade in equipment and an attendant decrease in the hardness of hard seat. On the *gaotie* bullet trains, "hard seat" simply means not-first-class. Hard seat tickets are the

Hard seat on a train from Hefei to Wuhu, in Anhui Province

cheapest kind you can buy ahead of time. There is also a class of ticket (**zhànpiào** 站票) below hard seat available during peak festival traffic that allows you on the train, but without a seat.

■ **Soft Seat ruǎnzuò** 软座

This term was more meaningful when hard seats were actually hard, but it still means "more comfortable than the hard seats," regardless of how hard the latter are. Prices on soft seat cars are slightly higher for hard seats elsewhere on the same train.

■ **Hard Sleeper yìngwò** 硬卧

"Hard sleeper" is the way to go for long-distance travelers on a budget... but a foreign budget. True budget travelers (such as jobless people and farmers) may spend the night in hard seat, but for most foreign travelers, hard sleeper is a good compromise between economy and comfort.

Hard sleepers are made up of three-tiered bunk beds, with different prices for each level. The cheapest is the top berth (**shàngpù** 上铺). It's cheap because it is so close to the ceiling that you cannot sit up and you are above the top rim of the window, so you can only see the ballasted roadbed below. The middle berth (**zhōngpù** 中铺) is also middle-priced. You can sit up if you stay hunched over, and the climb is not too far. You can also look out the window from this level. The bottom bunk (**xiàpù** 下铺) is priciest because you can sit on it like a chair by swinging your feet into the area between your bunks and the facing bunks. It is customary for the middle and top bunk people to sit on the bottom bunk until bedtime. If you are traveling with a companion, you can strategically buy tickets for the middle and bottom bunks in the same stack and limit the number of strangers using the bottom bunk as a seat. There are flip-up bench seats along the aisleway for people who like to look out the window and have their knees bumped into by the vending carts that are pushed back and forth by railway workers.

On older cars, hard sleeper berths are all open—if you walk down the aisle on the side of the car, you can see everything going on in all the berths... except the top berths, which are so high and close to the ceiling, it might as well be the attic. On newer cars, each pair of three-level bunks has its own compartment, albeit without a door. Thus, a bulkhead gives a little privacy by walling off the foot-end of each bunk. Another improvement in the newer cars is that the passengers in each compartment can store their luggage in an open cubby area that is built on top of the aisle and accessible only from within the compartment. On old cars, the aisle had a metal rack that ran the length of the car and it was everyone for themselves in terms of finding room for your oversized luggage and then physically getting it onto the rack. Some new sleeper cars have sockets for charging phones and computers, but don't count on it—make sure your electronics are fully charged before setting out.

In all sleeper cars, bedding is provided. Restrooms are found at one end of the car, usually two toilet chambers and one open sink area for rinsing your hands (BYO soap) or brushing your teeth (BYO toothbrush and toothpaste). On long trips, the water may run out before you reach the destination. Also at the end of the car (often the *other* end) is a water boiler for making tea and instant noodles.

Be forewarned: getting to the top berth requires considerable dexterity and flexibility; getting to the middle berth requires a little less physical acumen. If you have any mobility issues, stick to bottom berths, whether in hard sleeper or soft sleeper (discussed in the following section).

■ Soft Sleeper

Before air travel became common in China, soft sleeper was the height of luxury travel. In fact, soft sleeper compartments used to be hard to get without having the right connections. Nowadays, anyone who can afford the ticket can get a soft sleeper berth. Another recent development is the lowering of domestic Chinese airfare to the point that soft sleeper cannot always compete on any terms other than the fact that you do not have to leave the ground or check your liquids in your luggage. Soft sleeper from Beijing to Chengdu in August 2012 cost around ¥700 for a 30-hour trip, while airfare for the three-hour flight cost between ¥1010 and ¥1350, depending on departure time.

Soft sleeper compartments are private with doors, and there are only four berths per compartment. The newest soft sleeper compart-

Ticket counters in the Chengdu train station

ments have LCD TVs and are very nicely decorated. Older cars do not have TVs, but are kept just as clean. Like newer hard sleeper cars, soft sleepers have always had private luggage storage areas above the aisle ceiling.

Getting There, from Buying the Ticket to Leaving the Station

Before you can get on the train-or even on the station platform-you need to have your train ticket in hand. There are two main ways to do this: through an agency or at a train station. Buying from an agency saves you time and trouble but there is a service fee. No matter who you buy from, tickets for any given train are not released for sale until a certain number of days before departure. This number changes from year to year, station to station and from train class to train class. As of the time of writing, Beijing and Shanghai were issuing tickets 12 days prior to departure. There have been times in the past when certain tickets were sold beginning only three days prior to departure. Ask a Chinese person in your city what the time frame is while you are there. Some trains, like the Sunday night Beijing to Qingdao *gaotie*, sell out very quickly, so buy your tickets as soon as you can.

The cheapest and most direct method of obtaining a train ticket is to go to the train station. The location of the ticket windows varies by station, so it helps to be able to recognize the characters on signs pointing the way: 售票处 (**shòupiào chù**). At Beijing Station (the oldest and most centrally located of Beijing's several stations), the windows are located on the outside wall, facing the front plaza. At Shanghai Station, the ticket office is in a building that is across the street from the departure hall. At most train stations, the ticket windows are located inside the main lobby of the station. The railway bureau also has ticket offices sprinkled throughout urban areas and charge a minimal service fee (¥5 at last check). Do not expect much English ability on the part of ticket agents at either the station or railway bureau booking offices.

Travel agencies (**lǚxíng shè** 旅行社) that sell train-and often airplane-tickets can be found throughout major cities. They charge about 30 for obtaining tickets on your behalf, but it can save a lot of time and trouble. First, if you do not live near a railway bureau station or ticket office, they can save you a long trip across town. Second, they can tell you right off the bat when tickets for your train become available. There are few things worse than trekking across town to the train station only to find out that your tickets are not yet available. One thing that might be worse is to do that schlepping and then find out that there are no seats left on the day you want/need to leave. Maybe if you had gone to a local agent instead of spending an hour or two on the subway getting to the train station, you would have gotten the last empty seat....

Another advantage of buying through an agent instead of at the station is that you can avoid the crush of the station ticket windows. Whereas only people with a decent amount of cash can fly, *anyone* can take the train. "Anyone" can come in the form of someone butting in front of you because his trip is more important than yours; or it can come in the form of someone who takes your moment's delay in moving forward in line as indication that you have decided to get out of line entirely, and jump in front of you. Granted, most people take the lines seriously and wait patiently like you, but it is definitely an experience different from the airport.

Some agencies cannot issue *gaotie* tickets, even if they can issue regular train tickets. This is because *gaotie* tickets are sold with your ID number printed on it to reduce the possibility of counterfeit tickets being issued en masse. Just ask if the agency sells *gaotie* tickets and they will tell you. If you do not speak Chinese, just say "gow tee-ay?" and do an impression of a train, and they'll either smile and ask you to come in or frown and send you on your way. Or, show them the photo of a *gaotie* ticket below if you do not like embarrassing yourself.

If you cannot find a travel agent, or prefer to buy your tickets in English, you can go to any four- or five-star hotel lobby and ask the maitre d' for help. The service fee will be higher, and they will just use the nearest travel agent to buy your ticket, but at least someone else will take care of it for you, and the maitre d' will be able to communicate with you in English. Beijing Station, Beijing West Station and Shanghai Station have ticket offices for foreigners where the ticket agents speak English. Most stations do not have this service, however.

If you do some homework first, you should be able to buy train tickets wherever you want, regardless of your Chinese ability. There is a limited amount of information that needs to be communicated in order to buy a train ticket: date, train number, destination city, and seat class. If you come with this information on a piece of paper, as well as two backup options in case your desired ticket is sold out, you should be okay. If you are traveling with others and intend to buy sleeper berths, decide ahead of time if you prefer to have same-level bunks facing each other or bunks in the same "stack." One benefit of the latter is that fewer strangers will sit on your bottom bunk. If your party has a number of travelers who are not physically

A ticket for the gaotie from Shanghai to Suzhou. These, and some D train tickets, come in a shade of blue.

very mobile, they may need to be spread out across the lower bunks of several stacks, maybe even in different cars, depending on lower berth availability.

If you can read Chinese, train information can be found at www.huochepiao.com, as well as on large boards found next to railway ticket offices. As you do your research, keep in mind that major Chinese cities have more than one train station. In Beijing, for example, Beijing Station mostly serves points north; Beijing West Station mostly serves points south; Beijing South Station became Beijing's *gaotie* station when the Olympics came in 2008; there are also a few small stations throughout the city that serve slow trains and tourist trains like the one from Beijing North Station to Badaling Great Wall. Shanghai's main stations are Shanghai Station, Shanghai South Station, and the brand-new Hongqiao Station for *gaotie* and *dongche* trains. Shanghai Station also has some *gaotie* departures for trains on the line to Nanjing (including Kunshan, Wuxi and Suzhou).

Like most things in China, train tickets are sold for cash; make sure you bring enough cash with you wherever you get your ticket. Once your little rectangular paper ticket is in hand (see examples), protect it like you would cash. There is no electronic record proving that you bought it. If you lose it, it's gone. If you are planning to take the *gaotie*, bring your passport in addition to cash. You will hand your passport to the person issuing the ticket and he or she will have it printed on the ticket. This is probably the last time you will need your passport in connection with taking the train. When you get to the station and see how many people are going to get on with you, you will see why no one checks each ticket against the ticketholder's ID. A certain study abroad guide author, (ahem), once made a 1.5-hour trip from his hotel in the suburbs to a downtown railway station to buy a gaotie ticket... having forgotten to bring his passport. The ticket agent let me use my U.S. driver's license number instead. While you should not count on every ticket agent being this flexible, you can give it a shot if you discover yourself in a similar situation.

Tickets for some D trains and all other trains are pink. What can you tell about this ticket using what you have learned and some common sense? Look on the following page for answers.

1. Where is this passenger going from/to?
2. What time does the train depart, and on what date?
3. What is the train number? What kind of train is this?
4. What kind of seating/bunking does the passenger have?

1. This passenger is going from Shenzhen to Ji'an (in Jiangxi Province).
2. The train departed Shenzhen Station at 6:55 p.m. on August 31, 2011.
3. The train number is K442, so as a K train, it is fairly slow and inexpensive.
4. The passenger has bought a lower bunk (下铺), the most expensive level. The bunk is in hard sleeper (硬卧), the cheaper of the two sleeper options.

The ticket also indicates that:

- The passenger will be riding in a new air-conditioned hard sleeper (新空调硬卧 xīn kōngtiáo yìngwò).
- The ticket is only good for that particular train on that day (with exception, see the following paragraph). There is no Chinese version of the Eurail Pass, probably because there are too many people taking the train to leave seating to chance.…

Some tickets have an additional line of text reading 在3日内到有效, which literally means "valid for arrival within three days." This is supposed to mean that if the ticket holder must leave the train in mid-trip for some reason outside of his or her control (e.g., illness), he or she may replace the ticket with one for the same destination as long as arrival takes place within three days. On the same ticket, however, is written "[this ticket is] only good for this train on this day." According to one survey, 75% of Chinese poll respondents also did not understand whether their ticket was valid for three days or only on the ticketed train and date.[1]

Your ticket also has an important piece of information for you—the location of your seat or berth:

Here, "04车" indicates that the ticketholder will be on car #04, and "006号下铺" means the lower (下) bunk (铺) in [stack] number (号) 6. We'll show you what this means once we get to the part where you actually get on the train. For now, just know that this information is on your ticket.

■ Getting to Your Train

As you prepare for your trip, keep in mind the following as you pack:

- There is no checked luggage on trains, so carry only as much as you can lug around all by yourself. Strangers may help you lift your luggage at times, but never

"Limited for use in boarding this train on this day"
"Valid for arrival within three days"

---

1 Xinhua.net 火车票规定有歧义 市民不懂 "三日内到有效" www.cq.xinhuanet.com/2008-06/06/content_13474407.htm

Monks eat instant noodles on the train, too.

- pack under the assumption that the milk of human kindness will run freely during your trip.
- Train food is expensive and mediocre. There will also be carts of snacks and drinks pushed back and forth. These items are also priced knowing that you are stuck on a train. Bring your own food–it's cheaper and more hygienic than the food that the train staff have been trying to unload for who knows how long. Good things to bring include: instant noodles; fruit with skins you can peel; dry snacks; bottled drinks; tea in a thermos.
- Even though motels and hotels will provide you with a toothbrush, toothpaste and comb, the train does not. If you have an overnight ride, you can either rough it until you get to your destination motel, or bring a travel bag for use on the train. The easiest thing to do is to bring an unused set of toiletries from your last hotel stay.
- Sleeper compartments have one small table between stacks and one hook on the wall next to each bunk. If you have things you take off to sleep (glasses, watch, etc.), you might consider bringing a little bag to hang on the hook.

When you are ready to leave, budget your time so that you reach the station 30 minutes before departure for a *gaotie* and 45 minutes before departure for other types of trains. This will give you plenty of time to find the waiting area for your train. Large urban stations share a similar design and smaller stations are simply scaled-down versions, so once you get a feel for how Chinese train stations are laid out, you should be fine.

When you get to the station, look for a sign that says 入口 **rùkǒu**. In major cities, it should also say "entrance" on it. At the doorway, there will be an x-ray machine and conveyor belt for feeding your luggage through the machine. There may be a metal detector, too. Getting through train station security is a breeze; before you know it, you're in the main hall.

If you are leaving from a large urban station, there will be numerous waiting areas for numerous platforms (which you cannot see from inside the station). Upon entering the main hall, look around for a large electronic board that lists the departing trains and the numbers of their attendant gates. *Gaotie* stations tend to be huge halls lined with numbered gates and seats for waiting. The gates (labeled 检票口 **jiǎnpiào kǒu** "ticket-checking entry") lead to the areas of the hall where passengers board the train cars.

The waiting areas in regular train stations may be more spread out, depending on the design of the station. Follow signs to your gate number, like in an airport. If you are leaving from a smaller city, there may be only one waiting area for only a couple platforms, and passengers for all trains wait in the same room until their train is called, shortly before it arrives.

Do not be surprised if you cannot see any trains from inside the station. The waiting areas and gates in many stations are located above the tracks and platforms. Once you find your gate and waiting area, wait until your train is called. In major cities, it will be called in Chinese and English; elsewhere, the announcement will only be in Chinese, so keep your eyes and ears open. Your train's number will be displayed at its gate, either on an electronic board or on a printed sign.

If you are taking a *gaotie* or *dongche*, it is likely that one or more orderly lines will form when ticket checking begins. *Gaotie* stations have turnstiles that use a laser to scan your ticket, like the self check-out at a grocery store; at some stations, a human will physically look at your ticket before allowing you to continue to the turnstile. If you are taking one of the slower trains, you know boarding has begun when a human wave dotted with luggage flotsam surges toward the ticket-checking lanes. If you have little or no luggage, feel free to wait until the crowd thins out a little bit so that you do not get jostled. If you a) have a suitcase and b) your ticket is for an un-air conditioned hard sleeper or less, you had better jump right into the fray so that you can lay claim to a spot on the luggage rack. The ticket checker will make sure you are boarding the right train and let you through.

Follow the masses up/down/out to the platform and start looking for your car. Each car has a number on one end; find the one that matches the number on your ticket before the 车 character. At the doorway, your car attendant will check your ticket to make sure you are at the right spot. If, for some reason, you are so late that you are in danger of the train leaving before you make it down the platform to your car, get on the train first and then walk through all the intervening cars to your own—they are numbered inside on signs over the vestibule doorway. If you board at an intermediate stop, you will usually only have a couple minutes to get on the train. Intermediate station stops are short unless your train has to wait for faster trains to overtake it by just running through that station.

■ Once You Are On Board

Each seat and stack of bunks is numbered—just walk along the aisle until you find your seat. If you find someone is in your seat or bunk, smile and show your ticket. If you speak Chinese, you can ask that person where the seat/berth on your ticket is, as if you are not sure. This saves your face if it *is* you who made the mistake.

If you are in a sleeper, you can put your luggage on the over-aisle rack or cubby or under the bottom berth in your stack. In coach, you can put your belongings overhead. When you are ready to get into a sleeper berth, remember to take off your shoes—it keeps the linens and footholds clean for everyone. It is common courtesy to tuck your shoes under the bottom bunk near the lowest foothold if you are in a middle or upper bunk. Because the berths are shared by strangers and ticketing is gender-blind, everyone sleeps in their clothes. I keep my laptop by my head when I sleep because my life is in it, but onboard crime is low. On un-air-conditioned green trains, open windows sometimes invite thieves during station stops, but since the windows on newer trains do not open, this is no longer a problem for most foreign travelers. There are railway police on each train—contact your car attendant if something criminal actually does happen.

In sleepers, your car's attendant will come through sometime after departure and exchange your paper ticket for a plastic chip that has your stack number and the Chinese character for upper, middle or lower berth on it. The attendant will keep your ticket in a folio until shortly before your stop, when he or she will come back and exchange your chip for the original ticket, waking you up, if necessary.

Chinese trains are nominally non-smoking now, and smokers respect this by grinning and bearing it or going to the vestibules and bathrooms to sneak a smoke. On trains slower than G and D types, station stops are sometimes long enough to get off to smoke a cigarette, stretch your legs, or buy some local snacks being peddled by vendors. If you do not speak Chinese, you have a good chance of having been discovered by your car's bilingual passengers by the time you reach a station and can ask him/her to help you ask how long the station stop is if you need to get off for something. Do not get left behind, though—there are too many people on the train for the conductor to wait for one tardy passenger!

Follow the exit signs to get out of the station.

■ Arrival

Sleeper passengers know their station is coming up soon when the attendant comes back with their ticket; if you are in coach, keep your ears open for a station announcement and/or ask your seat mate to tell you when your station is coming. This can be accomplished through showing your ticket and making funny gestures and faces if you do not speak Chinese....

Getting off at an intermediate stop can be stressful if the stop is short and a lot of people need to get off. Everyone who needs to get off always does, but many people express the natural fear that *they* are going to be the exception to the rule if they do not become anxious and shove-y. Get ready to go before the train stops and calmly bring your belongings to the closest vestibule.

Once off the train, follow the crowd to the walkway that goes over or under the tracks to the station and the exit, usually labeled in English, but some extremely rural stations may only write it in Chinese: 出站口 **chūzhànkǒu**. If you find yourself ahead of or behind the pack, follow the bilingual signs out.

Have your ticket handy because station staff check passengers' tickets on the way out to make sure no one snuck a free ride into their itinerary.

Congratulations! You've successfully completed a [virtual] train ride. Now that some of the fear of the unknown has been tempered, there are a couple of things that smart travelers need to know about Chinese train stations. Train stations attract all kinds of people, including those who see a major train station as a fertile hunting ground for unsuspecting travelers. As with any crowded area, pick-pocketing and theft of unattended items is always a possibility. A trouble-free trip goes to the vigilant: keep your belongings close and be aware of them at all times. Once you're on the train platform, you're safe.

At the station exit, you may run into another type of person of whom you should be wary, even though they are just trying to make a buck: unregistered "taxi" drivers and their intermediaries. Knowing that there will always be some portion of travelers who are unfamiliar with their destination, these folks approach people leaving the station who look like they do not know where to go next and ask if they need a taxi. Major city stations have an official taxi hailing area, so you can say 不用, 谢谢 búyòng, xièxie (I do not need one, thanks) and keep looking for signs to the taxi line. Small cities and towns will have taxies sitting outside the exit gate, and you can walk up to the first taxi in line if you are not taking a bus or getting picked up. If you do go with one of the taxi "agents," you will have to pay a little extra for the "service" of having a taxi hailed for you, and the taxi itself will not have a meter, so you will not know how much you were overcharged.

If you have taken a train somewhere and do not know how to get where you are going next, just show the name of your intended location in your guidebook (in Chinese) to a train station employee, and they should help you find a legitimate form of transportation.

Air Travel

Thanks to the growing *gaotie* system, rail travel now competes head-to-head with airlines on some key routes. It can be a lot less of a hassle to take a train from Changsha to Guangzhou than it is to fly, what with airports being located far from downtown, and having to go through check-in and security. However, for distances over 350 km, flying is still a convenient way to go, especially if you have large luggage.

If you reached China by air, then you are already well-prepared to fly domestically. For all intents and purposes, domestic air travel in China works the same as domestic travel in the West, except you can still check luggage for free in China, and they still feed you as part of the ticket price. Assuming you will have had at least one flying experience under your belt by the time you reach China, the following are a few things you should know when flying domestically.

- You can buy cheap tickets very close to the date of departure. Chinese people have to change their plans all the time, so Chinese flyers are not penalized for having to buy last-minute tickets. The cheapest flights may be sold out if you book late, but you can often pick up

Flying in China is basically the same as anywhere else.

deeply discounted tickets very close to the date of travel.
- You can save a lot of money by booking domestic Chinese tickets through a Chinese agency or website. Popular websites include www.ctrip.com and www.elong.com, both of which have English websites and accept foreign credit cards. American websites generally sell domestic Chinese airplane tickets at full price, while Chinese sites sell them at airline-offered discounts, which can sometimes be up to 80% off full price.
- If you have domestic Chinese travel that immediately follows international travel to China, it is more convenient for first-timers to book all the way through to your final airport, as this will get your luggage all the way there under international luggage weight & piece restrictions. If you book separately, domestic travel luggage restrictions may be applied to your domestic leg(s).

There was a time when domestic travel made within a certain number of days of international travel allowed the international luggage restrictions to carry over to the domestic portions of travel, but those days seem to have passed. If you want to try it, please let me know how it works!

- At some airports, check-in counters are divided by airline, while at others, they are divided by airline and flight number. In the former case, several flights are served by each counter; in the latter case, you will need to find your flight number

on a monitor to find out which counter to go to.
- To make check-in easy, give a copy of your ticket/itinerary to the check-in staff, along with your passport. The check-in staff speak English well enough to check you in, so don't worry about language.
- You will need to show your passport and boarding pass as step one of the security screening process.
- You do not need to take off your shoes for Chinese airport security, but everything else is the same as TSA security checks in the U.S.
- Delayed flights are becoming more and more common in China. Let other passengers on your flight become [uselessly] irate; you can be patient or ask an employee if there is another flight you can take if you are in a hurry. Good luck with that.
- There are very few regional jets in use in China, so do not expect free plane-side checking of carry-on size suitcases. What you bring on board will have to fit at your feet or in an overhead compartment.
- Air travel in China nominally follows the same procedures as in the West; the main differences are in the behaviors you may see during your trip. Air travel etiquette in China is less strict than in the U.S. Don't be surprised if you experience some or all of the following behaviors. Most of the time, the best reaction is no action. Leave it to airline staff or native speakers to say something.
  - People who board with no regard for which seating sections have been invited to board.
  - People reassigning their own seats if they were not ticketed to sit with their travel companions ... and not waiting for the original seat owner to board and asking his/her permission to switch. If you care about where your ticketed seat is, you can smile and stick to your guns. If you do not, you can go to where their original seat was.
  - People bringing on too many carry-on items and/or making inefficient use of the limited overhead compartment space, leaving you little room for your carry-ons. Either start rearranging things for your luggage, or ask a flight attendant for help.
  - People who do not try to get out of the aisle as quickly as possible so that people behind them can board.
  - People who do not turn off their cell phones when they are told to. NOTE: Chinese regulations state that you cannot use your cell phone until the plane is parked at the gate, unlike in the U.S., where you can start dialing as soon as the wheels hit the ground.
  - People who start gathering their overhead bin items while the plane is still taxiing.

The process for buying tickets for and boarding a long-distance bus is very similar to that of taking a train.

- People in aisle or middle seats who simply turn their knees to the side to let in a seatmate instead of getting up and standing in the aisle to make way.
- Many airports still have staff compare the airline-printed luggage tag on checked luggage with the corresponding little sticker that was put on your boarding pass at check-in to make sure you leave with your own suitcases, so do not throw it away during the flight.
- Avoid the guys offering taxi services outside of the official taxi waiting area, just like at the train station.

Travel by Long-Distance Bus

In most cases, the cheapest way to get from City A to City B in China is to take a bus. In small cities and towns, it can be the *only* way to get to City B. Bus travel is cheaper because the equipment is often dirtier, the schedules often slower, and the overall experience much less comfortable than other modes of transportation. Important exceptions include regional bus services in Guangdong, Jiangsu, Zhejiang and Shandong Provinces, which also happen to be the wealthiest provinces in China. Express buses between major cities in those prov-

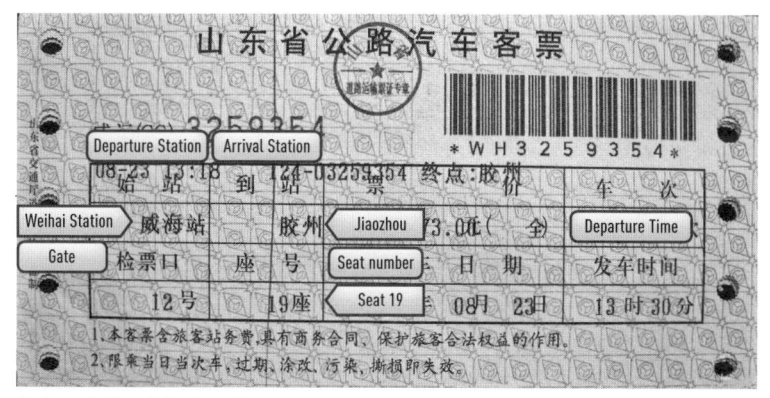

An intercity bus ticket from Shandong Province

inces are large, comfortable coaches with TVs and complimentary drinks or snacks. For other routes, however, taking a long-distance bus is a cultural experience on par with taking a slow train.

Major Chinese cities have more than one long-distance bus station, with different stations serving different routes. Find out from a guide book or a local friend which station you should go to for your intended destination. The Chinese names for long-distance bus station are **kèyùnzhàn** 客运站 and **chángtú qìchē zhàn** 长途汽车站.

You can find schedules and ticket prices online at www.piaojia.cn/changtu, www.keyunzhan.com, and www.ctqcp.com, but if you have time to take a bus, you have time to go to the station and check the schedule yourself, which will be more reliable than anything on the Internet (Chinese websites often provide out of date or inaccurate information).

Shorter routes are served by mid- and large-size coaches, while overnight routes are served by sleeper buses called **wòpù chē** 卧铺车. Instead of seats, sleeper buses have semi-reclined bunks. Tickets are sold from windows (and machines, in some places) at the bus station, and have specific seat assignments on them, even if the vehicle in question does not have numbered seats.

You can establish when you get on your bus if your ticketed seat assignment really matters or not by looking for seat numbers. It is not uncommon for buses to sell more tickets than there are built-in seats…because little fold-up stools can be put in the aisle of smaller buses that run like locals, but over a long distance.

At many stations, your ticket is checked shortly before departure at a door that leads to the parking lot in which the buses sit. At some stations, a ticket taker will check your ticket on the bus itself, and it is up to you to find your bus in the parking lot. It will be marked by a sign in/on the window indicating its first and last stops.

The nice big coaches tend to be used on long runs of hundreds of kilometers, with few stops between terminals. When these buses stop for gas, it's also a bathroom/snack break. Smaller buses are used for regional routes that take six hours or less to complete. That six hours includes stopping for every Tom, Dick, and Jane at the side of the road as long as there are seats or stools left on the bus, and then stopping at whatever village they're going to.

Even though many long-distance buses are dirty and uncomfortable, they are safe, so if you are on a limited budget and/or need mass transportation to or from a small town, taking a bus can be the best way to go.

Travel by Sea

There are a few intercity routes in *China* served by ships and boats, namely:

- Hong Kong to Shekou (Shenzhen), Macao, Zhongshan, Guangzhou
- Maoming, Guangdong to Haikou, Hainan
- Shanghai to Chongqing and points on the Yangzi River in between
- Yantai, Penglai and Weihai to Dalian

In addition, there are some intracity ferry services where rivers or channels separate parts of the city, including:

A car ferry between Qingdao and Huangdao

A Zhuhai-Hong Kong catamaran

- Xiamen to Gulangyu Island
- Putuoshan Island ferry in Zhejiang
- Cross-river ferry in Shanghai
- Ferries from Qingdao to Qingdao's Economic Development Zone in Huangdao

The two main kinds of intercity ferry are speedboats and large vehicle ferries. Speedboat ferries are usually sleek, low-profile affairs with no opening windows. This is good for keeping the spray out of the boat, but bad if anyone on board gets seasick. Large ferries, depending on the distance to be covered, may have only unreserved seat tickets (e.g., the car ferry between Qingdao and Huangdao), or may have several classes, as on the overnight trip between Yantai and Dalian, across the entrance to the Bohai Gulf. On the 6.5-hour Yantai-Dalian huge slow boat, ¥1,000 gets you a double with your own restroom, TV and refrigerator. At the other end of the spectrum, ¥180 gets you a ticket that simply gets you on the boat, and it is up to you to find a place to rest. In between, there are 4-person rooms, 6-person rooms and 8-person rooms.

Tickets can be bought in the ferry terminal, or online, though like with the *buses*, going in person is usually a better idea. You can probably obtain tickets through nice hotels' maitre d's, as well, with the addition of a service fee.

Private Taxi

Some trips call for personalized service, and for that, you can hire a taxi just for you or your party. This is handy when you have up to four people, will be returning to your home base by nightfall, and one or more of the following conditions exist:

- Member(s) of your party are physically unprepared for the rigors of mass transportation.
- You can afford to and prefer to avoid the "mass" part of mass transportation.
- Your itinerary includes stops that are not on the usual schedule, e.g., you are a birder and want to visit a marsh that is not conveniently served by public transportation, or you are an amateur photographer and need to be able to stop whenever you see a potential subject or location.
- You want to cover more ground in the day than scheduled mass transportation would allow you to reach, but you do not want to/cannot join any tour groups that may follow the same route (e.g., Great Wall plus Thirteen Tombs).

For the right price, many cabbies are willing to spend the day with you instead of trolling for fares. Try to establish some kind of baseline information before you approach a cabbie for a quote. You can ask your hotel's front desk how much it might cost to hire a taxi for the day to go to places X, Y, and Z; you can search the Internet; or you can ask a local friend.

Once you have at least a vague idea of what range the quote should be in, you can either approach a taxi driver outside your motel/university, or ask a staff person from where you live to help you do this. It is at times like this that having given a gift to this person when you first arrived comes in handy. You may be asked to pay part of the fee up front and the remainder at the end of the day. Do not pay the entire sum up front, no matter what. If they ask for that, find another driver. Once the driver has all your money, there is no reason for him to do anything for you other than for honor's sake, and honor does not always work.

If your party has more people (or more people and stuff) than can fit in a taxi, you can ask a travel agency to help you hire a mini-van (called a **shāngwù chē** 商务车) or larger vehicle. This will cost considerably more than hiring a taxi off the street, but if you cannot help it, you cannot help it.

You are now able to get out of the city! In the next chapter, we will introduce a number of places that are worth a visit in China.

Chapter 9
Sightseeing

There are a tremendous number of places in China worth seeing when you have several days of free time. Some tourist destinations have extensive infrastructure for supporting visitors; others are just catching on as destinations for Chinese tourists and are in the process of creating the hotels, shuttles, and so on that make going there easy. Some destinations are still diamonds in the rough, places that are either too remote or too "average" to attract Chinese tourists. Since even an average Chinese village can be fascinating to a foreign visitor, the main challenge is figuring out how to tour places that do not normally serve tourists!

In this section, you will learn about the places people visit in China, as well as some insider tips to help you decide whether or not you want to do more research and go there yourself. Even in the Internet age, it is still a good idea to bring the most recent copy of a comprehensive travel guide for China. Three popular printed guides are Fodor's, Frommer's and the Lonely Planet– my personal favorite because it is concise, humorous, and spot-on in

Places like Hemu Village in Xinjiang are way off the beaten path.

terms of useful information for people traveling on any budget.

Before we set out, this is a good time to remind you to try to time your travel so that it does not coincide with the rest of the country's vacations (e.g., Spring Festival and National Day). You really don't want to travel when everyone else is, if you can avoid it: everything will be packed, from trains, planes, hotels, and buses, to parks and restaurants. Most Chinese tourist destinations have the physical capacity to serve hordes of people, but crowd management systems in many places are still years behind Disney World, so the experience may wear you out. I once had the misfortune of visiting Sun Island Scenic Area in Harbin on the same hot summer day that was Family Day for a large local employer. The park is more than large enough to accommodate everyone comfortably, but the mini-trolleys that transported visitors from the parking lot to the park interior had been outsourced to multiple small companies that loaded the trolleys wherever there were enough visitors to fill the vehicle. Most visitors did not know this and patiently waited near the park entrance, where it would have been reasonable to establish an official boarding zone. The more enterprising visitors, however, realized that the trolley system was all-for-one and one-for-all. In a country as populous as China, it only takes a fraction of visitors being enterprising to run ahead and fill each trolley before it could reach the would-be de-facto boarding area at the park entrance. As each group of visitors realized that God and trolley drivers help those who help themselves, it became a scramble to get a seat on an empty incoming trolley, and enough seats for the whole party.[1] On a less crowded day, there would have been a long line of empty trolleys waiting for visitors to shuttle, and they would have gone right up to the park entrance to get visitors as soon as they arrived. Once we were inside, the park was pleasant, and the Squirrel Exhibit was a quaint counterpoint to the nearby tiger zoo where visitors can buy live animals to throw in the cages….

Popular Tourist Destinations for Chinese and Foreigners Alike

If you do an Internet search of "China Tour" and see where 10-day packages take you, you will find out where the top tourist hotspots are. Rest assured, they are perennial favorites for a reason, so don't feel like you're being too "touristy" if you go there. It would be like avoiding Yellowstone National Park because "everyone goes there." These hotspots include:

---

1 This also happened to me when trying to get a hotel shuttle at O'Hare a year later, so Looking Out for Number One is a skill useful in any country!

■ Beijing (Běijīng 北京)

Beijing is a huge and growing city that can keep you busy for a lifetime.

In terms of historical sites, you have the Forbidden City, the Summer Palace, the Old Summer Palace, the Altar of Heaven, the various gates that were part of the old city walls, and many more. Outside the city, you have the Great Wall, the Thirteen Ming Tombs, and Chengde (a mountain town where Qing emperors went to beat the Beijing heat), among many others.

For culture, there are numerous museums, a thriving art district in the 798 Art Zone, the universities in Haidian District, the National Centre for the Performing Arts, and a variety of teahouses. Laoshe Teahouse is a famous one that offers a classical environment and traditional performing arts, though some find it too touristy.

For nightlife, some popular spots include Houhai (后海), Sanlitun (三里屯), and Wudaokao (五道口). Houhai is centrally located and has great lakeside ambience; Sanlitun is where the foreigners used to congregate when Beijing was less cosmopolitan; Wudaokao serves the young college crowd.

Urban renewal has destroyed many old neighborhoods in Beijing, but a nice touristy treat is to take a pedicab tour if some **hútòng 胡同**, or alleys. The courtyard-style houses (**sìhé yuàn 四合院**) connected by hutong were often short on amenities (like decent bathrooms), but if you don't have to live there, they are very atmospheric.

■ Xi'an (Xī'ān 西安)

Capital of China during the Zhou, Qin, Han, Sui, and Tang Dynasties,

The city wall in Xi'an

the main draw of Xi'an is its history. The old city walls still stand as an attraction, Xi'an's flour-based snacks are nationally famous, and there are many ancient buildings to visit in the city. Outside of the city are the Terra Cotta Warriors and Huaqing Springs, where the famous Tang consort Yang Guifei took her baths. It is also the site where Chiang Kai-shek's allies kidnapped him and forced him to work with the Communists to fight the Japanese.

Trains between Beijing and Xi'an are often very crowded–try to book as far in advance as possible in order to get the accommodation you want.

■ Shanghai (Shànghǎi 上海) and the Yangzi River Delta (Chángjiāng sānjiǎo zhōu 长江三角洲)

If Beijing is like Washington, D.C., Shanghai is like New York City. It is a truly international metropolis. What it lacks in ancient history (it was built up as a result of Western colonialism in the nineteenth century), it makes up for in vibrancy and variety. Western visitors delight in finding familiar food, architecture and even worldviews in this city.

Top sights in and around Shanghai include Yuyuan Gardens, People's Square, the Oriental Pearl Tower, shopping (Nanjing Road, Xuhui, Huaihai Rd. and many, many others), the riverside Bund, the leafy lanes of the French Concession, and the Shanghai Museum.

Pudong ("east of the Pu"), on the east side of the Huangpu River, is where much of Shanghai's recent growth took place. Here, you will find gleaming skyscrapers and wide avenues that transition to industrial parks and Western-style housing subdivisions where homes cost two arms and a leg by any standard. Most residents of Pudong are from outside of Shanghai. Puxi ("west of the Pu") is where local Shanghainese tend to live. It is much more dense and lively and a good place to stay for those who are only in town for fun.

Called the "Venice of the East," Suzhou is a short 20-minute *gaotie* ride from Shanghai and is criss-crossed by canals. Suzhou's main attraction, however, are the gardens that were once the backyards of local gentry-officials. Now open to the public for a fee, these gardens are classic examples of Chinese landscaping, with garden-sized lakes, rivers and mountains and numerous places from which to observe the beauty. Do your best to avoid visiting on a fair-weather weekend when it is swamped with tourists. It can be hard to appreciate the serenity of the gardens when they are filled to the gills with people.

When dusk falls, head over to Shantang Street (**Shāntáng jiē** 山塘街) for the shops, fantastic night scenes, and maybe grab dinner next to the canal.

Outside of Suzhou are several small river villages that attract visitors for their quaintness. Examples include Zhou Zhuang (rather touristy now), Tongli (larger and quieter than Zhou Zhuang), Xitang (very

Popular Tourist Destinations for Chinese and Foreigners Alike | 233

A canal in Suzhou's Shantang Street area

scenic), and Wuzhen (the walls are darker than the other towns' walls; after seeing a gazillion river villages, this can make a difference). These villages require motorized transport to reach, so you will need to hit them on a tour or hire a taxi to get there if time is an issue.

Also nearby is Tiger Hill (**Hú Qiū** 虎丘), a naturally beautiful and historically significant spot. There is a thousand-year-old pagoda here, and it is the resting place of He Lu, king of the region around 600 BCE. If you are studying in/near Shanghai, this is a great place to go; if you have a limited amount of time in the area, you might want to pass it up in favor of more mountainous areas of China.

There is an old Chinese saying that goes, "Above there is heaven, below there are Suzhou and Hangzhou." Suzhou and Hangzhou have been centers of commerce and wealth for over a thousand years, so it is no wonder that they should have a special place in Chinese culture. Located less than 200 km southwest of Shanghai on the banks

Tiger Hill Pagoda

of Lake Xi (**Xīhú** 西湖), Hangzhou has gorgeous lake views, parks ringing the lake, pleasant walkways, the fantastic rebuilt Leifeng Pagoda (**Léifēng Tǎ** 雷峰塔), and the source of China's famous Longjing (Dragon Well) tea.

Visiting Hangzhou might be comparable to visiting San Diego–it's a beautiful and laid-back place that you tour while you are visiting a nearby metropolis.

■ Yangshuo (Yángshuò 阳朔)

It is difficult to choose one representative for all the tourist-attraction small towns of mountainous southwest China, but Yangshuo has come to be the king (queen?) of such places, thanks to ease of access, extensive guidebook coverage, and "discovery" by Chinese tourists. Visitors arrive via the city of Guilin, and then take a boat or bus to Yangshuo, a county town on the banks of the Li River punctuated by limestone karst peaks of the kind you see in Chinese landscape painting. Downtown's West Street (formerly called Foreigner Street) has been maintained to look like an old Chinese town, and it is lined with shops selling souvenirs.

The touristy-ness of Yangshuo makes it accessible for foreign visitors, though some may be put off by how commercialized things are getting there. If your research makes you think it is too touristy, rent a bicycle and head off into the hinterlands, or go next door to Guizhou Province, where few places have been fully commercialized.

Hangzhou

Rent a bike and see the countryside around Yangshuo.

Places Chinese Tourists Like to Go

Most American visitors to China only go once, and on that trip, hit some or all of the preceding places. You can spend a lifetime exploring Beijing alone, so rolling all the previous places into one trip leaves no time for China's thousands of other great places. Chinese people—and people studying in China—have more time to branch out beyond the Great Wall and the Terra Cotta Warriors. The following are just some of the top attractions for Chinese tourists not already covered.

■ Xishuangbanna (Xīshuāngbǎnnà 西双版纳)

Xishuangbanna is a semi-tropical region in southern Yunnan Province where the local plants, food, and architecture are all distinctly non-Han. In fact, Han Chinese account for only about a third of the population. Another third is composed of members of the Thai-related Dai minority, and the remaining third is composed of several small minority groups.

As is the case in many minority-populated regions, Han Chinese outnumber the local minority in the main city and in the business community, so after flying or bussing into Jinghong and getting your bearings (and a hotel room), head out into the surrounding villages to get a more local flavor.

■ Jiuzhaigou (jiǔzhàigōu 九寨沟)

This is a national park in Sichuan Province whose name means "Nine Stockades Gullies," after the nine ethnic Tibetan villages found in the

You know you're not in Beijing anymore when you go to the botanical gardens.

area's valleys. This park is known for perfectly transparent turquoise pools that punctuate a river as it flows down a mountain valley. The park is very well managed and maintained and is designed to accommodate large numbers of visitors while still protecting the natural beauty. To be honest, after two trips to Jiuzhaigou in ten years, I have been ruined for natural parks elsewhere.

Near Jiuzhaigou is a companion park, Huang Long (**Huánglóng** 黄龙 Yellow Dragon), where minerals in the water have been deposited over time to form natural stepped pools. At the top of the valley in which these pools are found is a temple in the most perfect setting imaginable. Even the ride to the park is amazing.

■ Hainan (Hǎinán 海南)

Tropical Hainan Island lies off the south cost of Guangdong Province and boasts many sandy beaches, palm trees, coconuts, and the southernmost point of uncontested Chinese territory. Hainan is mild in the winter and warm-to-hot in the summer, making it popular among Chinese

This is China, too!

Qingdao is famous for its German-inspired red-tiled roofs.

and Russians escaping cold weather up north. With little industry other than making Mazdas and growing sugar cane, Hainan's main economic engine is tourism, so it is easy to find leisurely diversions on the island.

■ Qingdao (Qīngdǎo 青岛)

Located on the south coast of Shandong's Jiaodong Peninsula, Qingdao began growing as a German colony in 1897, then became a Japanese colony after WWI, and finally reverted to Chinese control following WWII. Modern Qingdao attracts tourists for its extensive coastline, plentiful (if coarse-sanded) beaches, beautiful and religiously significant mountains (Lao Shan), and, not least of all, its colonial architecture. Qingdao's natural harbor and proximity to fertile agricultural land and manufacturing give this city economic strength well beyond its attractiveness as a tourist destination. Qingdao is also the largest city on the peninsula, making it a good jumping-off point for other tourist destinations in Shandong, including Confucius' hometown of Qufu, the former British colony ports of Weihai and Yantai, the pavilion in Penglai from where the Eight Immortals are said to be visible on the sea, and Mount Tai.

Qingdao is also famous for its beer and the annual beer festival in August....

■ Dali and Lijiang (Dàlǐ 大理 and Lìjiāng 丽江)

These two small cities are located in northern Yunnan Province, and are a popular alternative to Yangshuo and Guilin. Lijiang is about as beautiful as a mountain town can get, and it is overshadowed by snow-capped Jade Dragon Snow Mountain (**Yù Lóng Xuě Shān** 玉龙雪山 "yoo long hsway shan"). Lijiang has become quite commercialized, as well, but it is beautiful enough to be worth the trip, with creekside café's and quaint stone-paved alleys, as well as traditional food and art from the local Naxi minority (**Nàxī zú** 纳西族). South of Lijiang is Dali, located next to a long lake where local fishermen use cormorants to fish. The birds have rings around their necks so that they cannot swallow the fish they catch unless their masters want to feed them. Also nearby are a trio of pagodas built on the slope of the tall mountains that form the valley in which Dali sits.

Up the road from Lijiang is Qiaotou (**Qiáotóu** 桥头 "bridge-

Hiking through Tiger Leaping Gorge is a great way to recharge after a few months of Chinese classes in a major city.

head"), the starting point for visiting Tiger Leaping Gorge. Construction of a paved road through this deep gorge formed by a tributary

It is a pleasure to dine next to the creek that runs through Lijiang.

of the Yangzi River has made passage of the gorge much easier, but many still choose to hike their way through, a trip of two days or more.

■ Mountains

There are numerous mountains of historical and religious significance in China, and they have been significant for so long that "climbing a mountain" in Chinese generally means walking up centuries-old stone steps. Many, many, many stone steps. Thanks to economic progress, the most famous mountains can be ascended and descended by cable car. There are "Five Great Mountains," "Four Sacred Mountains of Buddhism," and "Four Sacred Mountains of Taoism." If you want to impress your Chinese friends with the mountains you have climbed, but do not have time to do them all (there are more than thirteen famous ones), here are some biggies to consider:

- **Anhui's Yellow Mountain (Huáng Shān 黄山 "hwang shan")**−famous for its stony peaks and pine trees growing from the rocky crags. Visitors can stay in hotels located on top of the mountains and get up early to see if they will be graced by one of Huangshan's famous sunrises. Sometimes, it is just clouds, however.
- **Shandong's Mt. Tai (Tài Shān 泰山 "tie shan")**−famous for having been a must-do climb for seventy-two Chinese emperors. The emperors were carried most of the way up, and you can be, too, for the right price. On top of the mountain is an impressive complex of temples and rentable cotton army coats for those who didn't dress for the cold damp air found at the top at night.
- **Sichuan's Emei Shan (Éméi Shān 峨眉山 "uh may shan")**−one of the Four Sacred Buddhist Mountains. Over seventy Buddhist monasteries are found on the mountain today; China's first Buddhist temple (now gone) was built here in the first century. Like the other mountains, steep peaks, stairs, and a cable car are found here.
- **Hunan's Zhangjia Jie (Zhāngjiā Jiè 张家界 "jahng jyah jyeah")**−

Zhangjiajie National Park

though not considered a mountain or mountain range, *per se*, it is a national park consisting of needle-like stone peaks and vegetation coming out of the rocks. This park was the inspiration for the "Hallelujah Mountains" in the movie *Avatar*.

Theme Tourism

With such natural, historical and cultural diversity from which to choose, it is easy to put together Chinese tours based on different themes. Here are some suggestions, but feel free to take the idea of a thematic trip to the library and put together your own.

■ Red Tourism

With the social angst that has accompanied fast growth and modernization has come a feeling of nostalgia for China's communist history, when almost everyone was equal. Equally poor, but equal. As a result, locations associated with Chinese Communist Party (CCP) history have become popular tourist destinations. These include:

- The birthplace of the CCP is in Shanghai, located next to the trendy Xintiandi shopping and restaurant district. What is considered the first congress of the Chinese Communist Party took place in a building located at 102 Xingye Road, Luwan District during the last week of July, 1921. Mao Zedong, then merely the representative for Hunan, was in attendance.
- Shaoshan (**sháoshān** 韶山), Hunan, Mao Zedong's hometown. Here, you can see Mao's humble beginnings, as well as infer why he might have believed that the power of China's Communist Party comes from the peasantry, unlike in European communism, in which urban industrial workers form the backbone of the party's strength.
- Huaminglou Village (**huāmínglóu zhèn** 花明楼镇), Hunan, the birthplace of Liu Shaoqi, Chairman of the People's Republic from 1959-1968, arrested by Mao for favoring economic liberalization and for being a threat to Mao's power. If you visit Mao's and Liu's family homes—only 30 km apart—one can see why Liu Shaoqi might have seen a healthy middle class as a strength instead of a threat... and why the neighboring Mao family might have begged to differ.

- Nanchang (**Nánchāng** 南昌), capital of Jiangxi Province and site of the August 1st, 1927 Nanchang Uprising, which was the first engagement between an organized Chinese Communist army and the army of the Nationalist Party under Chiang Kai-shek. Zhou Enlai, who played a key role in bringing President Nixon to China and establishing formal relations between the PRC and the U.S., also played a key role in the Nanchang Uprising. August 1st is still celebrated as the founding of the People's Liberation Army and is a holiday for members of the Chinese armed services.
- Jinggang Mountains (**Jǐnggāng shān** 井冈山), mountains in Jiangxi Province where Mao Zedong set up the first peasant soviet (a socialist government council) of the CCP following the violent suppression of urban communist activity in 1927 by Chiang Kai-shek's Nationalist forces. Here, you can tour the villages where the Chinese communists hid from the Nationalists and grew in strength until they were forced to move south by the Nationalists in 1929. Many important people in the CCP lived in the Jinggang Mountains, including Mao Zedong, Zhou Enlai, Zhu De, Peng Dehuai, Lin Biao, and Chen Yi.
- Ruijin (**Ruìjīn** 瑞金) is a small city in southeastern Jiangxi Province where Mao and Zhu De established the Chinese Soviet Republic in 1931 after leaving the Jinggang Mountains. Because it had its own bank, money, and taxes, some consider it to be the first instance of the existence of two Chinas. It is from Ruijin that the Long March started in 1934, when the Nationalists succeeded in again driving the CCP from its base.
- The Long March (**Cháng Zhēng** 长征) began as a retreat from the Nationalist Party's attacks in Ruijin, but soon became a winding trek under fire to Yan'an, in northern China's Shanxi Province. Of the 86,000 people who started the march, about 8,000 made it to Yan'an in 1935. Rather than following in their footsteps and walking the 9,000 km yourself, you can hit some major points on the trail: Xiang River Battle Martyrs Memorial in Xing'an, Guangxi Province (广西兴安县), where about half of the 86,000 were lost; Zunyi, Guizhou Province (贵州遵义), where Mao solidified his power in the party; Loushan Pass in northern Guizhou (贵州娄山关), site of a major victory for the CCP; Jiaoping Crossing of the Jinsha River in Yunnan (云南禄劝彝族苗族自治县皎西乡皎平渡), where 30,000 Red Army members crossed into Sichuan using seven boats over nine days and nights; the Shigu crossing of the Jinsha River by another portion of Long Marchers (云南石鼓), which is a lot easier to reach than Jiaoping; the crossing of the Dadu River northwest

The bridge across the Dadu River in Luding, Sichuan

of Shimian County Town in Sichuan (川省石棉县); crossing of the Snowy Mountains and the Grasslands of Sichuan (for a great description of a Westerner retracing those steps, visit www.redrocktrek.com); and finally…

- Yan'an, Shaanxi Province (陕西延安), where the CCP made their base when they arrived in 1936, and stayed there until 1948, when the communists abandoned Yan'an under threat of Nationalist attack… and ended up making Beijing their next home. The way Mao ran areas governed from Yan'an became a model for many of his actions after the establishment of the People's Republic.
- You can wrap up a tour of the founding moments of Chinese communism with a stop at Tian'anmen, where Mao proclaimed the founding of the People's Republic on October 1st, 1949. Considering the fact that many of the Red Tourism sites memorialize places from which the CCP was driven out, it may seem strange that the PRC was established at all. The sites of pivotal battles between 1945 and 1949 in which the Communists triumphed over

Nationalist forces have not yet been developed as tourist sites.

Really Ancient China

Once you have punched your top-tourist-sites card with the Great Wall and the Forbidden City, etc., you should have seen enough red-walled and glazed ceramic-tile-roofed Ming and Qing Dynasty architecture to last you for a while. Next, you can try visiting places that go much farther back in Chinese history than the founding of the Ming Dynasty in 1368 and get a sense of the kind of diversity that went into creating China as we know it today.

- Begin by touring the Warring States, the countries that were unified in 221 BCE to become the first "China." Each state had its own culture, parts of which continue to this day.
- Pre-Ming dynastic capitals: Xianyang (outside Xi'an); Chang'an (now Xi'an); Luoyang; and Kaifeng
- Qufu, Shandong Province, birthplace and home of Confucius. The buildings found there now were built in the

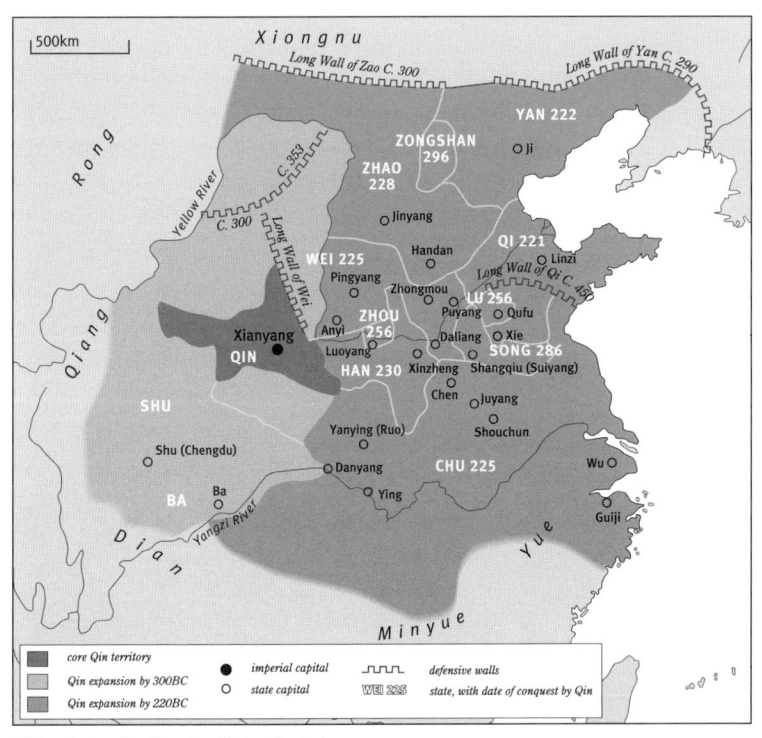

China during the Warring States Period

past few hundred years, so they resemble all your other "typical" ancient Chinese architecture, but Confucius himself lived during the Warring States Period, well before the buildings now found there.

- Sanxingdui, Sichuan Province, site of a 1986 archaeological discovery of a 3,500 year-old civilization with an artistic tradition dissimilar from contemporary cultures flourishing farther north at that time. Sanxingdui demonstrates how modern China is an amalgam of diverse cultural traditions that grew together over millennia, and not the descendant of a single cultural strain begun in the Central Plains.

Cast bronze head from the Sanxingdui Culture

- Traveling the Chinese portion of the old Silk Road(s) can teach you about the cultural and material exchange between Chinese civilization and Europe, Central Asia, and the Arab world, especially during the time of the Roman and Byzantine Empires. This route will

The Confucius Temple in Qufu, Shandong, birthplace of Confucius

The western end of the Great Wall, at Jiayuguan

take you from Xi'an, up the Yellow River valley in arid Gansu Province, through the last (or first, depending on where you're going) gate of the Great Wall at Jiayuguan, through the Buddhist grottoes of Dunhuang, through the melon fields of Hami, around the Taklimakan Desert, near the feet of the soaring Altai Mountains, through the Uighur-Han mixing bowl of Urumqi, and finally to Kashgar, where Central Asian culture still reigns supreme. For a detailed description of the things that were transmitted via the Silk Road, read *The Golden Peaches of Samarkand*, by Edward Schafer.

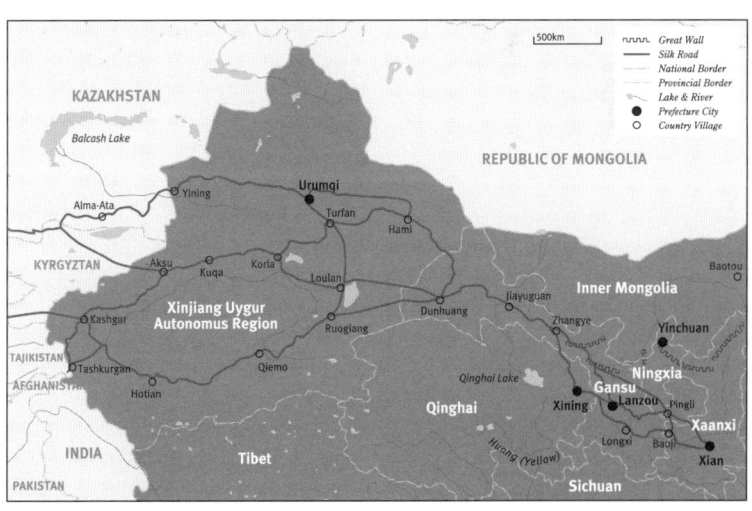

Route of the Silk Road

Tibetan prayer flags

■ Minority Cultures

Another way of experiencing the diversity of China is to visit regions where minority culture is still strong and observable. With 55 official minority ethnic groups, you could spend a lifetime visiting different minority regions. Here is a sample of minority groups whose areas of concentration are relatively easy to access.

- Miao and Dong peoples in Guizhou
- Yi peoples in Yunnan
- Dai peoples in southern Yunnan
- Tibetan peoples in Tibet, Sichuan, and Gansu (all of which were at times part of the Tibetan empire)
- Mongolians in Inner Mongolia
- Uighurs in western Xinjiang (Urumqi and points east have a lot of Han influence)

Miao women

If you do some research on each group first, visiting these places will be much more meaningful. For instance, once you know that the Miao believe that humans were born of a Butterfly Mother in their mythology, you will notice that there are butterfly motifs all over their crafts. Guizhou Normal University has partnered with The Ohio State University to help minorities in Guizhou maintain traditional aspects of their culture without commercialism twisting them into some-

Theme Tourism | 247

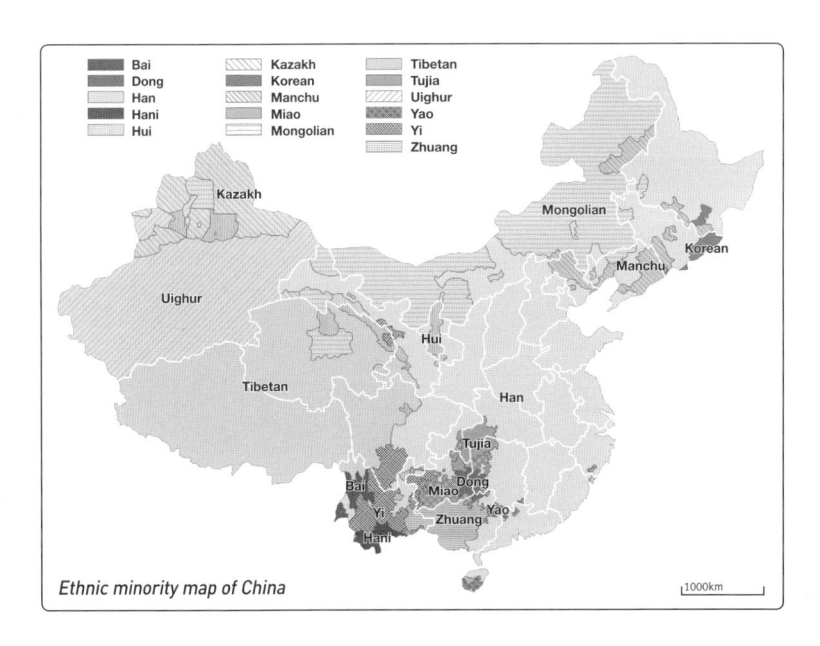

Ethnic minority map of China

Bai, Dong, Han, Hani, Hui, Kazakh, Korean, Manchu, Miao, Mongolian, Tibetan, Tujia, Uighur, Yao, Yi, Zhuang

1000km

This, too, is China.

Chapter 9: Sightseeing

thing unrecognizable to natives, as has happened in some other areas.

■ Economic Growth

While touring examples of China's amazing economic growth feels like work to me, you may want to visit parts of the country that are driving the "miracle" to get a sense for how it all works, and, especially, the people who make it go. If you are hoping to parlay your overseas study experience into a job in China, this tour might actually end up making money for you. If you plan it right, this trip can be a mixture of pure business and sightseeing, as many parts of the economic miracle are tied to major urban centers that are tourist destinations in their own right.

Especially if you speak Chinese, you can walk right up to factory gates and ask if there is anything you can do to help in the company while you are in town. This may work better if you look "Western," and some people may react to a cold-call offer of help with suspicion, but the worst that can happen is that someone says "no." Be sure to avoid businesses that produce what are called "dual use" products–things that have military as well as civilian applications, like laser targeting systems. Random foreigners looking for work at such places might be referred to the local authorities. In any case, what might start as a holiday lark could turn into a real resume-building job. You can try this in your home city, too, where you can show up more than just once or twice.

- You can start with visits to one or more of the Special Economic Zones that were begun in 1980. These areas, called

A small clothing factory in Shandong

Shenzhen, one of the first Special Economic Zones

SEZs for short, offer preferential policies to export-oriented and foreign-owned businesses, and were the original industrial drivers of Deng Xiaoping's economic reforms. The first SEZs, were Shenzhen, Shantou, and Zhuhai in Guangdong Province, and Xiamen, in Fujian Province. Xiamen is an old treaty port from Opium War days and worth a visit for its colonial architecture on Gulangyu Island, as well. Shenzhen is now one of the largest, most affluent cities in China, and it pretty much runs on ambition. Zhuhai is to Macao what Shenzhen is to Hong Kong—another border city created to capitalize on trade with the outside world ... except Zhuhai remains a sleepy little city in the shadows.

Since 1980, large swaths of China's coast have been allowed to offer preferential policies to businesses engaged in international trade, and, most recently, the city of Kashgar was granted SEZ status in 2010 to capitalize on its proximity to Kyrgyzstan, Tajikistan and the rest of Central Asia.

- China's industry is concentrated in three regions: the Pearl River Delta in Guangdong, the Yangzi River Delta in the east, centered on Shanghai, and the Beijing-Tianjin corridor. A tremendous amount of China's GDP is generated in these three regions, not coincidentally home to China's tier-one cities. In these areas, you can visit towns that are primarily composed of factories, blocks upon blocks of factories. To give you some starting points, here are some of the major factory towns in these

Guangzhou at night

regions, preceded by the major cities there.
- Pearl River Delta: Guangzhou, Shenzhen, Zhuhai, Dongguan, Bao'an (suburban Shenzhen), Zhongshan, Panyu, and Foshan
- Yangzi River Delta: Shanghai, Suzhou (home of the Singapore Industrial Park and Suzhou New District industrial areas), Ningbo, Hangzhou, Wuxi, Kunshan, Jiading (suburban Shanghai), Pudong New Zone (Shanghai), Zhenjiang, Yangzhou, and Changzhou
- Beijing-Tianjin Corridor: Beijing, Tianjin, Tangshan, and Langfang
- China's automotive industry is geographically diverse, thanks in part to Cold War policies of spreading out heavy manufacturing to avoid having all the country's eggs in one basket. That said, there are centers of auto manufacturing in Shenyang, Shanghai, Huangshi (Hubei), Wuhu (Anhui), and Guangzhou. As in the U.S., the auto industry is a pillar of the Chinese economy.

■ A Taste of Everything

In about ten days' time, you can actually get a taste of many different aspects of contemporary China by taking a trip around Shandong Province. You could probably recreate this trip in other coastal provinces, as well, but I have personally done this in Shandong with two groups of American students, and with very educational results. The following is a sample itinerary and the aspects of Chinese life represented by each stop.

- Stop 1, Qingdao 青岛 – a thriving tier-two port city. Attractions include German architecture and beer, former homes of many Chinese literati, Mount Lao, beaches and water sports.
- Stop 2, Yantai 烟台 – an attractive tier-three port city. Overshadowed by Qingdao to the north and Dalian to the south, it remains relatively affluent because of local industries and agriculture. Attractions include old colonial architecture and the former consulates of European countries and the U.S. (from when Yantai was the big man on campus, and not Qingdao), Changyu Winery.
- Stop 3, Mu Family Estate, Qixia (栖霞牟氏庄园) – a restored example of a pre-Revolution landlord's estate. It was because of the social structure supported by families like this that the communist revolution was successful in China. It is useful to keep in mind that the Chinese communist revolution succeeded because more people were sick of the status quo (the peasant class) than wanted to preserve it (the rural landlords and urban industrialists).
- Stop 4, Laizhou 莱州 – a provincial but affluent coastal county-level city. Here, you can see how much cash there is in places you have never heard of, driven by a growing national economy.
- Stop 5, Qingzhou 青州 – an inland county-level city that was an important place ... centuries ago. This is a great example of how many famous places of Ancient China are now forgotten. Attractions: Qingzhou National Museum, unexpected home to several important artifacts; Yunmen Mountain (云门山), a low-impact mountain climb with stunning views.
- Pass through Jinan 济南 – a large, inland industrial city. Jinan is also the capital of Shandong Province.
- Stop 6, Mt. Tai (泰山) – one of China's major holy mountains and the mother of all Stairmaster climbs. In the summer, I recommend starting your climb from the bottom around 11:00 p.m. in order to make it to the top by sunrise. It's cooler and seeing the temples at the top in darkness and light is rewarding.
- Stop 7, Qufu (曲阜) – Confucius' hometown. See where this Confucianism thing got started by visiting the "Three Kongs" (Confucius' surname in Chinese is Kong – the Kong Temple, Kong Estate, and Kong "Forest" (the family cemetery).
- Stop 8, Mengyin (蒙阴) – a tiny landlocked dot on the map that, though economically okay by national standards, can serve as an example of a place that is beyond the reach of much of China's meteoric economic growth, and a jumping off point for visiting any of the villages in the area. I have taken students to a peach-growing village near

Changlu Township 常路镇, northwest of Mengyin, where the richest people in town live in conditions that most Americans would find primitive. The irony is that these villagers themselves live in much better conditions than many people in remote mountain areas.

You could create an itinerary like this that incorporates wealthy urban areas, inland centers of industry, small towns and villages, and places of relative poverty in most Chinese provinces; consider making such a tour of the area in which you will study.

The goal of this chapter was to get you thinking about the types of places you would like to visit in China by offering some examples. Where you actually end up going will be informed by your personal interests, your budget, and a lot more research. Have fun and be open to the unexpected. You will encounter many unexpected things on your trip, both good and bad. Just remember, the biggest difference between a good experience and a bad one while on an overseas adventure is how much time must pass before you can tell the tale with a smile.

Chapter 10
The Key to Going Back: Making Friends

The first time I went to China, my class spent six incredible months there. We began with a fantastic study tour of three weeks, and then spent five months at Beijing Normal University. During those five months, we learned a lot of Chinese, learned a lot about living in a large Chinese city, and made some great friends…from Japan. In those days, Chinese schools were still very skittish about letting Chinese and foreigners intermingle, so we lived in separate dorms and Chinese students had to register at the front desk if they came to visit us. There were no activities organized by the school to introduce us to Chinese students with whom we might become friends, so few of us spoke with any actual Chinese people other than our teachers and the vendors on the street. I believe this was one of the primary reasons few–if any–of my classmates made a career out of their study of Chinese and their experiences in China.

Chinese schools have become

A cross-cultural social event on and off the court

much more open to creating opportunities for Chinese and foreign people to meet each other and become friends. Foreigners can live with host families, have Chinese roommates, take classes with Chinese people, participate in mixer activities to meet new people, and, sometimes, even live off campus in the local community instead of in the "foreign students dormitory." Today, the segregation that many foreigners experience in China is largely self-imposed. Many of us are afraid to leave our comfort zone, to use our broken (or nonexistent) Chinese to make friends, to participate in social activities in which we really do not know what is expected of us or how to leave the impression that we are the well-socialized adults that we think we are.

The key to making the most of your experience in China is to charge beyond your comfort zone and to make Chinese friends. Making friends in China is emotionally rewarding and the best way to keep your finger on the pulse of this constantly changing place. When I left China the first time, I didn't think I would care if I went back because I had made no friends there. The second time I left China, after an internship set up by the Ohio State University expressly designed to foster the establishment of relationships, I had already started looking for ways to get back and work with my friends in Shandong. This chapter introduces strategies for establishing and maintaining relationships in China in such a way that your newfound friends will see

Come back soon!

you as the adult you are and not the child you may sound like.

The Pillars of Chinese Relationships

The foundational element of relationships in Chinese society is so Chinese that there is no equivalent in English for it: **rénqíng** 人情. Literally "human sentiment," *renqing* is the positive feeling that exists between people who like and respect one another, as well as the behaviors that indicate the presence of this feeling. People between whom there is *renqing* have a relationship; people who do not express the existence of *renqing* are said to be cold.

So, how do Chinese express the presence of *renqing* and therefore the existence of a friendly relationship? Let's step back a second and ask how people differentiate between friends and non-friends. That is, how does someone go from being a stranger to being a friend? The Chinese and American answers to this question will shed some light on how *renqing* is expressed. Over the course of conducting pre-departure cultural training for over 70 American expatriates going to China, I have found that there is a typical American answer to what constitutes a "friend": shared interests and shared activity. If you recall from an earlier chapter that Westerners are sometimes characterized as single atoms bouncing around the social world, you can extend the metaphor to say that American friends are atoms that share some traits and who choose to be in proximity with one another for certain periods of time. Few people stop to think about what makes a friend, and most people assume the definition is universal....

The Chinese people with whom I have worked describe friendship as being constituted of three elements: shared interests, shared time, and reciprocity. To most Chinese people (who do not think about it, either), people with shared interests and activities are atoms that may bump into each other, but do not bond unless they share resources, like atoms do via their electrons. Chinese friendship is initiated when someone does something for the other person (and was not forced to). Before that point, people are simply acquaintances.

Actions that commonly indicate the presence of *renqing* and a friendly relationship in China include taking someone out to a meal, helping with a task without being asked, making sure that friends in your presence have what you want for yourself, and making an introduction to a third party who has knowledge or resources the friend could use.

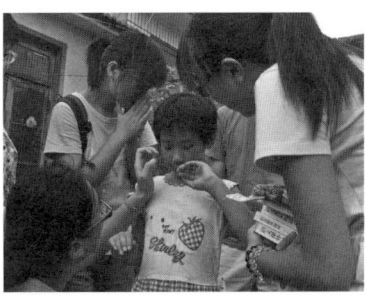

Chinese students donating school supplies to an underprivileged village girl whose mother had passed away

Going "Dutch" is common among Chinese students, but once in the professional world, it is common for one person to pay for meals, regardless of how many people are in attendance. This is an indication of *renqing*—the host indicates his or her positive feelings for the guests by picking up the check. We will talk more about banqueting as a medium for relationship building later in this chapter; here it is enough to say that even among friends, it is normal for them to take turns taking the others out to eat. Young people and professionals who work with many Westerners are often comfortable with going "AA" (制 **zhì**) as sharing the bill is called in Chinese, but it is considered to be a method of paying for food that is devoid of *renqing*.

Helping with a task without being asked is a frequently-experienced method of expressing *renqing* and initiating or continuing a friendly relationship. Notice that this does not say "offering to help with a task without being asked." If someone asks if help is needed, the polite response is "no," because the person in need should not inconvenience other people. Hence, the potential helper is expected to provide the help without asking about it. For example, you and a Chinese friend went to a bar on a Friday night and are ready to go home. Your friend's campus is between the bar and your campus, though not necessarily on a straight line. If you want to express your *renqing*, you can tell your friend you can have your taxi driver drop him/her off on the way to your campus. Your classmate may refuse, saying that it is easy to catch a taxi to the other campus, or that the bus comes frequently, etc., but if you continue to say "let's go," instead of "do you want to go together?", the classmate will likely join you. Your classmate may even offer to pay what is on the meter when you reach the first stop, and you may even have to communicate to the driver not to take your friend's money, but your friend will get out and thank you and make sure the driver knows exactly where you're going in Chinese. You have just demonstrated your *renqing* by going only a little out of your way (if at all) and sharing your resources. A portion of Chinese people really do not like this quid pro quo aspect of traditional Chinese culture and will insist on avoiding your paying for anything on their behalf. They will let you know who they are by their actions and their words. Don't be offended, be happy that you have found someone with whom you may be able to have an American-type friendship!

Another example of sharing resources that demonstrates the presence of *renqing* is to share things you want for yourself or to avoid partaking at all if there is not enough to go around. For example, if you are walking to class with a Chinese friend and want a soda, buy one for your friend, as well. It is considered rude to satisfy your own thirst without regard to your friend's needs. If you want to chew a piece of gum from a packet you have, offer it to the friends (or potential friends) around you first. If you do not have enough gum to share, then find a way to pop it in your mouth and dispose of the evidence when no one is around. Now that you know this, you can interpret some people's actions on long train rides: if your bunkmates offer you any of their food, it means they

Offering to others something you want to eat

consider you to be at least potential conversation partners (and therefore potential longer-term relations, depending on what comes out of the conversations); if they eat their food without offering you any, it probably means they see you as an "atom" that happens to be in proximity for the duration of the train trip. It doesn't mean you can't talk or you won't be polite to one another, it just means that, more likely than not, they perceive your presence to be a temporary one.

Another resource that may be shared to demonstrate *renqing* is other relationships, in the form of third-party introductions. Trust is the foundation of all solid human relationships, and a third-party introduction is a demonstration that the person doing the introducing trusts both parties enough to believe that bringing them together will have positive results for everyone involved. People who are generous with their relationships (*guanxi*) are considered to have a lot of *renqing*, and people who are stingy with their *guanxi*–rarely introducing people to each other directly and trying to keep their relationship resources to themselves–are often perceived as having little *renqing*, and therefore difficult to become friends with.

If you are studying in China for the first time, you may think that you do not have many such relationships to offer. Perhaps you feel that a student does not have relationships that would be valuable to a Chinese person, or that your lack of long-standing relationships in

Introducing people you know to each other is a good way to build renqing.

China means that you cannot introduce anyone helpful to your Chinese friends. In fact, who you know in the U.S.–especially your parents and immediate family–are important relationships that may be beneficial to Chinese people with whom you want to develop a relationship. Many Chinese with whom foreigners interact in China are middle class and upper middle class people who are either involved in Sino-foreign exchanges themselves, or have friends and relatives engaged in such projects. If you keep your ears open and hear that a Chinese friend has a friend who imports recycled PET plastic flakes, you can ask your family and friends in the U.S. if they know anyone who knows anyone in the recycling business. Even if they do not, a little Internet research and emailing in English can lead you to people you can introduce to your friend's friend.

If you haven't noticed already, a trusted relationship is a valuable thing. Relationships are created and maintained on the basis of reciprocity, and the medium of exchange is sometimes itself a relationship, when made by third-party introduction. In Chinese, social reciprocity is referred to by the term **lǐshàng wǎnglái (礼尚往来)**, meaning that socially-significant behaviors and objects are given in return for one other. Westerners just entering Chinese culture often feel like this social system is too economic, that friendship should be freely entered into without any expectation of reciprocity. If I give you a birthday present, it is because I want to give you a birthday present, not because you gave me one before or because I want you to give me one in the future.

Conversely, many Chinese people just entering Western society feel like there is no way to trust someone who will not commit any resources (time, money, introductions) to the relationship. They give someone a birthday present because they like them, and expect that if that person truly likes them back, a present will be given in return someday. So, though reciprocity is the basis of Chinese friendship, it is one based on sentiment (*renqing*), not economic exchange.

Moon cakes are the fruitcakes of the Mid-Autumn Festival: they get gifted and re-gifted until someone who likes them eats them.

It may take some time to get used to this system, especially if you feel like you are building up a lot of social debt to Chinese people who seem to come out of the woodwork to help you without your asking for it. Most of them just want to be your friend, and are expressing it in the way they know how. For your part, be clear about the people with whom you want to establish a relationship and keep mental notes about what they have done for you and what you can do for them. Repay kindness in a small way immediately, and in a greater way when an appropriate opportunity presents itself. Let's say you want to stay in China for three weeks after your program is over, but your visa expires immediately after the program ends, your local public security bureau requires that visa extension applicants appear in person, but you are in class during work hours. A Chinese friend uses personal relationships in the public security bureau to process your visa extension without your being there. First, you should give that friend a gift or take him or her out to dinner. Then, wait for an opportunity to do something for him/her that is really needed (unlike dinner, which is just to show you recognize you were helped). Maybe you can edit the friend's child's college application essay or introduce a foreign person who works in the friend's professional field.

With all these mental tabs to keep, relationship building in China can take some brain power, and it is further complicated by the great gaps between social classes that exist in China, gaps that are not as obvious in the U.S. In an example we gave previously, it is a good idea to give a gift to your dormitory night watchmen because it shows you respect them and they understand that there is an expectation that people who respect each other help each other…when one of them comes back after curfew. On the other hand, if the night watchman gives *you* a gift first, you might wonder what he has in mind for your relationship. The gap between your relative economic levels is such that it could be a highly unequal reciprocal relationship: by Chinese social expectations, if you establish a friendship you should help him to the best of your ability and he should help you to the best of his ability … except your resources likely far outnumber his. For every $10 dinner to which he treats you (and very possibly straining his own resources because he wants to treat you as well as he can), you might be on the hook for favors worth many times that much. Of course, you may be a very giving person and be comfortable with an imbalanced relationship, but it could possibly become a philanthropic one, which could in turn affect the nature of your interaction in the long term. Treat everyone around you with respect: most people in any country are good and can teach you a lot; just be sensitive about the reciprocal nature of Chinese friendship if you move beyond just chatting or having a pleasant service provider-customer relationship.

If the three things you need in real estate is location, location, location, the three things you need to successfully become a member of Chinese society is relationships, relationships, relationships. Now you know that relationships, or *guanxi*, are based on reciprocity and the expression of *renqing*. The debts and favors owed back and forth between you and the friends you make in China will tie you to Chinese society and be one of the main reasons you keep going back, physically and virtually. Once you have begun to develop *guanxi* in China, your relationship with the culture will fundamentally change from that of a spectator to one of a player.[1] You will have an emotional and economic connection with Chinese people like they have with one another, and will be able to negotiate interacting with Chinese people and organizations like they do, which means with a higher likelihood of success than those unfamiliar with Chinese culture.

Chinese people use *guanxi* to accomplish all kinds of things that Americans tend to do by themselves. In fact, some Chinese people use *guanxi* to do things they could do by themselves in order to begin or strengthen a relationship. Some examples include (for better and worse):

- Sending a piece of mail to a third party so that the intended

---

1 For more on levels of participation in a culture, read *Eat Shandong*, by Eric Shepherd (2005).

recipient has to meet the third party at pickup. The mail could have been sent directly, but that would have eliminated the opportunity for the third party and the recipient to meet, and the sender hopes that the two parties can get to know each other and develop their own reciprocating relationship.
- Obtaining license plates. Many Chinese cities limit the number of license plates they issue in order to limit the number of cars on the road. Wherever there are scarce resources, personal relationships create a gray market for goods: people with connections in the transportation bureau may get plates that other people cannot.
- Registering a new business or doing almost anything that requires approval from a government office. In the U.S., we assume that what government offices put on their websites is official and reliable; in China, not only is online information often out of date, it may not even be complete. The only way to know what materials are required is to go to the relevant office in person and inquire. If you know someone there, they may give you extra information that will save you a lot of work; if you do not, you may get the bare bones (though still accurate) version that leaves you guessing about what forms are needed when, what needs notarization and what doesn't, etc. If you have really good *guanxi*, your application may be reviewed and accepted even if it does not formally meet all the semi-published requirements! Keep this in mind when you see bad drivers on the road in China....
- Finding out what is going on in class. In Chinese universities, the professors often communicate information to the class via what is translated as the "class monitor" (**bānzhǎng** 班长), a member of the class chosen to be the go-between. If your *banzhang* knows who you are, you will get announcements about class cancellations; if you are a foreign student and not on the *banzhang's* radar at all, he or she may forget to include you in the communications. Not out of spite, of course, but simply because he or she is unaware of you.
- Getting "good" food from street vendors. Maybe the vendor

Buying watermelon from a street vendor in Penglai

knows which fruits are tastier or which vegetables have less pesticide on them; if you develop a rapport with a vendor by being a repeat customer, he or she may help you pick the better pieces in order to keep you as a repeat customer.

The necessity of having good relationships is by no means limited to Chinese society, but it seems to be important in more situations and at more levels of society in China than in the U.S., so being open to developing your own *guanxi* in China will be a key factor in your continued success there.

Any discussion of relationships in China has to include the concept of face or **miànzi** 面子. Face is the measure of an individual's esteem in the eyes of those around him or her. Face can be earned, given, lost and taken away. If *renqing* is the currency of interaction between two people, face is the currency of interaction in social situations of three or more people, that is, wherever there is an audience. Knowing how to give face and to repair it when you take it away from someone are useful skills for becoming a successful player in Chinese culture.

One earns face by doing things that result in observable expressions of respect from others. As you might imagine, people who consistently earn face are successful not because they want face, but because the things they do well are ones that earn them respect: winning salesperson of the year; being generous with one's *guanxi* and thereby getting invited to (and seen at) increasingly high-powered networking events; helping friends accomplish their tasks and dreams, thus earning them face and earning *renqing* for oneself that someday results in those friends repaying the help with face-giving support, and so on. If you invite a well-respected teacher to a social event and he or she shows up, that teacher is giving you face by being there: the other invitees see that your relationship with that teacher is so strong that the teacher—who surely had choices regarding what to do with that time—chose to attend *your* event.

In turn, you will have opportunities to give face yourself. As a foreigner, you may be invited to participate in events billed as "international," and the international component is you. If you go, you give the organizers face for making their event international, and they should repay the favor someday. There are many opportunities in daily life to give face, as well—if your language teacher introduces you to someone in China and that person compliments you on your Chinese ability, you should say you owe it to your teacher. If you attend a banquet at a nice restaurant and the manager comes in to ask what you think, if you have something good to say and say it in front of everyone, you have given the manager face. Simply giving credit to and complimenting others is an easy way to give face on a regular basis, and it is a habit that reflects well on you, as well. It demonstrates your modesty, and shows others that when you are around, you will make them look good!

The most common face mistakes foreigners make are ones in which the foreigner fails to give face rather than actually making someone lose it. Examples include not complimenting someone when it is ritually expected (e.g., touring a friend's home for the first time); not beginning a speech by greeting and thanking the leaders in attendance; not reading a friend's blog, Weibo, or WeChat posts. If you fail to do things like this, do not expect anyone to say anything to you unless a very good friend who is not involved in the situation pipes up. It would be rude for a Chinese person to say or imply "you forgot to give me face back there," so it is your job to make it happen.

Once in a while, people–of any culture–manage to create a loss of face for others and themselves. If you make someone else lose face, you also lose some yourself, just for making them look bad. Occasionally, superiors may intentionally cause a subordinate to lose face, but even in the heat of the moment, making someone lose face is normally not the best way to handle an issue. Some situations in which foreigners can create a loss of face include:

- Ignoring hierarchy when greeting, shaking hands, giving gifts, making introductions, and seating at banquets (see later section on banquets).
- Criticizing another person in a group setting, especially when out-of-group members are present.
- Contradicting or correcting a superior (including teachers) in front of others.
- Creating a situation in which it is apparent someone has insufficient funds for an activity (e.g., inviting Chinese students from different economic backgrounds to join, "AA-style," a costly outing like going to a bar or a Western restaurant, making it apparent that some can afford it while others cannot).
- Criticizing phenomena in China in public, especially without reference to objective challenges that cause those phenomena such as overpopulation, underemployment, etc.

When you have caused someone to lose face some repair work is necessary. Making up for *faux pas* is never pleasant, but there are ways to transmit your regret without making a scene. After all, if you were to make a big deal out of

Congratulations. You just made this an "international event."

publicly apologizing, it could very well simply remind everyone of the original slight instead of repairing anything.

Minor face issues can be repaired by following up the gaffe with compliments on a different topic. This directs the person's thoughts away from the error and makes them feel good about the compliment. This works for mistakes like offering small criticisms in front of others. Ignoring hierarchy can be made up for by paying special attention to hierarchy from the moment you realize your error: opening doors for ranking leaders/teachers, letting them walk first, listening intently when they are talking, finding things you can make sincere compliments about, etc. If at a banquet, a toast and a compliment can go a long way to covering up a previous insensitivity to rank.

For more serious mistakes, such as criticizing or contradicting someone of higher social rank in a non-debate public setting such as a forum, there are a few things you can do. First, you can see if there is an opportunity in that setting to affirm something the higher ranking person said, especially if the affirmation comes from a respected source other than yourself, e.g., "Professor So-and-So's thesis is supported by research at Fudan University, which says..." By itself, this is a face-giving kind of remark, so in following your social mistake, it helps to return the mood to equilibrium. Second, you can ask that person in front of others for his/her opinion on something and not argue with it, no matter what you think. This also helps show that you understand that he or she is of superior rank.

Finally, if you really offended someone—maybe you chose to attend one friend's banquet and refused another, even when you knew that the other friend had invited certain people specifically in order to meet you—then you may need to take the second friend out to dinner. Sometimes, a mutual friend is called in to invite both parties to dinner so that the offended person has a harder time saying "no," since the host was not the offender. In either case, if you are the one who made the mistake, you should make sure that you pay the offended person many compliments during the evening, make several toasts to him/her, and come prepared to offer ways to make up for having stood up your friend and the commitments they made to introduce you to the other guests at the original banquet.

Repairing a relationship can be a tricky affair in any culture, but you might have noticed that apologizing for making someone lose face, while also an available tool, is often not as effective as engaging in face-*giving* behaviors for repairing a relationship. Talk is cheap, but face-giving behaviors are meaningful. Saying you are sorry does not give the offended his/her face back, and sometimes it can just make you look like you still think it is all about you, not the person who was offended!

Banqueting

To many Americans, a banquet simply means a meal with many people in attendance and perhaps a theme such as "volunteer of the year." In China, a banquet is a team-based relationship-building meal taken at a round table. Few programs in China make a point of training learners to attend these all-important social events, though some students find themselves at banquets as guests of friends they have made during of the program. If you are a program director, you will partake in banquets during your trip, including welcome and farewell banquets with your host institution, and banquets involving Chinese partners who are part of the program experience (such as companies that provide tours to your students).

In order for a meal to be a formal banquet, there has to be a host team and a guest team. If everyone is on the same team, it is simply a large-scale meal among colleagues and friends. The host team consists of representatives of the group that wants something from the guest team. The "ask" may be a sale of goods or services, help with something, an introduction to a third party who could be helpful in accomplishing a task, help with negotiating a bureaucratic process (like getting license plates), or simply continued positive relations (like two universities engaged in a study abroad program). This last type of banquet is extremely common, as it is an instance of the reciprocity that keeps relationships in China fresh.

Banquet etiquette varies regionally throughout China, but the following things are universal:

This is not a banquet because everyone at the table is on the same "team."

- The host team pays for the banquet (though the host may in fact pay with money provided by one of the guests in certain situations).
- Seating is hierarchical.
- Toasting follows a sequence.
- The guest team does what the host team wants (with the understanding that the host team will try to make the guest team happy).
- Guest team members follow host team members in eating, drinking.
- Host team members look after the dining needs of guest team members, including refilling glasses, plates, replacing dropped utensils, etc.
- Regardless of what team you are on, make sure people around you have something you want before you think about getting any for yourself (e.g., refill seatmates' tea cups before your own).
- Alcohol is for toasting and is not a beverage for individual consumption.
- In cases where there are locals and outsiders, the outsiders are usually treated as guests. Therefore, foreigners are almost always guests.
- The "ask" often comes out near the end of the banquet, after up to three hours of socializing and sometimes as a private aside from a host team member to a guest team member.

If you are aware of these basic tenets, you can ask a local how they are expressed in the place where you will be banqueting. I once attended a lunch banquet with a potential education services client in Qingdao where the host was from a city in Henan Province in which I

Students practicing their toasting skills with tea

Cementing relationships at a banquet

was to participate in a banquet the following day. My host was able to give me advance warning of how toasting in that part of Henan differs from Qingdao (suffice it to say that it involved more drinking).

Banqueting can be tiring: you have to be on your A game, keep up with toasting or use a variety of tricks to successfully avoid it, be sensitive to the hierarchy of those present, pay attention to as many conversations as you can for information gathering, avoid focusing on eating instead of socializing (this can be hard when the food is really good), and make sure you are coherent enough at the end to respond appropriately to any requests that are made after all that drinking and eating. By being an outsider, you can avoid the highest tempo of banquet attendance that is found in China, but you should be prepared to participate in banquets if you want to have a long-standing professional relationship with Chinese culture.

For more tips on banqueting in China, read *Eat Shandong* by Eric Shepherd and *Chinese Business Etiquette* by Scott Seligman.

Using Your Foreign Identity to Establish Reciprocal Relationships

It is common for Chinese people to accumulate and repay *renqing* by taking others to dinner, but since foreigners are often not even allowed by locals to be hosts ("how can you take me to dinner in my own hometown?"), what does a foreign student have that he or she can use in the reciprocity game? The most common skill held by Westerners studying in China is native-level English language ability, which is a valuable commodity. As you consider what you can do for people to begin the cycle of reciprocity that defines relationships in China, do not be afraid of considering opportunities to help people with English language needs.

Most institutions frown on their students taking English teaching jobs during study abroad programs, and with good reason, as those jobs—and the associated paychecks—can easily push the original program goals to the back burner. That said, if your program offers an English teaching or tutoring opportunity, or if you are offered one outside of the program, discuss it with your program director. Teachers are respected individuals in Chinese society, and if you do a good job, many of your students' parents will feel indebted to you… and just like that, you have the potential for a friendly reciprocal relationship. If you teach students over a long period of time or repeatedly over multiple years, your students will eventually grow up and some will feel indebted to you for your help, as well. Helping Chinese people with English is an easy way to establish reciprocal relationships that can lead to ever-higher Chinese language/culture learning opportunities for you.

You can use your foreign-ness to build relationships in other ways, as well: editing papers, helping with speech contest performances or judging, doing short translations, or simply being the representative foreigner in a public event. One of my students helped a little girl's mom edit a song about Thanksgiving that she wrote for her daughter to sing in an English contest at school. Then, my student coached the girl through many performances of the song. My student got to practice her Chinese with both the mother and daughter, and got a couple good meals out of the deal, too!

If you are a foreigner of color (including Asian-Americans), you may find that your Caucasian classmates are offered more opportunities of this kind than you are. Instead of being angered by the racism you encounter—which isn't going to eliminate it, and will probably just confuse people, since most of them do not perceive their prejudice as being racism—try to demonstrate that skin color has nothing to do with helpfulness and a positive attitude.

Relationships to Avoid

Hopefully, you decided to go to China because you are open to the possibility of making Chinese people, language and culture part of your life. As we have described here, establishing relationships with Chinese people is the most important part of forging this bond. However, there are a few kinds of relationships that you should plan on avoiding as a student in China; some of them you should try to avoid forever, while one in particular you should just avoid until you have accumulated more experience interpreting what people mean in Chinese culture.

The one kind of relationship students should avoid establishing during their first couple of trips to China is a romantic one with a Chinese native. Being in a new place, experiencing new and exciting things every day, it is only natural for all the endorphins coursing through students' systems to intensify feelings of romantic interest in people from the culture students are there specifically to learn about. Furthermore, love and attraction are powerful and wonderful forces. The only problem is that it takes a fair amount of participation in a foreign culture to begin to be able to interpret intentions accurately. And, as China goes through tremendous social changes as a result of its economic and social policies, there is a wide range of possible intentions and means of conveying (or concealing) them.

First of all, the idea of casual dating is relatively new in Mainland Chinese culture. Traditionally, you "dated" the person you intended to marry, having already established compatibility through other means. Not too long ago, college students were forbidden from getting married, let alone being allowed to live together. Until recently, high school students could be expelled for dating. Casual dating has become common among young people in major urban areas, though many such people still do not introduce boyfriends and girlfriends to mom and dad until the relationship is serious and the possibility of marriage is on their minds.

Whether or not a foreign student's Chinese peer feels that there is such a thing as casual dating will depend on personal beliefs, informed in part by where that Chinese young person is from, how the family raised him or her, and how much exposure to Westerners they have already had, especially in this regard. Even then, with the concept so new in China, the standards for the dividing line between casual dating and a serious relationship may differ for the Chinese and American partners.

Female foreign learners rarely get into trouble over this issue during study abroad programs, so fellas, this advice is mostly for you.

Leave dating Chinese to the Chinese until you have much more time in country.

Avoid inviting a lone Chinese female on anything that she could construe as a date: meals, walks, movies, discussions over coffee, etc. If you think it is like a date, she probably does, too. Avoid accepting gifts from Chinese females in your age group who have no unromantic reason to give you one. Don't go to a bar in a group and lavish your attention on one particular young lady.

This draconian advice is to protect girls from having their hearts broken, to protect you from parents of heartbroken girls, and to protect the program in which you are a part from acquiring a bad reputation. Although you get to go home at the end of the program and leave your girl troubles 6,000 miles behind you, your school and your program director will probably be going back (if not staying there). If local parents say they have to lock up their daughters whenever your school sends a group of students to China, your school may eventually have to find a new home there, and you don't want to be the cause of that.

Okay, so those are the ways in which folks can hurt others as a result of not understanding the dating/courting scene in China. You can get hurt, too. Some young ladies in bars and discos target foreign men to become their boyfriends for personal gain. On one end of the spectrum are ladies who will expect to be paid at the end of a "romantic" evening, and you do not want to meet the guy she shares her take with. On the other end of the spectrum are women who are seeking long-term relationships with foreign men in the hopes of increasing their economic and social stations in life. These ladies are simply being practical, exchanging their resources for yours. If you are not able to tell the difference between someone who is interested in you as an individual from someone who is interested in the financial security you represent (or potential financial security, if you are still a student), you may find yourself in a relationship that isn't what you thought it was at the beginning. The vast majority of Chinese people who date foreigners are emotionally involved and not in it for economic reasons, but wouldn't you prefer to be able to tell the difference before jumping in?

The other kinds of people with whom you do not want to cultivate relationships, especially as a student, are those engaged in illicit activities. Such people include drug dealers, pimps, individuals in organized crime, smugglers, and people manufacturing pirated goods. There simply is no good ending to those stories for you or your program. Any Chinese circle of friends grows as they introduce their friends to you. Once you enter into reciprocal

There's nothing wrong with love; just wait until you know it when you see it.

friendships with people who break the law for a living, how do you get out? Not easily, so just don't start.

There is another group of people engaged in illegal activity with whom you will want to keep your distance while in a program, for the sake of the program: enemies of the state. Just because they are enemies of the state does not mean they are engaged in immoral activities, but your involvement with members of groups banned by the government such as Tibetan independence groups, Uighur freedom fighters and Falun Gong practitioners can pose a problem for you and your program. If your conscience compels you to build relationships with members of such groups, do so knowing that the potential consequences could include prison terms, and that your association with such groups could seriously jeopardize the continued operation of your study abroad program in China.

Many financially or politically successful people in China are or have been engaged in some activity of questionable legality, whether it is tax evasion or capitalizing upon inside information, taking/giving bribes or simply accepting gifts for the execution of one's normal work. In many cases, the law is in direct conflict with traditional Chinese culture, and most successful Chinese people adhere to their culture instead of the (often unenforced) law.

For example, it is common practice for families of sick people to give money and/or favors to doctors in order to establish a recipro-

Red envelopes, used to gift cash at weddings and during Chinese New Year, have become metaphors for extra payments given to obtain favorable service from bureaucrats, doctors, and other professionals.

cal relationship in which the doctor takes the gifts and in return takes good care of the patient. In a society in which people take care of in-group members and often ignore out-group members who are not potential in-group members (e.g., strangers on the street), are you going to trust your loved one's care to someone with whom you have no relationship? There is no Hippocratic Oath in the Chinese medical tradition—Chinese doctors are not honor-bound to save life no matter what the circumstances, and especially not if the patient cannot afford treatment. The closest equivalent, a monograph by a sixth century physician named Sun Simiao that is still read today, simply says that doctors should treat all patients equally.

Since you will want to build relationships with successful people, avoid asking about aspects of their lives that may highlight the differences between Chinese culture and Chinese regulation. Most of them will be pretty careful about not involving you in these affairs, anyway, because you will be an unknown commodity to them, and "loose lips sink ships."

This chapter has some pretty heavy information; even the sections on how to create good relationships with good people describe a social system that is so different from what many Westerners are used to that this chapter should give you some serious food for thought. When I went to China the second time, I had studied Chinese for three years and had already spent six months in country, but I honestly did not know how Chinese society runs on *guanxi*, *renqing* and *mianzi*. I had been seeing China through my own cultural perspective, unaware that speaking Chinese and physically being in China did not necessarily mean I was participating in Chinese society. It was only after I joined a program that made a point of breaking down the formal and informal barriers between foreign students and Chinese people that I learned a career involving China would mean a lifetime of building and maintaining relationships through reciprocal exchange, as well as a lot more socializing and public performances than I ever imagined as an undergraduate student of language.

So, get out there, make friends, be prepared to give and to receive (not necessarily in that order), and discover your own reasons for wanting to come back to China before you have even left.

Making local friends is the key to having a successful trip.

Chapter 11
Trouble, or "Ouch," "Oh, No!" and "Sorry"

Sometimes daily life throws you a curve ball, no matter where you live. A little scratch here, a misunderstanding there, and life goes on. Other times, life throws a big dodge ball right at you and you have a serious issue to take care of. Common sense, support from the people around you, and good travel insurance will get you through most situations; in others, there is very little you can do but hang tight and wait for help. In this chapter, we will look at three kinds of problems encountered by students in China: medical, legal, and large-scale events.

Ailments[1]

Visitors to China usually experience medical problems so small that no professional assistance is necessary. Everything that is needed to treat such minor issues is available in local convenience stores and pharmacies, and sometimes at much lower prices than in the U.S.

■ Diarrhea

Your best friend for the next 24 hours

For most visitors, the development of gastrointestinal discomfort is a matter of when, not if. Diarrhea[2] is

---

1 The advice given in this chapter is based only on experience and not professional training. The advice of a professional medical practitioner supersedes anything said here.

2 In Chinese, having diarrhea is literally "excreting my belly," so instead of saying "I have diarrhea," you say "I [am] excreting my belly": wǒ lā dùzi 我拉肚子 or wǒ xiè dùzi 我泻肚子。

a normal reaction to the microbes found in Chinese food that are foreign to our bodies. Developing a case of "Mao's Revenge" does not necessarily mean the food was unhygienic, as it takes time for all but the most iron of stomachs to acclimate to the food and drink of faraway places. The first thing to do is to let your program director and teachers know when you have diarrhea. In Chinese culture, it is not embarrassing to talk about diarrhea, so get used to being in an environment in which it is okay to bring it up and get helpful advice. As at home, drink a lot of fluids to avoid getting dehydrated. If you are vomiting as well, try to sip as much water or green tea as your body allows you to keep down. You may feel like the end of the world is at hand while your body purges itself, but most people are fine by the end of day two, if not earlier.

Chinese explanations for diarrhea are often based in traditional Chinese medicinal beliefs: your stomach became cool too quickly (**zháo liáng** 着凉) as a result of air conditioning, insufficient blanketing at night, or change in weather; you are under great stress; you are not used to the foreign environment (**shuǐtǔ bù fú** 水土不服). Many Chinese believe that no medicine is needed in these situations because your body simply needs to readjust. Americans tend to believe microscopic things are responsible for medical issues and thus seek pharmaceutical relief even when well-meaning Chinese friends think it was because the fan was blowing right on you while you slept.

Even if you are content with letting your body heal itself, medicine can help when it is inconvenient to make every trip to the bathroom demanded by your bowels (e.g., when you are traveling by bus, or you otherwise feel well enough to keep up with class). At these times, you can take the Pepto-Bismol or Imodium you brought from home. If you visit your local Chinese pharmacy and ask for diarrhea medicine (**zhì xiè dùzi de yào** 治泻肚子的药), they are likely to give you **huángliánsù** 黄连素. This is an herbal medicine, called Berberine Hydrochloride in English. In addition to helping with diarrhea, is also known to reduce blood sugar levels in diabetics. As an herbal medicine, it does not work as quickly as Pepto Bismol, but it is gentler on your body. If you show no signs of improvement after two days, a trip to a clinic for professional evaluation and/or stronger medication may be in order. Be sure to go with a bilingual friend or program staff member; you will owe that person some *renqing*, but don't worry about that now—get better first! The procedure for visiting a medical facility is described further later in this chapter.

■ Minor Cuts

Perhaps the second-most common self-treatable medical problem encountered by students in China is a minor cut. More often than not, such cuts are the result of poor judgment—itself often the result of intoxi-

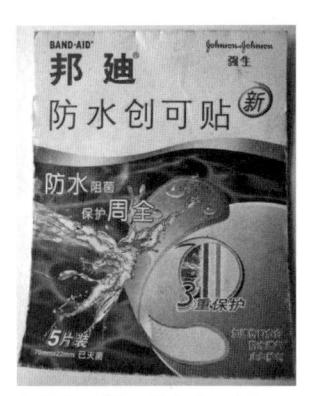

A chuàngkětīe will do the trick for many boo-boo's.

cation. Even if you take care of such a minor cut/abrasion yourself, do not allow shame to stop you from telling your program director or teacher about it. He or she can check in on you periodically to see how you are healing, and help you take action if an infection appears to be on the way. Just as at home, first disinfect the wound with a liquid disinfectant and then put on a self-adhesive bandage (**chuàngkětīe** 创可贴). Some students, knowing that alcohol can disinfect, pour beer on their boo-boos, but the alcohol content of beer is not high enough to do the trick. Rather than wasting good liquor on simple medical treatment (it hurts a lot, too), wash the wound as soon as possible with soap and water (bottled water, if possible; cooled-off boiled water if not), apply a disinfectant bought at a pharmacy such as 75% or higher content rubbing alcohol (**jiǔjīng** 酒精) or "red mercury" (**zǐgǒng** 紫汞). Red Mercury is the go-to disinfectant for many Chinese families—like Bactine to Americans.

For really deep or wide cuts, go to the hospital and get professional help. You might be able to heal on your own, anyway, but they will thoroughly disinfect the wound, and will know if you will need stitches to avoid a nasty scar.

■ Allergies

Students in China also occasionally need treatment for extreme allergic reactions. Food allergies are rarely discussed in China; whether this is because Chinese people have fewer allergies than Westerners or because they ascribe discomfort to other causes is unclear. The upshot is that students need to communicate to program staff and teachers what allergies students have before arrival in China because food preparers very rarely even think about the possibility of serving people with allergies. This is especially important for students with severe allergic reactions to peanuts (**huāshēng** 花生), shellfish,[3] and, most of all, MSG (MSG is called "flavor essence" **wèi jīng** 味精 in Chinese). MSG is also the chief ingredient of chicken bouillon **jījīng** 鸡精.

Peanut oil is used to make stir-fries more flavorful, and kitchenware used to prepare dishes with

---

3 "Shellfish" as a single category does not exist in Chinese. It is composed of 贝壳类海鲜 **bèiké lèi hǎixiān** (seafood with hard shells) and 甲壳类动物 **jiǎké lèi dòngwù** (crustaceans), the latter term being a scientific one used much less frequently than **xiā lèi** 虾类 (shrimps), which includes all kinds of shrimp, crayfish and lobsters.

peanuts and peanut oil is used to make other dishes, as well. Without specific and careful attention paid to the presence of peanuts in the kitchen, an allergic reaction may take place. The most dangerous part of Chinese cooking for those with allergies to shellfish may be the use of small dried shrimp (**xiā mǐ** 虾米) as a flavoring. Because they can be ground up and practically disappear into the dish, it is important to make sure that no dishes being served to a person with a shellfish allergy contain them.

Small dried shrimp

Unless you ask the preparer to do otherwise, nearly all Chinese dishes will have MSG in them. Many Chinese cooks will even add MSG (or chicken bouillon) to dishes consisting only of fresh ingredients, believing that it will taste even better. Fortunately, even if few people in China really care about their MSG intake, it is commonly known that there can be negative effects associated with its consumption. As a result, if you clearly and calmly ask the cook (or wait staff) to not use MSG, they will understand what you mean (as opposed to saying you are vegetarian, which many people in China do not understand). To stop the use of MSG in your food, just say to the server or cook "**qǐng bú yào fàng wèijīng**" 请不要放味精, which literally means, "Please do not put in MSG."

■ Feminine needs

You will find a full range of products and medicines for feminine needs in China, though like many other areas related to personal hygiene, if you prefer a specific brand or product, it might be a good idea to pack it in case you cannot find it in China. Maxi-pads (still called "sanitary napkins" on the bags found in hotels for their disposal) are more popular in China than tampons, so keep this in mind as you pack. Discomfort associated with your period can be treated with over the counter Western-style medicine such as the one pictured below, or slow-acting Chinese medicines. The easiest thing to do is to bring from home a box of the over-the-counter medicine you normally use in the U.S.

Chinese-made Western-style medicine for feminine discomfort

■ Miscellaneous

There is a liquid called **Fengyoujing** fēngyóujīng 风油精 that seems to be used for all kinds of ailments. As the box indicates below, it is good for "cooling off, pain relief, dispelling wind, [and] soothing itchy feeling." It is used when people feel overheated, over-exerted, tired, headachy, dry, and for mosquito bites. The bottle is about an inch tall and it costs next to nothing, so give it a try. Your Chinese friends probably all own a bottle or two....

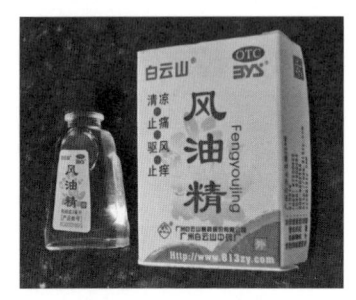

Fengyoujing, the wonder potion

Medical Treatment

If someone in your group has a severe allergic reaction, he or she probably knows better what to do than those around, and it may involve the use of an EpiPen, an automatic epinephrine injection device that can be jabbed into the stricken person's thigh in an emergency. EpiPen or no, a trip to the nearest hospital is probably a good idea.

Professional medical treatment of minor problems is very, very inexpensive in China, as the healthcare system is set up to make such treatments economically feasible for as many people as possible. The process of seeing a doctor in China is a bit different from the in the U.S., and you will do well to focus on the cleanliness of the sterilized instruments and not the overall condition of the facilities. First of all, if you need to go to a hospital, you might as well splurge on a taxi. No one wants to take a crowded and bumpy bus ride when they're not feeling well. Be sure you're not going to bleed all over his seats before you hail the cab, though. When the driver asks "where to?" respond by saying "**wǒ yào qù zuìjìn de yīyuàn**" 我要去最近的医院, which means "I want to go to the nearest hospital."

Some hospitals in major cities have clinics for foreigners where the medical staff are bilingual; some taxi drivers will even take you there without asking if you look foreign, are alone, and sound like your Chinese ability might not go far beyond "*ni hao*." Hopefully, you have a Chinese-speaking person accompanying you, though—hospital trips are not fun at any time, so your companion can provide linguistic as well as moral support.

Once you arrive at the hospital, you first "get a number" or **guà hào** 挂号 at a service window (always labeled appropriately, so learn to recognize those two characters). When you get your number, you pay the price of seeing a doctor for a diagnosis. The price you pay varies depending on the medical specialty

A hospital in Shenzhen

you need, but it is usually $2-$10 U.S. dollars. Yes, the cost of seeing a Chinese doctor for a minor issue is about the same as dinner at Taco Bell. After you have your number, you go to the waiting area for your specialty (e.g., internal medicine, ENT, gynecology, etc.) and wait to be served.

When it is your turn, a nurse will bring you back to see the doctor or just tell you what room number to go to. In the room, you may find the previous patient (and family) still receiving a diagnosis, or even two doctors serving two parties in the same room at the same time. Privacy is unusual and expensive in Chinese hospitals. In many neighborhood hospitals, the physical infrastructure is primitive by American standards: wooden stools, flimsy paper, aging desks, and so on. If you think about it, though, as long as the doctors are professionally trained and the drugs come in sterile media, who cares how expensive the chairs are?

The doctor will make his or her diagnosis and send you to get any prescription medicine you need. Here is where it gets complicated. You take the prescription to the pharmacy, where they issue you invoice tickets for your medicine that you then take to the pharmacy payment window. There, people who are authorized to handle money take your payment and stamp your ticket(s) "paid." You then take the tickets to the pharmacy dispensary window, where they take one copy as proof of payment and then give you your medicine. This process sometimes requires a lot of walking and/or elevator rides.

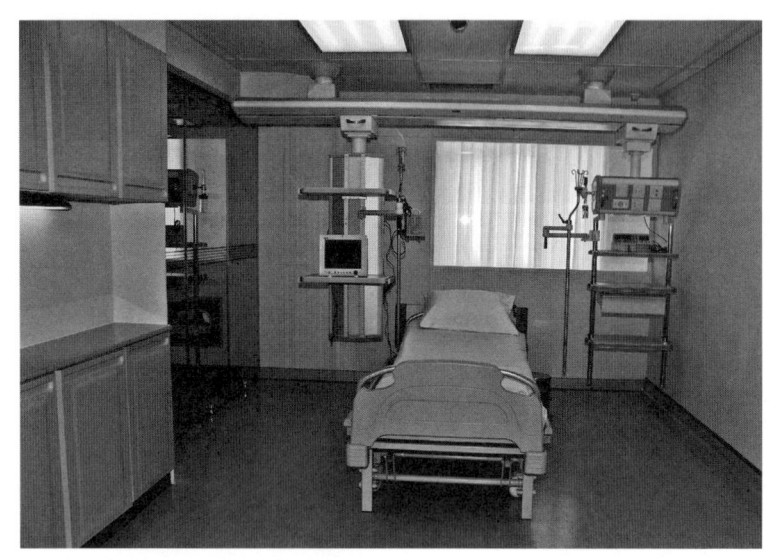

A modern hospital room in a major Chinese city

Because the medicine is also highly subsidized, by the time you leave the hospital, you may have dropped only $20 on the whole thing. Many students choose not to take the time to submit receipts and reimbursement forms to their travel insurance provider because the time spent on it would not be worth the money recovered, but you do have that option. If your condition is such that you have time to do some research before you head out, you can search your travel insurance provider's website for the nearest hospital that is in their system. Other hospitals' fees should be covered by your plan, as well, but it may make paperwork a little easier if you can use a facility that is in the insurance company's database.

Very occasionally, students studying in China will encounter serious unexpected medical problems. In these cases, step one is to get to the nearest hospital. If a taxi is practical (e.g., the patient can be moved), take a taxi–they often arrive faster than an ambulance, and Chinese ambulances are simply minivans with a couple of orderlies riding in the back, anyway. If the patient should not be moved (e.g., he or she has been struck by a vehicle and the extent of the injury is unknown), have a Chinese speaker dial 120 for emergency medical assistance.[4]

Step two is to call the program director and tell him/her where to meet the patient (on the scene if nearby, at the hospital if not).

---

4 For police emergencies, dial 110 and for fire, dial 119. When in doubt, just dial 110 and they will figure out what help you need.

Step three is to get access to cash. This is probably going to be the program director's responsibility. Chinese hospitals may assume that a foreign patient is able to pay and go ahead and begin treatment, but it is quite possible that the hospital will ask someone associated with the patient to begin a process of paying the bill or at least a deposit while treatment is being started. There isn't enough credit in China to let people receive treatment and then figure out the bill later, so it is a good idea to bring at least ¥1,000 to the hospital, just in case. At the very least, medication will need to be paid for. Staying in the hospital (**zhùyuàn** 住院) is an additional expense, and food is not provided, either.

Step four is for the program director or a friend to contact the student's travel insurance provider and get advice concerning next steps. This should happen as soon as possible, ideally while still at the hospital.

All this is much easier if the student can be immediately transported to a hospital that caters to foreign expatriates such as those in the United Family Hospitals system in Beijing, Shanghai, Guangzhou, and Tianjin.

Legal Issues

The most likely legal problem a foreigner would encounter in China is a visa problem, and the most common visa problem is working while in China on a tourist or student visa, which is common…and illegal. The public security bureau periodically cracks down on such employment, focusing mostly on foreigners with full-time jobs over those making some cash by tutoring a few hours a week. You cannot convert a tourist or student visa into a work visa without leaving China, so the solution to this kind of visa problem tends to be quitting the job.

If a student has seriously overstayed his or her visa—which should only happen after a program is over and the program is no longer responsible for the student's actions—a student may try asking the program coordinator to call in some *renqing* and look for someone who is a fixer. The student must remember that he or she would owe a huge favor to the coordinator in this case, as the coordinator would then owe a favor to the fixer. Such fixers know people in relevant government offices who can be relied upon to accept and approve visa applications that are submitted outside of the requirements of the law. If a friend of yours is able to find a fixer to solve your visa problem, but the friend does not tell you how much the fixer's services cost, then you owe that friend twice over, since that friend spent money and/or *renqing* to obtain the fixer's services on your behalf. This is in addition to any application fees that need to be paid to the government.

Periodically, one or more foreigners in China do something particularly egregious like rape a Chinese girl, and then the authorities (and the public) become strict about enforcing rules regarding public behavior and visa status. At times like these, public drunkenness might lead to a fine instead of just a slap on the wrist and a meeting with representatives from the Chinese host university and the American study program. To be clear, neither of these are good for a student, as they are sufficient cause for expulsion from most programs.

Too much of a good thing

Most student legal problems in China, from destroying property to crossing the street without regard to traffic, are a result of excessive drinking. Such problems are extremely easy for mature adults to avoid… but not so easy for many American students. With no legal drinking age on the books, it is easy for American students in China to make a habit of getting drunk on inexpensive beer (and expensive liquor). Chinese dorms have a no-alcohol policy, which helps keep trouble off-campus, but it also means students are more likely to get in trouble some distance away from home base and away from where the program director lives. Program directors should be prepared for some late-night calls from students in need: one unfortunate program director was called out to compensate the owner of a property on which his drunken students had urinated; I have myself been called to deal with students who nearly started a brawl with Korean exchange students. In both cases, however, the authorities were not called and the issues were resolved privately (**sīxià jiějué** 私下解决), as is often preferred. In the Chinese tradition, it is commonly assumed that the only people who find themselves in court are guilty ones, so people try to avoid calling the police if they can.

The best way to avoid these kinds of problems is to drink in moderation and to always socialize in groups of friends that will look out for each other (read: stop each other from doing stupid things). I once had a student who told her also-inebriated friends that she wanted to take a nap under some roadside bushes. They let her do that, and she spent the rest of the night passed out on the side of the [on-campus] road. It sounds like a funny story now, but it could have ended up quite differently.

If a student is caught by authorities using, or worse, selling drugs, there isn't much that the program can do for him or her. Even if *guanxi* can be found in the Public Security Bureau to help the student, it may only be able to reduce the punishment or allow for a speedy expulsion from the country instead of serious jail time. Dealing drugs can be a capital crime in China. Don't get anywhere close to the drug trade while you are there, and if someone approaches you asking you to help with something that seems sketchy, it probably is.

Long-term expatriate residents of China—such as year-round resident directors—can encounter the full gamut of legal issues from broken contracts to traffic accidents, but students, with their limited and regular regimen of school and local socializing, are usually not exposed to such liabilities.

Damage from the Wenchuan Earthquake of 2008

Dangerous Events, Natural and Manufactured

Some events are simply so large in scale that there is little you can do to protect yourself other than to leave the affected area as soon as possible. Such events can take place anywhere in the world, but there are a few that seem to strike China on a more regular—or at least more severe—basis than in the U.S. Among natural disasters, there are earthquakes, floods, snowstorms, and typhoons. Fortunately, these things rarely strike major cities on a scale that can do serious damage.

China's most recent earthquakes have done most of their damage in rural areas that, though still highly populated, are home to few foreigners and few or no formal study abroad programs. The last time a major earthquake struck a large city in China was in 1976, when Tangshan in Hebei Province was leveled and possibly 500,000 people died. If you are indoors when an earthquake strikes, get away from any glass and under something sturdy like a table so that falling objects are deflected; if outdoors, move away from buildings and wires.

Flooding is a regular problem in many parts of China, and controlling seasonal flooding was one of the reasons the Three Gorges Dam was built on the Yangzi River. Torrential rains can sometimes make city life dangerous as well; in July 2012, one day of rain in Beijing led to the deaths of 79 people. Some of those killed were in rural areas outside of the city proper, but others were trapped by floodwaters in roadways. If you encounter an urban flood, stay away from rivers and canals and never try to cross flowing water more than a few inches deep. If you cannot tell how deep it is, do not go in at all.

Northern China regularly experiences dust storms, but they are more of an inconvenience than a personal threat, as are the occasional snow and ice storms that strike normally-mild southern China. Coastal southern China is regularly subject to typhoons (called hurricanes in the Atlantic). The wind and rain of a typhoon are inconvenient to pedestrians, but unless you are in a shack or are on a fishing boat, typhoons pose little threat to students in China.

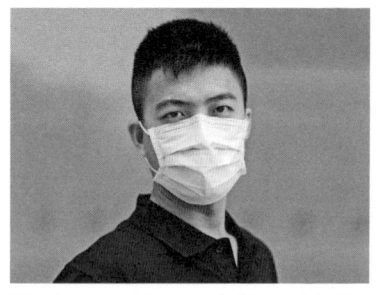

Wearing a mask to prevent airborne infection

Another occasional threat to personal well-being is communicable diseases. Other than STDs (mentioned earlier), there are also periodic outbreaks of diseases that begin among livestock in the warm climate of South China and then jump from the animals to their owners living in close proximity (the Chinese character for "home" is a pig under a roof). When these viruses adapt to human hosts, they have the potential to mutate into a particularly nasty strain, as was the case with Swine Flu and Bird Flu. When Swine Flu (AKA H1N1) struck China in 2009, individuals with a fever were quarantined until they recovered. Individuals near those with a fever were also quarantined. This happened to many American students arriving on flights with passengers found to have a fever, as well as students already in China who may have been exposed to ill people. Many China summer programs were canceled that year just to be safe, leaving a relatively small number of year-long program participants to experience the anxiety felt by a billion Chinese people during the epidemic. Thanks to lessons learned in 2009, subsequent flu outbreaks have been dealt with more efficiently and with incrementally more transparency in media coverage.

One threat to health and safety that is entirely man-made is the release of industrial pollution into the environment. The level of pollution that is found on a daily basis should have no immediate effects on any but the most sensitive visitors to the country, but every once in a while, an industrial accident causes the release of particularly nasty chemicals, such as has happened a couple of times in Northeast China. Like the other threats mentioned above, residents of major metro areas are protected fairly well from industrial accidents, as the government is able to efficiently provide aid and protection to the highly dense urban populations. People living in villages immediately adjacent to the industrial accidents may not be well-protected, but the likelihood of anyone reading this book living in one of those places is very, very low.

Finally, there are periodic instances of mass unrest that turn violent. The most common of these events fall into one of three categories: unhappy farmers; unhappy factory workers; unhappy ethnic groups. Westerners studying in China are unlikely to be based in an agricultural village, a factory town, or a city with a large population of ethnic minorities (specifically, Tibetans and Uighurs, as the other minorities have not rebelled in a couple hundred years). The only real opportunity a foreign student has of coming across a violent protest (assuming he or she does not unwisely seek it out) is if it occurs during a trip to the beautiful areas where Tibetans and Uighurs live. All three of these forms of unrest happen quickly, so it is hard to know which areas to avoid ahead of time, but if you ever hear that violence has started in a place you are visiting or plan to visit, save yourself a lot of hassle and change your plans. If you're already there, catch the next train back east; if you haven't yet departed for the troubled area, try to return your tickets or just chalk the loss up to "insurance."

There are also periodic mass protests by Han Chinese against the Japanese. Such protests are manifestations of the ongoing animos-

That's not fog outside, it's the air.

ity the Chinese feel toward Japan because of World War II (called the "War to Resist Japan" in Chinese), and are sparked by different events each time. The most recent one is over territorial rights in the South China Sea, where several countries assert sovereignty over an area with a variety of economic resources. In 1999, there were nationwide protests against the U.S. and NATO (but mostly the U.S.) after the Americans bombed the Chinese embassy in Belgrade; McDonalds' windows were smashed and some people advocated the boycotting of American-branded goods and services. While these protests rarely result in physical injury, they can be scary to be in, and you would do best to steer clear.

This has been the chapter about what could possibly go wrong. Once in a while, bad things happen to innocent people, and there is very little that could have been done to prevent them; all we can do is try to react calmly and appropriately and minimize the suffering incurred. When someone is hurt, get professional medical help; if a crime has been committed against a student, call the police or ask a Chinese person for help in calling the police.

Other times, a little prudence goes a long way toward avoiding problems. Any study abroad program coordinator can tell you that alcohol is the leading cause of trouble while overseas. Drinking to excess and its attendant impairment of good judgment can lead to a wide variety of legal and health problems, most of which mean bad news for the student, the director, and the program. Each

Don't be afraid to ask for help when you need it.

program will have its own way of trying to minimize the risk of alcohol-induced trouble, and its own reasons for doing so. High school programs tend to have a zero-tolerance policy for alcohol consumption while programs for college students and adults tend to stress personal responsibility. My own experience has been that many college students and adults will drink a lot in China, regardless of how many horror stories you tell them, so it is better to impress upon them the importance of sticking together so that most sober of them can look out for the others, and hopefully avoid being robbed, pick-pocketed, left in the gutter, etc. In my programs, we have a rule that students are generally allowed to pursue any social activities they want to on their own time as long as it does not negatively affect their participation in or the operation of the program. This tends to align with Chinese attitudes toward alcohol consumption, as well. Excessive drinking is very common among adult Chinese, but because it is socially expected, it only becomes problematic when the drinking negatively affects the drinker's responsibilities as a member of society or reflects poorly on his or her in-groups.

As we close this chapter, the most important piece of advice is to be ready to deal with the unexpected. That means not trying to anticipate everything that could go wrong—you can't—but, instead, being flexible and keeping your head on your shoulders if something does.

Chapter 12
Going Home

Depending on the nature of your program, getting ready to go home can be as simple as packing your suitcases and tchotchkes, or there may be a long list of things to do before you go. In this section, we will describe the full list of things that may need to be done before you leave China; you can decide for yourself which of them apply to your particular situation.

You should start getting ready to go home about two weeks before departure for programs of two months or longer; for shorter programs, one week or less should be sufficient. During this phase, you will be showing your Chinese friends that you will not forget them, preparing to bring back objects that demonstrate to your friends and family back home that you never forgot them, and wrapping up loose ends in terms of accounts and items that you no longer need.

The first order of business is to start scheduling your farewell events. For students in programs that are short and/or highly regimented, it is possible that few local friends were made between all the traveling and activities. Even during short programs, students still often feel like they make friends at local bars and with owners of small shops near campus or near the hotel in which they lived. Such relationships are, by nature, fleeting, and so a farewell dinner or gift exchange is really not necessary; just mentioning when you are leaving and saying you will miss them/their dumplings is sufficient. There is a Chinese saying that says "no one is ever offended by an unnecessary gift," so it is perfectly fine to give a small memento to local friends made during short 1 or 2 month programs. Such things might include small school-branded merchandise or a developed photo of everyone together.

For program directors and participants in longer programs, farewell activities will focus on dinners and the obligatory end-of-program banquet/variety show. Farewell dinners are usually hosted (or at least paid for) by the party that is leaving, the assumption being that they were themselves treated to a welcome banquet when they first arrived. These farewell dinners can be divided into formal banquets and friendly social occasions.

Formal farewell banquets are commonly organized by the program staff and their Chinese part-

In Shandong, it is traditional to serve dumplings to people who are preparing to leave home, even if it is an adopted home.

ners and signal the official end of the program. This dinner may be coordinated by the host institution, as the location and the food will probably be provided by the Chinese side, but the tab will be picked up in part or in full by the foreign side, depending on the agreement the program has with the foreign affairs office they work with. Some programs share the cost of the farewell banquet, with the foreign side picking up the tab for its teachers, students and guests (if there are any local people unaffiliated with the host institution who helped with the program), and the Chinese side paying for their own employees.

Like the welcome banquet, end-of-program banquets often include a variety show. This time, since the foreign students are more familiar with China and have ostensibly expanded their comfort bubbles to include being ready to perform for Chinese observers (since they are essentially doing this every day anyway), they can perform skits, sing songs, recite poetry, and do just about anything they want to demonstrate what they have learned during the program. If the program included Chinese room-

Celebrating the end of the program

mates or classmates, this is the perfect time to for students to work together on cross-border performances. Stage-ready performances take time to prepare, so it is important that program staff and students begin planning their gigs at least two weeks before the farewell banquet. Program staff may need to make this a class requirement, since many foreign students are not used to artistic performances being socially expected, as it is in China.

The teachers celebrate, too.

In addition to the formal programmatic farewell banquet, program staff and students in longer-term programs will want to start planning their informal farewell dinners a couple weeks before departure. The more friends you have in your host city, the more meals it may take to say goodbye to them all. Since the person leaving should make an honest effort to pay for the meal, it is okay to combine a couple farewell dinners into one and introduce Chinese friends of yours to each other. These Chinese friends may refuse to let you pay because, as a foreigner, you are semi-permanently stuck with the "guest" role, and guests never pick up the tab, but eventually, your friends will let you pay. Maybe not this year, but someday. One sneaky way to make sure you pay the bill is to slip out to "use the bathroom" and pay when no one is looking. This is a common trick, so some people may call you on it if you try it. Another reason you may not be allowed to pay is if you are not well off, or at least poor relative to the Chinese friend in question. If you have made friends with someone who is well-off, it is unlikely that they will allow you to pick up the check. Nevertheless, it is good form to invite that person and his or her family to the nicest restaurant you can reasonably afford; if he or she lets you pay the bill, you can! If your friend commandeers the planning of your farewell dinner—which may happen if they want to eat better than you can afford, or if they want to invite people who you do not know—it's okay. You should still offer to pay, but you do not need to insist if the friend says twice that they will pay, especially if you are new friends. Arguing over paying the bill is okay among good friends, but where there is an in-group and an out-group (e.g., people who would not be expected to pay because they are "guests" instead of "friends"), it is unseemly to force the issue of money.

You do not need to take out to dinner everyone you met during the program; you only need to have farewell meals with people with whom you expect to keep in touch: people you got along with exceptionally well; any host families with whom you lived; people you will be seeing in the U.S. in the near future; people who gave you great help when you needed it and thus earned "friend" status. If you have not given gifts to these people yet, it is appropriate to give them a gift at the farewell dinner. If you are all out of gifts from your home, it is better to leave it at treating them to dinner than picking up something Chinese that they can get themselves. The very fact that you are taking them to dinner means that you intend to see them again someday, and will have more opportunities to give them "meeting gifts" (**jiànmiàn lǐ 见面礼**), gifts you give when meeting them for the first time or after a long distance or long-time separation.

If you leave your farewell dinner planning to the last few days, your Chinese friends will start organizing the dinners for you (and them, since they may have more friends of their own who they would like to introduce to you), and there could be scheduling conflicts. You would hate to have to tell one friend that you don't have time to see them because another friend is taking you to dinner, right? You may encounter a situation in which someone you do *not* want a long-term relationship invites you to a farewell dinner. In this case, you can thank that person very much for their kind invitation, but apologize for the fact that others have already arranged your little time remaining. This shifts the burden to someone else; if you say you are sorry because you have arranged all your remaining farewell dinners, then you are telling the person, "I have the power to change these plans, but since I won't, you can interpret this as meaning I don't like you." Even if that is true, it helps no one to leave an unpleasant impression.

Pace yourself.

For adult (college age and above) men, farewell dinners often involve a fair amount of toasting. As you now know, toasts are a mechanism for articulating reasons why two or more people have or should have a long-term relationship, and the farewell dinner is the ultimate platform for giving these toasts. As with any banquet at which you would be expected to toast, either tell your companions ahead of time that you will be toasting with a non-alcoholic beverage because of allergies or an early-morning flight, or rely on your ability to digest alcohol. The former never works for me, but I have seen older government/party officials whose job descriptions include nightly banqueting very skillfully avoid drinking more than they want and yet still convey all the depth of

Your packing should be much further along than this by the time you go out to dinner on your last night in China.

emotion that the toasts are intended to convey.

Since it is nearly impossible to avoid attending a farewell dinner the night before you finally leave China, try to be all packed and ready to go *before* you go to dinner, even if you have a late flight the next day. Especially if you are an adult male, you may not be firing on all cylinders the next morning… or even the next afternoon, depending on which liquid fueled the toasts. Even if you abstain from drinking, these dinners can go quite late into the night, sometimes being followed by one last trip to the karaoke parlor for old times' sake. So, do your packing while you are still awake and sober so that you don't miss something the next day.

Be sure to say thank you to your local Chinese teachers; even better, pool funds in your class to buy them a nice little gift to say thank you. They have worked hard for you, and if you show the proper respect and gratitude, they will be happy to treat you as a friend in the future, as well. If there were front desk people, gate guards or cleaning staff with whom you interacted every day, tell them when you are leaving and thank them for being your conversation partner or whatever they did for you (open the dorm doors after hours on the weekend?).

Even if you already gifted some of these people at the beginning of the program, it is appropriate to thank them once again on your way home.

Another thing to start doing a week or two before departure is accumulating the souvenirs that you want to bring home as gifts for friends and family and for yourself. During your travels in China, you will have seen many trinkets sold at tourist sites, and, undoubtedly, will have picked up some as impulse items. Here is an important piece of advice: except for a few items that are manufactured expressly for individual tourist attractions, most of the items you see for sale near these places are made in factories far, far away, and can be bought in the trinket markets that exist in all major cities. Therefore, limit your travel souvenir purchases to items that are clearly tied to the attractions you visit (e.g., post cards, miniatures related to that site, etc.), and do your non-location-specific souvenir/gift shopping in your base city.

Shopping for souvenirs in your base city is preferable for several reasons: 1) You can visit the souvenir market more than once and learn by eavesdropping what things sell for. The prices at these markets are usually much lower than at tourist attractions, and for the exact same green glass Buddha on a red string. 2) You can search for higher-quality versions of the things you see at tourist sites. When you are excited to be visiting a famous site, it is easy to overlook the quality shortcomings of low-cost, high-volume manufactured art goods. In your base city, you can go to where locals buy art pieces for their own homes, pieces that are supposed to stand on their own as art rather than a cheap

You can get a nice silk scarf in any Chinese city.

reminder of having visited the Great Wall. It is possible that you are just looking for a cheap reminder, but some people prefer to buy a smaller, finer piece of art (e.g., a jade pendant) than a larger piece of green glass. 3) By shopping in your base city, you can bring along a Chinese friend to help you tell the difference between good and mediocre, the difference between expensive and just right. Don't worry; there is plenty of jade-like green glass to be had at urban gift markets, too, if that is what you are looking for.

Here is a short list of things visitors to China commonly buy:

- Scroll watercolor paintings
- Jade or glass Buddhas
- Lacquer or imitation lacquer plastic bodhisattvas (the "laughing Buddha")
- Fancy chopsticks
- Painted snuff bottles
- Fans
- Liuli glassware
- Chop seal with your Chinese name
- Green tea
- Things related to Peking Opera masks
- Bamboo tchotchkes
- Pins associated with a college or school

It is common to engage in re-gifting in China, so feel free to re-gift to friends at home things that Chinese friends gave to you. Even though re-gifting is common, do not tell the original giver you re-gifted their gift to you. Some will not mind, but some will.

If you do not plan on returning to China for a year or more, there may be a few other things to do before going home, like closing accounts.

If you opened a bank account and deposited money into it, you can withdraw your money and close the account. These days, most people just withdraw cash directly from their U.S. accounts via ATM, but you may have opened a Merchant's Bank account in order to buy things from Taobao.com, China's equivalent of eBay.

If the SIM card you bought for your phone still has money on it when you leave China, you can give it to a local friend. This should not be your going-away gift, but merely a supplement to it. If you do not have any friends to whom you are giving a gift, ask if one of the staff in your dorm or hotel would like to have it. Start by saying how much money is left on it and ask if they would be able to give it to someone who can use it. That way, they come off as helping you without appearing greedy or selfish. If your card has less than ¥4 or 5 on it, you may not find any takers, but there's no reason to donate that money to the phone company.

If you have a gym membership and you are not going to use part of a month due to going home, ask the gym if you can transfer that remaining time to a friend. It may not be possible, but if you give the time to someone who has not used that gym before, the gym may be more willing to let you do it, as it could mean a new customer. Similarly, you may have a monthly member-

Daily life images can be nice reminders of your routines in China.

ship to an Internet café or some other establishment that you can leave with a friend or even another student who is not going home, yet.

Back when I was at Beijing Normal University in the late 1990s, some Japanese and Korean students would stay for years at a time and accumulate a variety of kitchen and daily goods like clothes drying racks. They generally just gave these items away to students not going home, and these items, in turn, found their way into the hands of later students. The washing machines we used that year were actually hand-me-downs from previous Japanese students. Beijing Normal University later installed industrial-grade washer-dryer sets in the foreign students' dormitories.

The last of the things you should start doing a couple weeks ahead of time is keeping a blog, diary, or photographic record of your life in China if you haven't done so already. And, while text is great, make sure that you take a lot of pictures. When you pull out your camera to start taking last-chance photos of things that had become routine, they have a way of becoming special again. Don't be afraid to take pictures of the unique as well as the mundane—back at home, nearly everything you see in China appears unique and exotic.

If your program has arranged for everyone to go home together, just relax and let them do the heavy lifting of getting you there. If not, make sure you have all your ducks in a row. A week before departure, check your itinerary again and check online to see if there have been any changes in your flight, including departure time, flight number, or even cancellation. Make absolutely certain that you have the right date and time for your outbound flight. It would be pretty embarrassing to show up at the airport a day early, or worse, a day late.

If you have to get yourself to the airport, plan on arriving at the airport at least two hours before departure. Three or four days before leaving, ask your classmates if anyone else is going to the airport (or train station) around the same time as you so that you can arrange for van transportation and share the cost. Because of luggage, it is usually impractical for more than two people to share a taxi to the airport. If you do plan to take a taxi, arrange with a taxi driver you used previously to pick you up at your dorm or hotel on departure day instead of trying to hail one on the street. When you're hailing a cab to go to a club, you don't notice so much if it takes 15 or 20 minutes to get one; when you're already late for the airport because you missed packing some things or you are hung over from the farewell banquet(s), waiting an extra 20 minutes or more can really destroy your schedule. Furthermore, you may be going to the airport at a time when you have not previously taken a taxi and do not even know if there are many taxis going by at that hour.

To minimize the unknown elements in your trip to the airport, get the phone number of a taxi driver days before you leave and arrange for him to meet you at your dorm or university gate. You can enlist a bilingual Chinese friend to help you, if you like. Some drivers will go to the airport at a discount if you agree not to run the meter (which reports the fare to the taxi company and the tax bureau), but you will need someone with pretty good Chinese and an understanding of the standard meter fare to the airport in order to make sure you don't figuratively get taken for a ride.

You may have made friends who are willing to take you to the airport, as well. You should politely refuse their offer once and say that you can easily get a cab. If your program has helped you get transportation, or if you are sharing a van with classmates, you can continue to refuse but thank the friend(s) for the offer. If you were only going to take a taxi by yourself anyway, and if you really like the friend who is offering to drive you to the airport, go ahead and accept the offer after your first polite refusal. This indicates that you agree to continue the cycle of reciprocity in which you do favors for each other. Once you accept the offer, prepare a gift for that friend and his/her family and give it at the last social event you have with them or when you arrive at the airport. Later, when that friend emails you asking for advice regarding school applications or editing a paper, you will agree, because that is what friends do.

A day or two before you start packing, check the websites of each airline you will be flying with to find out what their luggage limits

Many visitors pick up souvenir weapons in China. Call your airline to find out how to get it home.

are. Your initial carrier's checked luggage and carry-on luggage limits are critical; check the carry-on limits of any intermediary airlines you are flying, as well. Your checked luggage should go to your final destination based on the initial carrier's limits, but each airline in between might apply their own standards to your carry-ons. If you have any questions, call the airline; they will have English-speaking staff.

As you are packing (and shopping), keep U.S. Customs restrictions in mind. Things you absolutely cannot bring back include fresh fruits and vegetables, and most meat products. There are dogs that walk around sniffing luggage at the customs inspection section of international airports, so trying to sneak something through is a matter of playing the odds. To be on the safe side, just don't bring these things home. If you do, declare it on your customs form to let the customs officials look through your stuff with a smile on their faces instead of a frown. I declared dried donkey meat on my way back from my first trip, and a customs official threw it in a garbage can, along with an entire case of oranges that a woman had actually *not* declared on her arrival form! Despite many rumors to the contrary, you *can* bring moon cakes into the U.S., as long as they do not have egg yolks or meat products inside. Some Chinese think that you can only bring home a certain brand of moon cake, or that they are all illicit, but U.S. Customs is just worried about poultry and meat problems. You can bring home all the lotus seed paste pastries you can fit in your suitcase. You might have trouble packing the Häagen-Dazs ice cream moon cakes, though....

Last, but certainly not least, you may bring home up to 1 liter of alcohol duty-free. You are allowed to bring as much alcohol home as you wish—provided you are over 21—but U.S. Customs has the right to tax liquor over 1 liter in quantity,

Pack it wisely.

even if for personal consumption. To be honest, paying import taxes on alcohol is the least of your worries if you are bringing some home with you. Since you cannot bring large bottles of liquid in your carry-on luggage, you have to pack it in your checked luggage. As with any liquids in your luggage, wrap the bottles in two layers of plastic bags, and then pack them snugly in clothing that will cushion the impacts when the baggage handlers throw your suitcase around (and they will literally throw it). I learned this the hard way on my second trip back from China.

Everything else related to packing is the same as when you left home, except now you have a lot more stuff. On the day you leave, be sure to have all of your luggage ready to go before the time you are getting picked up, and be waiting at the pick-up point a few minutes early. Regardless of who is taking you to the airport, you want to leave on time, for your companions' and your own sake. Once you reach the airport, the process is the same as at any airport around the world, except in Chinese airports, the luggage carts are all free.

It is normal to have mixed feelings about going home. You want to see your friends and family again. No matter how great Skype is for keeping in touch, it's no substitute for literally being able to reach out and touch someone. At the same time, you have had an unforgettable experience in China. Even if you are among the few who had a negative experience, it was still unforgettable and it will be a part of who you are forever. If you had a positive experience, this trip will hopefully be the beginning of a long-term relationship with China and its people. Even if you do not get a chance to go back to China for a long time, the friends and memories you made there will continue to touch you in many ways. In the next chapter, we will talk about some ways you can keep the memories alive, as well as how you can use your experience to enrich the lives of people who haven't had the good fortune to visit China.

I'll be back.

Chapter 13
After You Return

You made it home! Hopefully, having read this book increased the chances that the biggest problem you had between leaving and returning home was figuring out how to unload all the pocket-sized packs of tissue you accumulated. In this chapter, we will talk about some things you can do to make sure that you get the most out of your recent trip, by keeping in touch with friends in China, making new friends at home with others related to China, and by sharing your experiences with people who have not had a chance to learn first-hand about what modern China is like.

Is that dinnertime 5:25 or sunrise 5:25?

You have earned a little rest, but don't let yourself fall asleep until after 9:00 p.m., local time. Most people start to fade around 3 or 4 o'clock in the afternoon; if you let yourself take a "nap" then, you'll have to start the jet lag recovery process a day or more later. Stay active and busy until nightfall: go visit your grocery store and get reacquainted with the overabundance of choices in the cereal and toothpaste aisles; go for a walk; just *do* something. If you sit down and watch or listen to something passively–even your family–you may just conk out right then and there when your body decides it has had enough of this all-nighter nonsense, even though it's the middle of the day at home.

If you force yourself to stay awake until nightfall, your recovery process will be much faster. You may still wake up at 4 or 5 o'clock in the morning for a few days, but that is better than being awake all night long, and you may discover that you can get a lot of things done before most people get out of bed. Try to eat at mealtimes that are appropriate for your home time zone, and consider taking some kind of homeopathic cold-prevention supplements such as Cold-EZ or vitamin C tablets. Many people catch cold in their weakened, jet-lagged state, especially after having breathed the same dry air as 300 other people on the flight(s) home.

After doling out the gifts you brought back for everyone and eating foods that you couldn't get in China (gyros?), one of the first things you should do is let your friends in China know that you made it home okay. It shows that you are still thinking about them, which makes them feel good, and shows them that you understand the importance of *renqing*. You don't have to say a lot, just tell each one you got home safely and that you will keep in touch. You can post pictures of you at home on your Renren page (like a Chinese Facebook), your Weibo, or just send them via WeChat.

A month before the next major Chinese holiday, you can send a small care package to your closest friends in China, including some of the things from home or your home school that you would have given them had you had them over there. You can print out a photo of an activity you did with that friend and frame it before sending over, too. When each major holiday rolls around, send an e-card to your Chinese friends by email and let them know how you are doing. It is nice to send a holiday e-card even if you have been keeping in touch via email or social media since you got home.

After returning home, keep your eyes peeled for organizations that attract local people who have been to China. Building *guanxi* with others who have China experience is a good way to keep your knowledge fresh and to be counted among those who are sought out when China experience is needed. Even though everyone and their neighbor may tell you they know someone who has been to China recently, it is really a small portion of Americans who have been there, and your experiences are valuable, no matter how short a stay you may have had.

You can find people with China experience at university activities organized by language departments, the international affairs office, the business school, and the China/East Asian center. You do not have to be a student at that university to attend most of such events—their organizers will welcome anyone with an interest in the subject! Off-campus, you can look into participating in events organized by local business organizations such as the chamber of commerce or economic development office, by the

Great, she made it home okay!

nearest overseas Chinese association, heritage school or chamber of commerce, and your nearest city with a sister-city relationship in China. If any of the events you find have a high cost of admission, ask the organizer if you may participate as a volunteer. That way, you can build your resume and your *guanxi*–and you may get a free meal out of the deal!

If your city has a Chinatown, that might be an easy place to start making connections.

You will have a lot of stories you can share with people stateside; the people you will meet at China-focused events will often have similar experiences and will be able to visualize what you describe as you relate your own experiences to them. The more time you spend in China and in Chinese communities, the more stories you will accumulate and the more expertise you will acquire. As your stories grow in number–including stories you hear from others who have gone–you will be able to differentiate between the commonplace and the unusual, and be able to distinguish between what is appropriate speech and behavior in different contexts. In a sense, you can borrow experience from others who have gone to China and share their stories with you, adding their stories to your extended repertoire. Eventually, you will come to learn things like when Chinese people are indirect (with out-group people) and when they are direct (with in-group people) and who spits phlegm on the sidewalk (older people with limited education) and who does not (everyone else).

In addition to establishing relationships with people who have gone to China, read more books about China. Having been there once will make each book you read or documentary you watch that much more relatable and informative. Even if you reread this book after your trip, you may find several references or pieces of advice to be much more relevant once you already know what I was talking about. For example, if you come back and read *China Road* by Rob Gifford, you may be able to better relate to the part where he says you are never far from people when in eastern China. Before you go to China, it may be difficult to imagine being in a place where even the most back-of-beyond places have been under regular cultivation for thousands of years. Once you have gone, though, you can appreciate the density of the population of eastern China…and thus you can appreciate it when Gifford writes that the deserts of Gansu and Xinjiang in western China offer the first feelings of absolute remoteness. When I train corporate managers prior to being sent to China on multi-year expatriate assignments, the trainees who get the most out of the training are those *who have already been to China once or twice*. So, jump right into reading and watching more about China—it will make a lot more sense now.

Now, imagine trying to tell someone who has never been to Asia a story about the first time you had to use a "squatty potty." If, as you read this, you have not yet seen or used one, you simply cannot imagine what the experience of using such a commode consists of. When you get back from China and have a million stories to share with people who have *not* been to China before, you will have to use your judgment and your storytelling abilities to tell your stories in a way to which your listeners can relate. If too many of your stories require the listeners to picture what they cannot picture or understand something with which they have had no personal experience (e.g., being in a rural area hundreds of miles from anywhere of import, and still finding a village every half mile apart), your listeners may develop China Story Fatigue. I am obviously making up this term, but the possibility of giving your friends and family CSF is very real.

Sufferers of CSF find their eyes begin to glaze over when they hear another story about how rush hour bus riders are crammed like sardines; they start to play with the buttons on their shirts when they are told about the fifth time you haggled down the price of a fake jade Buddha; their cheek muscles cramp from smiling about another taxi ride you took at high speed on the wrong side of the street. The remedy for CSF is to pick your stories wisely, choosing ones that you have taken pictures of, or ones that have some corollary in your listeners' experience. Everyone has had hair-raising experiences on the road at home, so describing how your taxi drivers dodged a variety of obstacles (inanimate and living) is something most people can relate to, even if they have never had to avoid pedestrians, bicycles, tricycles, overloaded trucks, unmarked construction areas, stopped cars, cars driving the wrong direction, and cars making left turns from the right lane all in the same trip.

Similarly, some of the foods you will eat in China may have no corollary whatsoever in the Western dining experience, but if you talk about them in a category people can understand—"interesting foods I saw/ate," then most people can relate, even if they cannot imagine exactly what it was like. Naturally, different foods will fall in differ-

The only people who know what Haw Flakes are have eaten them before.

ent places along the spectrum of culinary-experiences-I-can-imagine. If you tell someone you ate a spicy cuttlefish kabob, they can probably get the gist of it (once they know what a cuttlefish is); likewise, if you say you ate braised pork flavor Pringles potato chips, there is enough information in there for the uninitiated to guess what it tasted like. On the other end of the spectrum, you have things like Haw Flakes (**shān zhā piàn** 山楂片, candy made from the berries of the Chinese hawthorn bush) and the hard husks of berries of the prickly ash tree (**huājiāo** 花椒, a spice that is the hallmark of Sichuan cuisine and that makes your mouth numb). You can try to describe what these things taste like, but what your listeners will hear is "foreign flavors that I can't imagine." It only takes a few instances of this to creep into CSF, so either limit your stories about these unknown items, or pick some up from a Chinese grocery store near home. Your family may just have to go to China and find out for themselves what deep-fried scorpion tastes like…

Some experiences might be better left for discussions with others who have been to China, like the "strange bathrooms I have used in China" narrative, which is much less taboo for people who have been there and seen it all. As you tell stories like "bathrooms I have seen," it is important to put them into context for your listeners. Each time you share your China stories, you are building your listeners' repertoires of stories they have about

Some things are best left to the annals of history.

China. Each story informs how they think about the place, and if they have never been there before, it is easy to get the impression that China consists entirely of the things that stuck out in your mind (like the breezy wooden outhouse perched over a ditch next to a dumpling restaurant in a rural part of Heilongjiang Province), when in fact, such things may be unusual for contemporary urban Chinese people, too. The hotel in which our group stayed in on that trip had broadband Internet in each room, and this was in the year 2000, when broadband was just catching on in the U.S. When you take the Internet for granted and only talk about the two wooden planks propped over a ditch, it can lead to an imbalanced impression.

Which brings us to the last piece of advice I have for what you should do after you return: create a narrative about your experience, add images and video, and share it with *groups* of people in your community. Many people who are curious about China have not had a chance to go there, or at least not since the great changes that took place after

1949. We see China in the news nearly every day, and, for the most part, the Western media covers the same kinds of stories in China that they cover in their own countries: tales of misfortune, misdeeds, and politics. When we read our own news, we know that daily life is different from what is considered newsworthy; when we read news about China, it is easy to think that daily life there consists of what we read in the paper. The same is true of Chinese reading about the West—many Chinese think that random violence is a regular occurrence here, and that many foreigners are drug-addled sex addicts. If all you knew about your country was what you saw on your news, these would be reasonable conclusions.

Hence, you have some responsibility to building world peace and understanding by sharing your observations about daily life in China with your community. You can do this cheaply by asking your local library, schools, and civic organizations (e.g., Rotary Club, Veterans of Foreign Wars, Knights of Columbus, the chamber of commerce, neighborhood association, etc.) if you can give a short 20-minute presentation on your experience in China, and take questions afterward. You do not need to be an expert on China to do this—though the time following your first trip to China is probably when you will [naively] feel most like an expert about the subject—you just need to share your personal experiences and let your audience add your experiences to their knowledge.

Converting your experience in China into a short presentation will help you organize your thoughts and perspectives, as you will need to create a narrative framework for your experience. Will you tell it as a chronological story, giving highlights from day one to when you returned? Will you present your experience thematically, perhaps describing what you saw in the city versus what you saw in the countryside? Will you talk about gender roles as you saw them? The framework will depend largely on your audience. If you are speaking to an audience in the VFW, you might concentrate on how China seems to be changing, as some members of the audience may actually have lived in China…60 or more years ago. If you speak to your neighborhood association, folksier subjects such as food and family life might be more appealing. In any case, try to relate as many human aspects as possible. Even if your trip was a short one and you essentially skimmed along the surface, you still saw people living their lives. What were they doing? Were their goals and aspirations very different from those of people in your own community? If not, what about their lives seem different?

Precisely because many people come back from China thinking they "get it," it will be a good idea to run your presentation by someone who has been there many times over the course of many years. That person will be able to make sure that when you present interpretations of what you saw, you are

What does it mean when roadside buildings are marked for demolition?

making accurate interpretations. I once had a student who, when presenting his understanding of our class trip through the countryside, explained that the ubiquity of the character 拆 (**chāi** *tear down*) on roadside buildings meant that the economy must have been bad. He interpreted mass destruction of buildings as widespread business failures, when, in fact, these buildings were being torn down in order to widen the road and facilitate the movement of more goods and people in a *growing* economy. The student could have simply said that there were many buildings along the road with the *chai* character on them, and left it at that, but as human beings, we always interpret what we experience, and do so using the stories we have in our repertoires. His repertoire had not yet added the knowledge that buildings that are torn down in China get replaced with bigger, newer buildings or bigger, better roads, but just by sharing his presentation with someone who has spent more time in China, he was able to add that knowledge to his repertoire. You, too, can turn your presentation into a double-learning experience by sharing it first with an experienced China traveler.

As you design your presentation, be sure to include as much multimedia as possible, especially photos and graphics. While choosing your images, keep in mind what relationship your audience has with the people in them, if any. A picture of you and your classmate in front of a fog-enveloped valley may bring back memories of you two hiking up a mountain, but to people who do not know you, it is just a photo of two strangers with a gray background. Conversely, a picture of you and a random Chinese tourist who asked to have his or her picture taken with you in front of that same foggy valley might lead to a discussion about what kinds of people you saw at tourist sites, and which kinds of tourists asked to have a picture with you and which did not. You do not need to know that the growth of the Chinese middle class and their discretionary spending has driven a tremendous increase in domestic tourism in the past ten years; you can simply show your audience a tourist site overrun by Chinese visitors and they will know that tourism is big business. You can show them a photo of the tour bus parking lot and your audience will know that group tours are more popular in China than in the U.S. You can show them a photo of a tour group all wearing matching baseball caps and your audience can deduce that many Chinese people do not mind moving in identifiable groups. Many of your photos and videos can speak for themselves, and then you can add an interesting anecdote to how or why the photo was taken.

If you are a shy person and giving a presentation like this poses a challenge, I encourage you to pick up the gauntlet and do it if you want to be involved in China for a long time. As a foreigner in China—and even more so if you are learning the language—you will always be on stage. For better or worse, people will watch what you do and say. People from Beijing and Shanghai don't care so much about what foreigners are doing, but these cities are full of people from smaller places where foreigners are still intriguing (when someone in Tiananmen Square wants to have their picture taken with you, it is a good bet that person is a tourist from elsewhere in China and not from Beijing). Giving a presentation on your personal experiences and letting your audience reach their own conclusions is a low-pressure way of getting used to being in the limelight.

What next? Start thinking about how to get back! With your first China trip under your belt, you can start considering less-structured ways to go back—independent travel, direct enrollment in a Chinese university's classes for foreigners, or even jobs and internships. One common way for foreigners to get back to China is to take a job teaching English. There are websites dedicated to ads for English teaching positions, as well as agencies that place English teachers throughout the country. If you look for work in China, try to do it the way Chinese people do—through references by people you know. For one, many jobs in China are filled by word of mouth and via expatriate websites. Job hunting through connections will also increase the reliability of the employer. Some English teachers have been stiffed on their pay, sent to a school different from the one they hired on for, made to teach more hours than was promised, etc. You don't need to be frightened, just informed. China is, after all, a developing country, and there are some risks that come along with all the amazing opportunities.

So, get out there delivering pizza so you can buy your plane ticket back to China!

Appendix A
Measurement Conversion

China	U.S.
1 centimeter	0.393 inches
1 meter	1.093 yards
1 kilometer	0.62 miles
1 square meter (used in real estate)	1.196 square yards
1 mu (traditional measure of land area)	0.16 acre, or 7175 square feet
1 liter	0.26 gallons (about ¼ of a gallon)
1 kilogram	2.2 pounds
1 jin (traditional Chinese weight, used in produce markets)	1.1 pounds

U.S.	China
1 inch	0.304 m
1 foot	1.093 yards
1 mile	1.6 km
1 square foot	0.092 square meters (You can simply divide the square feet by 10 for a rough estimate of the square meters, e.g., a 2000 square foot home is about 200 square meters.)
1 gallon	4.54 liters
1 pound	0.45 kg

Celsius - Fahrenheit
(°C x 9/5) + 32 = °F
(°F - 32) x 5/9 = °C
Freezing 32° F = 0° C
Boiling 212° F = 100° C
A pleasant 75° F = 23.8° C

A hot 40° C = 104° F (Chinese law says that companies must let their workers off if the temperature gets above 40° C, so official urban weather reports rarely exceed 40°, while private thermometers may have higher readings)

Appendix B
Reference Books

Background

China: A New History, Second Enlarged Edition, by John King Fairbank and Merle Goldman

China Airborne, by James Fallows

Another book by a former China-based journalist, this one looks at modernizing China by analyzing the frenzied growth of the air travel network in China.

China in Ten Words, by Yu Hua, translated by Allan Barr

One of the few books in this list written by an actual Chinese person, a concise look at contemporary Chinese culture.

China in the 21st Century: What Everyone Needs to Know, by Jeffrey Wasserstrom

Chinese Lessons: Five Classmates and the Story of the New China, by John Pomfret

Pomfret wrote about China for the Washington Post, and this well-written book describes where his Chinese classmates at Nanjing University in the early 1980s are now.

Factory Girls: From Village to City in a Changing China, by Leslie Chang

Lao Tzu: Te-Tao Ching – A New Translation Based on the Recently Discovered Ma-wang-tui Texts, by Lao Tzu, translation and commentary by Robert G. Henricks

Though Daoism is not experienced on a daily basis quite like Confucianism is, it runs deep in Chinese thought.

Mencius (Translations from the Asian Classics), by Mencius, translated by Irene Bloom

These are the writings that comprise the basis of Confucianism, the prescriptions for daily life that have informed over two thousand years of Chinese civilization.

On China, by Henry Kissinger

Kissinger had access to levels of Chinese power that few others in the U.S. did, and was present for the reestablishment of U.S.-China relations. However, this book is not without its critics. Take it as one perspective on China from the outside.

Pretty Woman Spitting, An American's Travels in China, by Leanna Adams

This book describes an American woman's experience teaching English in a tier-three Chinese city, a place where few tourists go and yet represents the experience of many city-dwelling Chinese.

Selected Stories of Lu Hsun, by Lu Xun, translated by Yang Hsien-yi and Gladys Yang

Lu Xun is one of the greatest modern Chinese authors, and he is often felt to have expressed the tensions created by China's breaking from its thousands of years of tradition.

Story of the Stone (or, The Dream of the Red Chamber), by Cao Xueqin, translated by David Hawkes

This novel is one of the great novels of late imperial China. Following the lives of a declining aristocratic family, it is as popularly known in China as *Gone With the Wind* is in the U.S., and is referred to often.

The Analects, attributed to Confucius, as translated by Arthur Waley, D.C. Lau, or James Legge

The Chinese Century: The Rising Chinese Economy and Its Impact on the Global Economy, the Balance of Power, and Your Job, by Oded Shenkar

The Good Earth, by Pearl S. Buck

A classic novel about the experience of the Chinese peasant in pre-WWII China, written by an American woman who was born and grew up there.

The Living Tree: The Changing Meaning of Being Chinese Today, by Tu Wei-ming

A well-informed self-reflection on Chinese identity by overseas Chinese scholars, written shortly after the Tiananmen incident.

The Search for Modern China, by Jonathan Spence

An excellent survey of Chinese history and culture.

Understanding China: A Guide to China's Economy, History, and Political Culture, by John Bryan Starr

Every book by Peter Hessler

Hessler first went to China to teach English in a little-known (outside of China) part of Sichuan. His writing is excellent and balanced.

Travel and Travelogues

China Road, by Rob Gifford

This great read describes the former NPR China correspondent's trips on National Road 312, from Shanghai to Urumqi, artfully combining stories about the people he met with the highlights of what you need to know about Chinese culture to begin to understand it as it is today.

China Survival Guide: How To Avoid Travel Troubles and Mortifying Mishaps, 3rd Revised Edition, by Larry and Qin Herzberg

Any of the Lonely Planet, Fodor's, Frommer's, or Rough Guides guidebooks on China and places in China.

News From Tartary: A Journey from Peking to Kashmir, by Peter Fleming

Written by the brother of Ian Fleming of James Bond fame, this is Peter Fleming's account of his trip to western China in 1935.

Riding the Iron Rooster, by Paul Theroux

Theroux is a well-known travel rider, and this year-long trek through China in the late 1980s, largely by rail, is still a popular read.

Phrasebooks

Essential Mandarin Chinese Phrase Book. by Philip Yungkin Lee.

Instant Chinese, How to Express 1,000 Different Ideas With Just 100 Key Words and Phrases! by Boyé Lafayette De Mente.

Mandarin Phrasebook, (Lonely Planet) by Charles Qin and Justin Rudelson

Survival Chinese: How to Communicate without Fuss or Fear–Instantly!, by Boyé Lafayette De Mente.

The Rough Guide Mandarin Chinese Phrasebook

Appendix C
Popular Chinese Movies

These are movies that were popular in China and are important parts of popular culture:

A Better Tomorrow is a good representative of John Woo's Hong Kong action movies starring the Chinese megastar Chow Yun-fat. The movie, as is common for Chinese movies, has a complicated plot in which characters are unaware of other characters' true identities or intentions, and in the end, fate steps in.

A Journey West, a comedy version of the classic Chinese story *Journey to the West*, starring the Hong Kong comedian Stephen Chou. This movie is very popular among younger Chinese people.

Big Shot's Funeral, a comedy by one of China's other famous directors, Feng Xiaogang, starring Ge You with Donald Sutherland. This is a "New Year Movie," a comedy produced to celebrate the Chinese New Year.

God of Gamblers is another Stephen Chou comedy, about a gambler who suffers a brain injury but can continue to gamble for his friends.

Hero, an exciting Zhang Yimou movie about relative merits of independent states and a unified China.

If You Are the One is another Feng Xiaogang comedy starring the megastar Ge You. Ge You plays a man who returns to China after years abroad, and, having become wealthy, seeks a wife.

Infernal Affairs is another excellent example of a Hong Kong organized crime action movie (see *A Better Tomorrow*) in which there is a complicated plot, mistaken identities and a deep Buddhist meaning. This is the film that Martin Scorsese adapted for American audiences as "The Departed," starring Leonardo DiCaprio, Matt Damon, Jack Nicholson, and several other famous actors.

Not One Less, a movie by the famous Chinese director Zhang Yimou about a village girl who goes to the city to track down a pupil she loses track of.

Police Story is a good example of Jackie Chan's work during his rise to fame in Hong Kong and his development of the kung fu comedy genre.

Raise the Red Lantern, another Zhang Yimou movie, this time about the intrigues among concubines belonging to a wealthy man in Republican-era China.

Yip Man is a poplar recent kung fu movie that describes Bruce Lee's master's life story.

Appendix D
Useful Websites

These websites are provided as a starting point only, without endorsement or assurances of accuracy—websites change quickly!

China News and Background

CIA World Factbook: China:
https://www.cia.gov/library/publications/the-world-factbook/geos/ch.html

Official Chinese English language newspaper, China Daily U.S. Edition:
usa.chinadaily.com.cn

Official Chinese news website:
www.china.org.cn/index.htm

Chinese News in the Developed World

NPR:
www.npr.org/sections/asia

South China Morning Post (Hong Kong):
www.scmp.com

The Guardian (UK):
www.guardian.co.uk/world/china

The New York Times:
topics.nytimes.com/top/news/international/countriesandterritories/china

The Wall Street Journal:
blogs.wsj.com/chinarealtime

Washington Post:
www.washingtonpost.com/world/asia-pacific

English Language Information about Life in Specific Cities

Beijing:
www.thebeijinger.com
www.beijingexpat.com
www.cityweekend.com.cn/beijing

Nanjing:
nanjingexpat.com,
www.hellonanjing.net

Qingdao:
www.myredstar.com

Shanghai:
www.cityweekend.com.cn/shanghai
www.thatsshanghai.com

www.shanghaiexpat.com
www.seashanghai.org
www.shfamily.com

Tianjin:
tianjinexpats.com
www.tianjinplus.com/tjplus

Xi'an:
www.echinacities.com/xi'an
talkxian.com

Travel

A China travel wiki:
www.china-travelguide.com

Airfare to China:
www.flychina.com

Airline ticket information aggregator:
www.kayak.com

Domestic travel reservations:
www.ctrip.com
www.elong.com
www.qunar.com

Fodor's travel guide companion site:
www.fodors.com/world/asia/china

Frommer's travel guide companion site:
www.frommers.com/destinations/china

Rough Guide travel guide companion site:
www.roughguides.com/destinations/asia/china/

The Lonely Planet travel guide's companion site:
www.lonelyplanet.com/china

Youth Hostels China:
www.yhachina.com

Study Abroad Program Listings

www.cucas.edu.cn, a listing of Chinese universities' program offerings

www.goabroad.com, another study abroad search engine

www.iiepassport.org, a study abroad search engine

www.studyabroad.com, a listing of mostly U.S.-based programs abroad

Appendix E
A Sampling of Language Programs

Short-Term English Programs

- Alliance for Global Education International Business in China (1-4 months)
- Artis China Traditional Chinese Arts (3 weeks)
- Eastern Illinois University Plant Usage & Culture in China (3 weeks)
- Ohio State University Multicultural Southwest China Program (1 month)

Short-Term Chinese Programs

- ACC (Beijing)
- CET (Beijing, Shanghai, Harbin, Kunming, and Hangzhou)
- CIEE (Beijing, Shanghai, and Nanjing)
- EducAsian language/culture and internship programs (Shanghai)
- Global Professional Service Corps (nationwide internships)
- IUP (Beijing)
- OSU Intensive Chinese Language (Qingdao)
- Princeton in Beijing (Beijing)
- School Year Abroad (Beijing, for high school students; summer and year-long programs)

Long-Term English Degree Programs

■ Bachelor's Degree

- Beijing Foreign Studies University, International Business (Beijing, 4 years)

- China University of Petroleum, Mechanical Engineering (Qingdao, 4 years)
- East China Normal University, International Communication (Shanghai, 4 years)

■ Master's Degree

- People's University of China, Public Administration (Beijing, 2 years)
- Shandong University, Chinese Economics (Jinan, 2 years)
- University of International Business and Economics, Finance (Beijing, 2 years)

Long-Term Chinese Degree Programs

These are programs that have taken or want to take foreign students.

■ Bachelor's Degree

- Beijing Forestry University, Landscape Architecture (Beijing, 4 years)
- China University of Geosciences, Petroleum Engineering (Wuhan, 4 years)
- Guangxi University, Aquatic Farming (Nanning, 4 years)

■ Master's Degree

- Harbin Institute of Technology, Statistics (Harbin, 3 years)
- Shanghai Jiaotong University, MBA-Finance (Shanghai, 2.5 years)
- Wuhan University, Financial Engineering (Wuhan, 3 years)

Index

A
accessibility 71, 169
accidents 272-276, 278
activities *see* sightseeing
adjusting 72-79
air travel 90-94, 98-99, 221-224
airport transfers 100-105
alcohol 196, 202-204, 280, 289
allergies 274-275
ambulances 278
ancient China 28-33, 243-245
Anhui 21, 175
apartments 117
arriving in China 98-105
ATMs 191-192

B
bái kāi shuǐ (boiled water) 181
banqueting 264, 286-288
bānzhǎng (class monitors) 137-138, 260
bargaining tactics 197-198
behavior expectations: clothing and 145-147, 188-190; for students 134-148 *see also* alcohol; relationships (*guanxi*)
Beijing 16-18, 35-38, 40, 54, 231
bikes 170-171
boats 226-227
Border Control 99, 295
buses 103-104, 160-163, 224-226

C
campuses 112-119
cars 104-105, 172-173
cell phones 192-193
Central China 22-23
Chang'an 33-34
Chángjiāng sānjiǎo zhōu (Yangzi River Delta) 232-234
Cháng jiāng (Yangzi) 12
Cháng Zhēng (Long March) 37, 241
Chiang Kai-shek 37
Chinese: Communicating in the Culture (Walker) 82
Chinese Business Etiquette (Seligman) 266
Chinese-language programs 53-70
Chinese relationships 32, 78, 254-264
Chinese writing 79-82
Chongqing 24
chop sticks 129-130, 185
chuàngkětiē (bandage) 274
chuànmén (conversation) 62
chūnqiū shíqī (spring and autumn period) 32
chūzhànkǒu (exit) 220
civil war 38
class monitors (*bānzhǎng*) 137-138, 260
classroom experience 69, 137-140
climate 14-15
clothing 145-147, 188-190, 198-199
coaches 104
communications 106, 192-194 *see also* Internet access
Communism 37-41
computers 96, 111, 114-115, 193-194
Confucius 12, 32
conversion chart 306
credit cards 192
credits 64-65
crime 269-270, 280-281
cuisine types 174-188
Cultural Revolution 38-39
culture shock 72-76
customs duties 99, 295
cuts, minor 274-275

D
dà bízi (big nose) 151
Dali 237-238
dangerous events 270, 281-285
Daoism 32-33
dàpāi dàng restaurants 177-178
dating 97, 115-116, 268-270
degree-granting programs 68-70, 314-315
Deng Xiaoping 39
dental hygiene 194-195
diarrhea 272-273
dìgōu yóu (ditch oil) 179
directions, asking 167-168
dongche trains 208
dormitories 113-119
driving 104-105, 171-173
drug use 280-281
Dynastic Cycle 29-37

E
East China 20-22
Eat Shandong (Shepherd) 259, 266
economic growth 248-250

economic opportunities 42-43
electricity quotas 115
electronics 95-97 *see also* specific types
emailing 194
Emei Shan 239
emergencies 278
enemies of the state 270
English-language programs 51-52, 67-68
English tutoring 149-150
èr lù chē (number 2 bus) 166
ethnic minorities 26, 238, 246-248
exercising 199-200

F

face, saving 132, 143, 219, 261-263
feminine needs 275
Fēngyóujīng medicine 276
food: banqueting 264-267, 286-288; cuisine types 174-188; with host families 129-132; regional 14-15; tourism for 250-252
foreign influence 35-38
friendships *see* relationships (*guanxi*)
fù èrdài (rich second generation) 204
Fujian 23, 175
fun activities 196-204 *see also* sightseeing
fúwùyuán (waiter) 186

G

gàijiāo fàn (lunch special) 177-178
Gansu 26
gaotie trains 207-208

geography 10-28
gifts 96, 123, 128-129, 196-199, 289-290, 298
The Golden Peaches of Samarkand (Schafer) 245
government 16-18, 37-41
Great Wall 231, 244
greetings 152
group tours 47-48
Guangdong 23-24, 55, 174-175
Guangxi 23
Guangzhou 250
guānxi (relationships) *see* relationships
guests, tips for 124-132
Guizhou 24, 26

H

Hainan 236
hair cuts 195
Han Dynasty 33-34
Han ethnicity 12
health insurance 87-88, 278-279
Hebei 282
Heilongjiang 20
Henan 30-31
history: ancient 28-33, 243-245; Communist 37-41; dynastic 33-35; foreign influences on 35-38
homestays 124-132
Hong Kong 36, 89, 104
hospital (*yīyuàn*) 276-279
host families 124-132
hosts, tips for 267
hotels 106-112, 133
Huabei (North China) 19-20
Huai River 14-15

huājiāo spice 301
Huaminglou Village 240
huángliánsù (diarrhea medicine) 273
Huang Long 236
Huáng Shān (Yellow Mountain) 21, 239
Hubei 22-23
human sentiment (*rénqíng*) 254-259
Hunan 22-23, 175
Hú Qiū (Tiger Hill) 233
hútòng (alley) 231
hygiene 112, 131, 179, 194-196

I

illness 272-279, 282-283
immunizations 85-88
independent travel 45-47
infections 274, 282-283
Inner Mongolia 19
insurance 87-88, 278-279
intercity travel *see* transportation, intercity
Internet access 96, 111, 114-115, 193-194

J

Japan 38, 283-284
jet lag 297
jiǎgǔ (shell-and-bone writing) 30
Jiangsu 20-21, 175
Jiangxi 20-23
jiànmiànlǐ (meeting gifts) 289
jiǎnpiào kǒu (ticket-checking entry) 218
jié zhàng (check please) 186
Jilin 20

Jinan University 62
Jinggang Mountains 241
jīn (unit of measure) 188
jiǔjīng (rubbing alcohol) 274
Jiuzhaigou 235-236

K
karaoke 84
kōng chē (empty car) 164
kōngtiáo yìngwò (air-conditioned hard sleeper) 216
kuài (people's money) 100

L
language pledges 66
language practice 79-82
language programs 51-70
lǎo wài (foreigner) 151
laundry 188-190
legal issues 270, 279-281
Léifēng Tǎ (Leifeng Pagoda) 234
liǎng zhī láohǔ (Two Tigers song) 154
Liaoning 20
light rails 104
Lijiang 237-238
línshí kèchē (temporary passenger trains) 209
lǐshàng wǎnglái (social reciprocity) 258 *see also* reciprocity
liúlí (glassware) 198
living spaces: campuses 112-119; homestays 124-132; hotels 106-112, 133; during language programs 61-64; roommates for 119-124
local transit 104, 157-174
Long March (*Cháng Zhēng*) 37, 241

Long River (*Cháng jiāng*) 12
long-term programs of study 67-71
Lu Gully 38
lǚxíng shè (travel agency) 213

M
Macao 89
Maglev 104
mǎi dān (check please) 186
màn chē (slow trains) 207-208
Mao Zedong 37-39
markets 187-188, 197-198
medical care 272-279
Mencius 32
mental preparation 72-79
miànzi (social face) 132, 143, 261-264
Ming Dynasty 35
minority cultures 26, 238, 246-248
mò chē (last bus) 162
money 95-96, 100, 106-107, 187, 190-192, 255
Mongolia 19
motorcycles 171-172
mountains 239-240
movies 310-311
Mozi 33
MSG (monosodium glutamate) 184

N
Nanchang 241
National Grand Theater 18
national security 194
natural disasters 281-282
Naxi minority 238
Needham, Joseph 14

negotiating prices 197-198
Netizens (online people) 194
nightlife 202-204
Ningxia Hui Autonomous Region 16
North China (*Huáběi*) 14-16, 19-20
Northeast China 20

O
Opium Wars 14, 36
oracle bones 29-30

P
packing 94-97, 290
Pangu 28-29
pedestrians 166-170
performance skills 82-85, 287-288
Performing Monkey Syndrome 153-155
personal property 127-128
philosophy 32-33
photographs 292
physical differences 151-155
pinyin Romanization 79-82
pollution 283
population density 26-28
preparing to travel: flights 90-94, 221-223; immunizations 85-88; language practice 79-82; mental preparation 72-79; packing 94-97, 290; performance skills 82-85; visas 88-90, 279-280
privacy 127-128
programs for travel: list of

314-315; long-term 67-71; short-term 51-66; tourism 45-51
prostitution 196
protests 283-284
public transit 104, 157-163

Q
qiáo (bridge) 38
Qiaotou 238
Qin Dynasty 33
Qingdao 237
Qing Dynasty 35
Qinghai 26
Qin Shihuang (First Emperor) 33
qiú yǒu (ball friends) 146

R
racism 144, 267
rail travel 205-221
reciprocity 122-123, 131-132, 257-258, 267
Red tourism 240-243
reference books 307-309
relationships (*guanxi*): banqueting and 264-267; Chinese and 32, 78, 254-264; dating 97, 115-116, 268-270; establishing 267; maintaining 297-304; repairing 263-264; at school 115, 119-124, 135-137; types to avoid 267-271
rén (kindness) 44
renminbi (people's money) 100
rénqíng (human sentiment) 254-259
rental cars 104-105
resident directors 59-61, 191, 204, 278-279
restaurants 174-188
returning home 286-304
romance 97, 115-116, 268-270
roommates 115, 119-124
ruǎnzuò (soft seat) 211
rùkǒu (entrance) 218

S
Sanxingdui culture 15-16, 244
Schafer, Edward 245
Science and Civilisation in China (Needham) 14
scooters 171-172
sea travel 226-227
seating class 210-212
Seligman, Scott 266
Shaanxi 31, 37, 242
Shandong 19-20, 174, 237, 239, 244, 250-252
Shang Dynasty 30-31
Shanghai 9, 19, 20-21, 55, 232-234
shàngpù (top berth hard sleeper) 211
shāngwù chē (mini-van) 228
Shāntáng jiē (Shantang Street) 232
Shanxi 19
shān zhā piàn (Haw Flakes) 301
Shaoshan 240
shèng shì period (prosperity and growth) 41
Shenzhen 249
Shepherd, Eric 259, 266
Shǐhuáng (First Emperor) 33
shoes 199
shopping 196-199, 291-292
short-term programs of study 51-66
shǒuchē (first bus) 162
shòupiào chù (ticket window) 213
showering 131
shuttle buses 103
Sichuan 15-16, 24, 55, 175
sightseeing: with host families 131-132; for leisure 200-202; theme destinations 240-252; tourism programs 45-51; tourist destinations 230-240
sìhé yuàn (houses) 231
Silk Road 34, 244-245
smart cards 163
social expectations 144-146, 202-204
social face (*miànzi*) 132, 143, 261-264
social reciprocity (*lǐshàng wǎnglái*) *see* reciprocity
Song Dynasty 34-35
South China 14-16, 19-20
Southeast China 23-24
Southwest China 24-26
souvenirs 196-199, 291-292
street vendors 178, 260
students 134-156; classroom experience of 69, 137-140; expectations for 134-148; physical differences of 151-155; role of 148-150
study tours 48-51
subways 104, 158-160
Sui Dynasty 34
syllabi 139

T

taiji quan (tai chi) 49
Tài Shān (Mt. Tai) 239
Tang Dynasty 34-35
Taoism 32-33
taxis 101-103, 106, 163-166, 227-228
teachers 135-144
television performances 154-155
text messaging 192-193
theme destinations 240-252
Tiananmen movement 40
Tianjin 208, 249
Tibet Autonomous Region 26-28
Tiger Hill Pagoda 233
tipping 106-107, 187
toasting 203, 289
topography 12-14, 16
tourism *see* sightseeing
tourism programs 45-51
trains 205-221
transportation, intercity: boats 226-227; buses 224-226; flights 221-224; private taxis 227-228; trains 205-221
transportation, local: airport transfers 100-105; bikes 170-171; buses 103-104, 160-163, 224-226; cars 104-105, 172-173; motorcycles 171-172; subways 157-163; taxis 101-103, 106, 163-166, 227-228; walking 166-170
travel programs 45-71, 314-315

U

U.S. Customs 295

V

vaccinations 85-88
vegetarians 184
visas 88-90, 279-280

W

Wade-Giles Romanization 79-82
wàibàn (foreign affairs office) 60
wàiguó rén (foreigner) 151
wàimào fúzhuāng diàn (export clothing stores) 199
Walker, Galal 82
walking 166-170
wǎngmín (online people) 194
wars 36, 38
websites 194, 312-313
Wēixìn (WeChat) 193
West China (*Xīzàng*) 26-28
wòpù chē (sleeper buses) 225
World War II 38

X

Xià Dynasty 30
xiā mǐ (dried shrimp) 275
Xi'an 231-232
xiàpù (bottom bunk hard sleeper) 211
xièxie (thank you) 187
Xīhú (Lake Xi) 233-234
Xinjiang 26-28
Xishuangbanna 235
Xīzàng (West China) 26-28
Xunzi 32

Y

Yangshuo 234, 235

Yangzi River 12, 232-234, 239
yèxiāo (snack) 178
Yin and Yang 28
yìngwò (hard sleeper) 211-212
yìngzuò (hard seat) 210-211
Yong, Lang 82
Yuan Dynasty 35
Yù Lóng Xuě Shān (Jade Dragon Snow Mountain) 238
Yunnan 24-26, 233, 237-238

Z

Zhangjia Jie 239-240
zhànguó shíqī (Warring States period) 32
zhànpiào (no-seat class) 211
zhāo liáng (cool stomach) 273
Zhejiang 20-21, 175
zhì (sharing the bill) 255
Zhongguan Cun 19-20
Zhōngguó (Middle Kingdom) 14
Zhōnghuá mínzú (Chinese people) 12
zhōngpù (middle berth hard sleeper) 211
Zhōu Dynasty 31-32
zhùyuàn (to be hospitalized) 276-279
zǐgǒng (Red Mercury disinfectant) 274

Photo Credits

CanStockPhoto: zhuzhu 231

Dreamstime: Alexandr Vlassyuk 150; Angela Ostafichuk 198; Ashwin Kharidehal Abhirama 197; Baiploo 76; Bartlomiej Magierowski 92; Beercates 105; Cczbb 126; Cheng Zhong 281; Dryly75 249; Edward Lemery Iii 48; Edyta Pawlowska 145; Elian Kars 80; Elwynn 298; Flashon Studio 49 (top); Flytosky11 81; Fox007 229; Gan Hui 139, 204, 210, "green skin train" (4 color inset on 26 bottom); Gang Wang 296; Grandboat 25, 237 (bottom); Graphictools 293; Hanhanpeggy 185 (bottom); Howard Hong 174; Huang Huang Jian 246 (top); Huating 54, 62, 102, 127, 146, 181, 192, 227; Hupeng 18, 21, 111, 132, 136 (top), 207, 212, 245, 284; Hxdbzxy 205; Imtmphoto 137; Ivan Sinayko 187; J6789 278; Jacetan 269; Jackq 85; Jerryway 239; Ji Zhou 295; Jiang Qing 103; jindong 20; Jinlide 204 (bottom); Jjspring 46, 170; Jpldesigns 49 (bottom); kchen 22 (bottom); Kenjaychen 42; Kingalex1208 242; Koscusko 217; Lee Snider 55, 74, 173; Leung Cho Pan 254, 282; Liangfeng 122; liouyuyaho 19; Llz0511 236 (top); Lovell35 121; Mamahoohooba 115, 222; Marek Uliasz 129; Maria Barski 290 (top); Mario Savoia cover (4th from top left); Monkey Business Images 141; Mosessin 184 (right); Natalia Bratslavsky 299; Nicholas Burningham 97; Pa2011 97; Pavel Losevsky 250; Payphoto 287; Peter Kim 130 (bottom); Pniesen 247; Queenfather 224 (top); Rafal Cichawa 238 (bottom); Raywoo 136 (bottom); Robert Findlay cover (2nd from bottom right); Robert Paul Van Beets 114, 233 (bottom); Ryflip 271; Sebastian Czapnik 153; Song Yang cover (top right), 240; Songquan Deng 91; Stanko07 163; Suprijono Suharjoto 270; Tanawat Pontchour 189; Tangducminh 262; trix1428 15; Typhoonski 172; Uptall 24, 73, 128, 169; Venusangel 258; Vivian8529 238 (top); Waihs 180, 195, 277; Wavebreakmedia Ltd 138; Wayne Zhou 116; William Perry 64; Wisconsinart cover (5th from top left); Wxin 184 (left); Xi Zhang 41, 53, 58; Xiaofeng123 191, 224; Yang Yu 291; Yinan Zhang cover (3rd from top left); Ying Liu 246 (bottom); Zaramira 235; Zhanglianxun 226; Zhaojiankang 234; Zheng Bin 124; Zheng Xiaoqiao 168; Zhiqian Li 63; Zhudifeng 75, 257

Na Na 113 (top)

Patrick McAloon: cover (top left; 2nd from top left; bottom right), 4 color inset (except "green skin train" at 26 bottom)

Shutterstock: Antonio Abrignani 14 (bottom); hjschneider 14 (top); Ssguy 9

Sydney Chinese Consulate 99

Tom Mason 39

Zi Lan 220

All other photos by Patrick McAloon

The Tuttle Story: "Books to Span the East and West"

Many people are surprised to learn that the world's largest publisher of books on Asia had its humble beginnings in the tiny American state of Vermont. The company's founder, Charles E. Tuttle, belonged to a New England family steeped in publishing.

Immediately after WW II, Tuttle served in Tokyo under General Douglas MacArthur and was tasked with reviving the Japanese publishing industry. He later founded the Charles E. Tuttle Publishing Company, which thrives today as one of the world's leading independent publishers.

Though a westerner, Tuttle was hugely instrumental in bringing a knowledge of Japan and Asia to a world hungry for information about the East. By the time of his death in 1993, Tuttle had published over 6,000 books on Asian culture, history and art—a legacy honored by the Japanese emperor with the "Order of the Sacred Treasure," the highest tribute Japan can bestow upon a non-Japanese.

With a backlist of 1,500 titles, Tuttle Publishing is more active today than at any time in its past—inspired by Charles Tuttle's core mission to publish fine books to span the East and West and provide a greater understanding of each.